Language and Interracial Communication in the United States

June 20, 2009

To my dear Aunt Connie,
Thanks for your
interest in my work.
It means a lot to me.
Love,
George

Language as SOCIAL ACTION ▶

Howard Giles,
General Editor

Vol. I

PETER LANG
New York • Washington, D.C./Baltimore • Bern
Frankfurt am Main • Berlin • Brussels • Vienna • Oxford

George B. Ray

Language and Interracial Communication in the United States

SPEAKING IN BLACK AND WHITE

PETER LANG
New York • Washington, D.C./Baltimore • Bern
Frankfurt am Main • Berlin • Brussels • Vienna • Oxford

Library of Congress Cataloging-in-Publication Data

Ray, George B.
Language and interracial communication in the United States:
speaking in black and white / George B. Ray.
p. cm. — (Language as social action; v. 1)
Includes bibliographical references and index.
1. Intercultural communication—United States. 2. United States—
Race relations. 3. Communication and culture—United States.
4. Communication—Social aspects—United States. I. Title.
HM1211.R39   305.896′073—dc22   2009005918
ISBN 978-0-8204-6245-5
ISSN 1529-2436

Bibliographic information published by **Die Deutsche Bibliothek**.
Die Deutsche Bibliothek lists this publication in the "Deutsche
Nationalbibliografie"; detailed bibliographic data is available
on the Internet at http://dnb.ddb.de/.

Contents

Preface

In the late 1980s, I joined the faculty in communication at Cleveland State University and agreed to teach an existing course with the title "Interracial Communication." I was a "middle-aged, white guy" who had grown up in a rural, virtually all-white area in the Midwestern United States. In my previous experiences in life, I had attended racially integrated universities, served in the U.S. Air Force in integrated units, lived for two years in a large, culturally diverse city, and taught for a number of years at Berea College, an institution with a historic commitment to interracial education. Thus, I had some relevant background experiences upon which to draw, at least as far as living and working in racially integrated environments. Yet, I felt a great challenge in teaching at an urban commuter university within a metropolitan area that had a checkered past in race relations.

As I began teaching, I found there were some extremely useful books that had been published in the 1970s. Arthur Smith's *Transracial Communication* (1973), Andrea Rich's *Interracial Communication* (1974), and Jon Blubaugh and Dorothy Pennington's *Crossing Difference . . . Interracial Communication* (1976) were three such texts that helped shape my thinking and teaching about race and communication. Although there was not a great deal of current research on interracial communication, these texts provided useful starting points for me.

In the classroom, a significant concern arose: European American and African American students had plenty of stereotypic information about themselves and each other, but they had relatively little direct experience interacting with each other as individuals. Furthermore, the course I was teaching fulfilled a diversity requirement in the university's general education curriculum. I had students from all over the university and some students had little interest in interracial communication, other than to fulfill a course requirement. One of my early realizations was that understanding interracial communication could be facilitated by black and white students learning more about each other's ways of using language and cultural patterns of communication. It has also been my experience that African Americans understand more about mainstream European American culture than do European Americans about African American culture.

I discovered Thomas Kochman's *Black and White Styles in Conflict* (1981), which was very beneficial in my teaching, and over time I assembled articles by various authors from communication, education, psychology, anthropology, sociology, linguistics, and other fields. The more I taught the course, the more I realized that communication between blacks and whites occurred within a complex context. There were a number of factors that seemed to influence interracial communication, but there seemed to be no single dominant influence. Language and speech style were clearly significant. Educational experiences also seemed important. Stereotyping was obviously a crucial factor, although the more I studied racial stereotyping the more I realized this was an incredibly complicated psychological process. Furthermore, as my readings and teaching experiences showed, there was a history of race relations in the United States, awareness of which always seemed to be operating just below or right at the surface of interracial interaction.

Over the last 20 years, a lot has changed about me, society's awareness of race relations, and interracial communication as a field of study. I have appreciated living in a racially integrated neighborhood within a racially diverse community in the Cleveland area, and my children have attended public schools, primary and secondary, which are racially integrated. Interest in race relations has heightened in the United States, especially in 2007 and 2008 with the candidacy and then election of Barack Obama. Current events in race relations have not only provided a constant source of examples that have been valuable in teaching but also helped clarify the evolving nature of race relations in the United States.

It has also been important that a growing number of scholars are writing and conducting research in the area of race and communication. The 1993 book *African American Communication: Ethnic Identity and Cultural Interpretation* (Hecht, Collier, & Ribeau, 1993) was an excellent synthesis of research on language, cultural identity, and communication style. This book has appeared in a second edition (Hecht, Jackson, & Ribeau, 2003) and remains most useful. In 2001, Mark Orbe and Tina Harris published *Interracial Communication: Theory into Practice* (now in its second edition), a volume that not only provides a fine review of scholarly literature but also develops a coherent discussion of interracial communication for those of us conducting research and teaching in this field.

The theoretical insights and reviews of research from the Orbe and Harris text as well as from the monographs by Hecht and associates have not only helped me in particular develop my own ideas about the impact of race in communication but also stimulated additional research in the field of communication in general. A goal of this book is to contribute to scholarship in race and communication, adding another source of which readers, scholars, teachers and practitioners can take advantage.

As will be pointed out in Chapter 1, this book focuses on the importance of black/white relations in the United States. Yet, it is clear that the United States has become quite diverse and that African Americans are only one of several notable ethnic minorities.

Although it might be desirable to integrate research and theory that would more generally apply to intergroup relations between the still dominant European American culture and other minority groups, I argue for a focus on black/white relations. The status of African Americans in the United States, both historically and in the present, remains highly distinctive and constitutes what may be termed black exceptionalism (Sears, Citrin, Cheleden, & van Laar, 1999; see also Chapter 1). Although there are parallels between black/white relations and other interethnic dynamics in the United States (e.g., relations involving Hispanics, Asians, Native Americans, etc.), this book approaches black/white relations as a significant subject in its own right and as deserving the specific treatment developed herein.

In my opinion, race relations truly have changed for the better in the United States, not only over the last 200 years, but even over the last 20. In my teaching, I still encounter conflicts and dilemmas; at times, it is difficult to avoid a grievance-centered approach that dwells on negative experiences. However, in my classes I try to stress that there are notable signs of progress in race relations. It is my aim that this book will be useful to anyone wanting to understand how race affects communication. My experiences in the classroom make me believe that there is an important educational role teachers need to play in addressing contemporary concerns about race. Therefore, this book presents a review and synthesis of research and also reflects my experiences teaching, reading about, and thinking about interracial communication.

Race relations in general and communication effectiveness between blacks and whites in particular will improve only when individuals break away from dysfunctional patterns of the past and present and accept others as co-equal partners in social interaction. Such a change must be based on understanding how race functions in communication—the primary goal of this book.

Acknowledgments

I have received the assistance and encouragement of many individuals, without whose support I could not have completed this project. Howie Giles has been supportive every step of the way, and whatever favorable qualities this book is judged to have will directly reflect his guidance. I owe Howie a huge debt of gratitude. At Peter Lang, Mary Savigar was great at keeping me on track, nudging me toward deadlines, and helping me stay focused. I extend my heartfelt thanks to Mary.

In addition to Howie, there are various scholars from whom I have benefited over the years through discussions about race, language, and communication. Walt Wolfram, of course, has considerable expertise in linguistic issues, but he also has excellent insights into communication and social interaction. I deeply appreciate the opportunities to meet with Walt during his many visits to Cleveland State University. The late Howard Mims, through his knowledge and teaching, and by virtue of his character, was a wonderful source of ideas, many of which were due to his life experiences, both within and outside of academia. It was also useful for me to discuss portions of this book with audiences at Bowling Green State University and John Carroll University, as well as with colleagues at Cleveland State University.

Teaching interracial communication has given me a significant depth of experience, both intellectual and personal. I, therefore, want to thank the many Cleveland State students who have taken classes from me over the years. My interracial interactions in the classroom have helped me develop a far better understanding of interracial communication.

Finally, I wish to thank my family, Eileen, Bryan, and Lesley. You not only encouraged me to keep pushing ahead on this book but also added to my knowledge by discussing your own interracial experiences with me.

CHAPTER 1

Introduction to Interracial Communication

This is a book about the nature of interracial communication, the goal being to help readers understand the historical background of interracial communication in the United States; some patterns that often occur when blacks and whites communicate; several critical variables such as language, education, employment, stereotyping, and discourse; and, finally, some strategies that can help improve communication effectiveness when racial differences are present.[1] This chapter explains some primary issues that help frame our study of interracial communication and also previews the chapters that follow.

Primary Issues in the Study of Interracial Communication

Consider the results of two experiments in social psychology, both conducted at universities within the United States. In the first study, white and black student participants completed questionnaires about several interracial issues (e.g., wanting more friends who are white [or black], likelihood of seeking out friends who are white [or black], etc.). Questionnaires also contained this description (Shelton & Richeson, 2005, p. 95):

> You enter the dining hall for dinner. You are alone because your close friends are in a review session. As you look around the dining hall for a place to sit you notice several White [Black] students who live near you sitting together. These students also notice you. However, neither of you explicitly makes a move to sit together.

Half of the participants imagined that the students in the dining room were white, while the other half imagined that those in the dining room were black. The participants then responded to several questions about fear of rejection because of race, lack of interest in getting to know the others, and the others' lack of interest in wanting to get to know the participant.

---

[1] This book will interchangeably use the terms black and African American, and white and European American.

Among the findings were these patterns: (1) whites and blacks were interested in having contact with one another, but they tended to believe those of the other race did not want to have contact with them; (2) whites believed they were more interested in having contact with blacks than they believed blacks were interested in having contact with them; (3) whites felt there were factors that would probably prevent themselves and blacks from initiating contact; and (4) participants felt that their own inaction was based on fear of rejection, but that inaction by those from the other race showed a lack of interest (Shelton & Richeson, 2005).

Next, consider a second study involving communication expectations and race (Shelton, Richeson, & Salvatore, 2005). Participants consisted of minority students, half of whom were African Americans, approximately half of whom also had white roommates. The participants completed questionnaires with items related to interracial encounters with their roommates, including: liking, negative emotions, self-disclosure, and authenticity. Later, participants read several newspaper articles, one of which referred to ethnic minorities experiencing prejudice and discrimination. Participants then interacted with other participants (mixed ethnicity and no prior acquaintance) during an exercise in which they were instructed to take a few minutes to get to know each other.

Among the findings: (1) ethnic minorities anticipating prejudice during their interactions with whites tended to have negative experiences during their interactions with white partners (more negative emotions, liked their partner less, felt less authentic); (2) after interactions with minority participants who were anticipating racial prejudice, whites had more positive feelings about the interaction and liked their partner more (Shelton, Richeson, & Salvatore, 2005).

Given the approach this book takes, these two studies offer an excellent introduction to key concerns in the study of interracial communication. In these two studies, we can see that blacks and whites often have different perspectives toward interracial communication, that whites and blacks have different expectations about interracial encounters, that blacks and whites may experience the same communication encounters differently, and that what one expects to happen during an interaction can affect how one behaves during and later feels about a communication encounter.

Let us note three intriguing findings from these two studies. First, we see that blacks and whites would like to have contact with those from the other race. Yet, these students said they do not believe those of the other race want to have contact with them. Second, white students said they did not initiate contact with blacks because they feared the black students would reject them because of their race. However, the same white students felt that the black students did not initiate contact due to a lack of interest. Third, in the second study we see that when minority students expect to experience prejudice from whites, they tend to have more negative experiences during their interactions. However, whites tend to have a positive experience while interacting with minorities who are expecting prejudice. As Shelton et al. (2005) note, minorities who expect prejudice may engage in compensatory strategies, behaviors that lead to a cordial interaction and dispel negative racial stereotypes. Thus, a minority person may act to present him or herself in a more likable manner, the result of which can make the interaction more pleasant to the other. The provocative results from these two studies open our eyes and expose our thoughts to some of the intricacies of communication processes involving race.

Components of Interracial Communication

During the first 250 years of black/white interaction in North America, interracial contact was largely governed by rules, customs, and laws that severely restricted spontaneous, natural forms of interaction. Over the last 100 years, blacks and whites have increasingly interacted more freely. Yet, black/white interactions display dysfunctional outcomes too much of the time, leaving many of us feeling perplexed and dissatisfied. Our approach to interracial communication begins with an examination of some fundamental issues that can help us orient our thoughts about race and communication: interracial communication, race, racism, and notions of ethnic diversity and distinctiveness.

The Idea of Interracial Communication

From a casual perusal of news and publications in the popular press, let us note the following: (1) the American Medical Association formally apologized for its past policy of excluding African American physicians from its membership (MSNBC.com, 2008); (2) a prominent radio personality was vilified for making racist and sexist slurs about black members of a women's basketball team (Kosova, 2007); (3) a black comedian, Paul Mooney, vowed to stop using the word *nigger* in his comedy performances (Asim, 2007); and (4) a black professor of law writes that many claims of racial injustice are often trivial complaints in reaction to unintended slights (Ford, 2008). These examples are but a tiny sampling of literally thousands of race-related news items that could be noted. What these incidents have in common is that they are all a part of the process of interracial communication.

Orbe and Harris (2008) define interracial communication as "the transactional process of message exchange between individuals in a situational context where racial difference is perceived as a salient factor by at least one person" (p. 6). This is a broad conceptualization and, as Orbe and Harris (2008) note, it is a working definition. For present purposes, we can adopt this definition while also commenting on some of its features. The idea of transactional process is important because communication involving race invariably entails interactants' claims of their identities, as well as negotiation of their identities. The notion of context is also important. Many discussions in this book will examine face-to-face interaction in specified settings. Interracial encounters in school, in the workplace, in community dialogues, and other settings exhibit patterns that are shaped and constrained by rules and customs that apply to the given situation. Although there are also patterns of interracial communication that transcend context, certain settings consist of distinct circumstances that affect communication outcomes.

Finally, in defining interracial communication we must call attention to the awareness of racial difference as a matter of crucial importance. Chapter 2 reviews the history of race relations in the United States, one main point of which is to argue for the significance of race and its existence at the sociopolitical core of American history. Identity, of course, can have many influences (e.g., gender, age, occupation, etc.), but we must recognize that race is capable of shaping identity in a highly distinctive manner. Race has a way of sharply intruding into social interactions, as shown in this incident described by Shipler (1997, p. 65):

> When they did a play at one of our elementary schools in Brookline and a black boy tried out, recalled Jean Maguire, the voluble director of Metco, the principal said: "You can't be that. You're black." It was a Shakespearean play. He couldn't be in it because he was black. And he was furious.

There is a great deal of social interaction in the United States during which the race of the participants exerts a notable impact on identity. When one's identity has a strong racial character, we can say the identity is "raced" (Rawls, 2000) — meaning the category of race stands out and becomes an important influence on identity and the ensuing interaction. Race has a range of complicated influences on communication and affects whites as well as blacks. However, as the dominant group in the United

States, European Americans typically face fewer disadvantages associated with being "raced."

The definition of Orbe and Harris (2008) helps us see that identities, messages, context, and racial identity (avowed or ascribed) all function together during interracial communication. This book examines a number of variables that enter into interracial communication, even when the context is not a face-to-face meeting. For example, Chapter 5 discusses racial stereotypes and images from the mass media. At first glance, media images may not seem pertinent to face-to-face communication. As will be shown, however, stereotypes from mass media affect how we perceive, categorize, and interact with others, therefore, indicating how such group-related identities are influential in face-to-face communication.

Race

One of the most enduring, consequential, and far-reaching concepts in modern life is that of race. There is a long history associated with race, and thoughts of race have evolved as a result of trends in science, culture, and politics. In a most basic sense, race means a group of people who share characteristics based on cultural heritage and physical appearance. This notion of race connotes a visibly identifiable group that can be thought of as a people. Two important properties have been traditionally associated with race: culture and heredity. In ordinary, customary usage, race has referred to human groups with shared cultural characteristics including social customs, religion, language, and other qualities that contribute to ethnicity. For example, Chapter 2 notes how 18th-century ethnologists identified major groups (e.g., Mongolians, Malays, etc.) who were thought to be relatively intact and homogeneous and were also differentiated by their appearance (e.g., skin color, hair, facial features, etc.). That such groups were differentiated by appearance was presumably due to inherited biological traits. Thus, characterizing a group as a race incorporated the ideas of cultural patterns and biological traits.

The concept of race was always problematic, but its shortcomings have become glaringly apparent in the age of modern biology and genetics. The essential difficulty is that so-called races exhibit so much variety, that the differences within groups are greater than the differences between groups (Blum, 2002). Biologist Richard Lewontin has stated, "Of all human genetic variation, 85 percent is between individual people within a nation or tribe" (1995, p. 123). Thus, genetic characteristics vary so little between the traditionally classified racial groups that they render the concept of race meaningless. As Graves (2004) observes: "In other words, the variability that makes one African-American person different from another is greater than the variability between African Americans and Swedes or Tibetans or Amazonian tribes" (p. 10). From a biological standpoint, there is one human species and the genetic similarities among all humans far outweigh the differences. This is not to say there are no genetic differences whatsoever among humans. However, to maintain that there are significant and defining genetic differences between groups does not hold up to scientific scrutiny. On the basis of scientific evidence, there is no such thing as race.

Yet, there is such a thing as race in the sense that people use it in a nontechnical way to refer to human similarities and differences. To cite just one case in point, a recent survey (Pew Research Center, 2008) reveals that 31 percent of whites and 48 percent of blacks say that race of a candidate is an important consideration in how they would vote in an election. In this sense, it could be said that race exists because individuals find the concept and term useful, in some way. Race exists in our language and communication because we collaborate in perpetuating its use. In effect, race remains in our vocabulary and thoughts, not because it has scientific validity, but because we socially construct a sense of race (Montagu, 1997).

As a social construction, race may be thought of as arbitrary and given to shifting meanings, as opposed to something that has a verifiable existence in nature. For example, male and female may be thought of as natural categories in that there is a verifiable, biological basis for this distinction. Masculinity and femininity, however, do not exist in nature. Femininity (or masculinity) refers to behavior that is prescribed in a given culture (Wood, 2009). Therefore, one could say masculinity and femininity are socially constructed. Similarly, when one refers to European Americans as white, the reference makes use of a social construction. Blum (2002) observes that it is incorrect to refer to an ethnic group as a race, when what is actually meant is a racialized group. Races do not exist, but racialized groups do.

In this book, there are many references to race, race relations, and various race-related phenomena. Such uses of the word "race" are understood to conform to the socially constructed sense of the term. It must also be emphasized that our culture has been so infused with the notion of race that it must nevertheless be recognized as real and consequential. Furthermore, let us note that some individuals still maintain belief in a biological basis for race—an orientation that interferes with interracial friendship formation and leads to feelings that the disadvantaged status of racial out-group members is justified (Williams & Eberhardt, 2008). In several respects, therefore, notions of race are ever-present, and it is unrealistic to believe that in the foreseeable future we can somehow overcome or get beyond race: As Omi and Winant (1994, p. 55) assert:

> A more effective starting point is the recognition that despite its uncertainties and contradictions, the concept of race continues to play a fundamental role in structuring and representing the social world. The task for theory is to explain this situation.

This book fully acknowledges the presence of race in our culture. By conducting an analysis of race and communication that is based on important theoretical insights, this book attempts to make sense of the many influences of race on communication and social interaction.

Racism

Racism is defined by Fenton (1999) as "ideas which claim to classify different races and view these races as fundamentally different and unequal; and it refers to the reproduction of a racialised system of inequality itself" (p. 62). This definition, as with most definitions of racism, includes notions of power and hierarchies. By recognizing groups of people in a racial sense and assigning differences in status to these groups, racism enables those of higher status to exert social, political, and economic dominance over groups of lower status.

Defining racism is difficult because it has cultural, political, and historical dimensions that give it different meanings at different times and in different places. As an analysis of interracial communication in the United States, this book considers the role of racism in its U.S. American context. Fredrickson (1988) concludes that in the United States racism has existed in two forms: ideological and societal. As an ideology, racism in the United States did not fully develop until the 19th century when pro-slavery forces defended the institution of slavery against attacks from humanitarians who wanted to abolish it (Fredrickson, 1988). By the 18th century, however, societal racism had already emerged as various forms of discrimination were aimed at maintaining a white-dominated society with blacks in the lowest socioeconomic position.

Fredrickson (1988) notes that even though the 20th-century civil rights movement succeeded in eliminating or greatly diminishing the presence of ideological racism, societal racism has been and remains embedded deeply in American culture. Many references to racism in this book are influenced by Fredrickson's concept of societal racism, a component of American culture whose presence continues to be felt.

Diversity and Distinctiveness

When blacks and whites are discussed in the following chapters, we must note that the terms are meant to apply generally. However, it is readily acknowledged that these terms encompass great variations within groups. African Americans and European Americans are groupings that include tremendous diversity owing to socioeconomic, cultural, linguistic, regional, and other variations. Thus, a reference to one group or another must be taken in a general sense, meaning what is typical or mainstream. Few if any research findings about blacks or whites apply to every single person so identified. However, research findings in the following chapters attest to the fact that a significant number of blacks and whites, separately and in interaction, can be meaningfully described in general terms.

It has recently been forecast that by 2042 European Americans will constitute less than 50 percent of the population of the United States (Dougherty, 2008). The United States is steadily becoming more ethnically diverse, and one may question this book's emphasis on black/white race relations. Are not black/white relations becoming less distinctive and, therefore, less important in an era of increasing national diversity?

One reason for this book's focus is that black/white relations have been the most significant domain of interethnic relations in American history. As Marger (2009) states:

> The experience of African Americans is unique among American ethnic minorities. No other group entered the society as involuntary immigrants, and no other group was subsequently victimized by two centuries of slavery. The vestiges of these social facts account for the uninterrupted, if vacillating, conflict between whites and blacks throughout American history and the agonizing nature of adjustment of blacks to a predominantly white society. (p. 164)

Marger's quote underscores what can be called black exceptionalism, the distinctive status of African Americans as a minority group in the United States (Sears, Citrin, Cheleden, & van Laar, 1999). For example, across a range of issues including affirmative action, housing, and stereotypes related to employment, researchers find that African Americans are more likely to be treated negatively than Latinos, Asians, or Native Americans (Skrentny, 2002). In their study of white attitudes toward public policies affecting various minorities, Sears et al. (1999) note: "In brief, white

Americans do not treat all outgroups equally. Specifically, anti-black attitudes have a disproportionate influence over whites' preferences about policies relevant to any minority group" (p. 63).

Furthermore, rates of intermarriage with European Americans are far higher for Latino and Asian Americans than African Americans (Jacobs & Labov, 2002). Skrentny (2002) also notes that children from intermarriages involving Latinos and Asians generally do not result in the offspring exhibiting an Asian or Latino identity, unless the child chooses to do so. Yet, a child from a black/white marriage is more likely to be classified as black. In these instances, we see evidence for the main argument for black exceptionalism, that compared to other minority groups in the United States, the African American experience shows a distinctiveness that sets it apart.

A second reason for this book's black/white focus lies in the necessity of examining the contemporary status of interethnic relations in the United States in terms of race. Now, in the early 21st century, the United States may be taking significant steps toward becoming a post-ethnic, or post-racial society (Hollinger, 2000). As already noted and as will be further discussed in Chapter 6, there is increasing diversity within the United States for all cultural groups, including African Americans. Yet, a defining feature of minority status in the United States has been and remains blackness. Hollinger (2008) asserts: "Blackness is the pivotal concept in the intellectual and administrative apparatus used in the United States for dealing with ethnoracial distinctions" (B8). As the chief marker of racial classification in the United States, blackness must be accounted for as it functions in its contemporary sense. Race relations in the United States have evolved over nearly 400 years of black and white interaction. With each evolutionary turn, race and race relations changed into something somewhat different from what these were in the past but still remained related to the past. As a review and synthesis of research, this book examines the current state of interracial communication and helps clarify how race is operating in contemporary society.

Organization of the Chapters

This book attempts to systematically analyze the most relevant topics that bear on the discussion of interracial communication. The focus is on key issues involved in face-to-face interaction, with emphasis on language and patterns of communication in specific settings. Stereotyping and related social cognitive processes are also discussed, the point being that presuppositions and expectations have important effects on interracial communication. The first five chapters explain some of the important background issues in history and language and also discuss some common patterns of interracial communication, thus laying the groundwork for the concluding chapter that considers models of race relations. A final discussion presents two proposals for communication practices that can lead to more effective interracial communication. Here is a brief preview of the contents of each chapter:

Chapter 2 takes a historical perspective on American race relations. Interracial communication in the United States has a unique character; however, there were important European influences on race relations in the American colonies and in the early days of the United States. One of the points of Chapter 2 is to argue that race relations constitute a fundamental component of American history.

One central topic in Chapter 3 is African American Vernacular English (AAVE). In examining AAVE, we find not only that this dialect has distinctive features but also that its distinctiveness shows how it contrasts with Standard American English (SAE). This chapter also discusses speech style and some important sociolinguistic variables that enter into interracial communication. One goal of Chapter 3 is to show how different ways of speaking English can affect interracial communication.

Chapter 4 examines how interracial interactions can result in particular patterns of communication in two important settings: the school and the workplace. Language is emphasized in the discussion of interracial communication in education, with attention given to learning outcomes directly affected by language. Expectations and self-fulfilling prophecies are also key issues in interracial communication and education. In employment, not only does communication affect individuals in one-on-one situations, but also workplace communication patterns reflect underlying predispositions toward race and diversity present within organizational structures.

The nature of stereotyping is the main topic in Chapter 5. This chapter discusses some basic aspects of the stereotyping process — the cultural and social cognitive origins of racial stereotypes — and contains examples of the influence of stereotyping in interracial communication. This chapter also discusses some prominent discourse themes that illustrate how race and race-related events are often discussed in contemporary society.

Chapter 6 examines several models of race relations and discusses how communication plays a role in the production and reproduction of racial discrimination. This chapter also argues for multiculturalism as a viable model for the overall improvement of race relations. A final section focuses on interracial contact as a critical variable in race relations and also shows how two communication strategies can promote more effective interracial contact.

Conclusion

Interracial communication involves identities, messages, contexts, and, of course, race. Because race does not refer to human groups with unique characteristics that are scientifically demonstrable, we use race in an arbitrary manner. The way we use the term "race," therefore, is the result of a social construction. By recognizing the idea of race in our language and culture, we can better understand racism and its effects. *Language and Interracial Communication in the United States: Speaking in Black and White* analyzes the history of race relations in the United States, as well as several related issues in language, education, employment, stereotyping, and discourse. This book concludes by examining models of race relations and offering proposals for practices that could improve interracial communication effectiveness. As we read, think about, and discuss these various subjects we can attempt to reach our primary goal, which is to understand the nature of interracial communication.

CHAPTER 2

An Overview of Race Relations in the United States

Chapter 2 argues that a valuable perspective on interracial communication is gained by surveying the development of race relations throughout American history. The historical perspective is worthwhile and necessary in two respects. First, as noted by Husband (1977), it is important to contextualize intergroup relations in their own historicity. In the case of African Americans, there are unique circumstances surrounding relations with the dominant society that must be understood in their historical contexts. Second, as noted in Chapter 1, understanding race relations in the United States is fundamental to the American experience (Marable, 2002). Throughout American history, everyone in the United States has been directly affected by race relations, appreciation of which helps us understand how race relations came to be what they are today.

This chapter shows how race-related attitudes in the United States originated and grew out of events and trends over 750 years in European history. After discussing some European influences on race and racism, this chapter then outlines the course of race relations in the history of the United States, including the Colonial Era, the Antebellum Era, the Civil War, Reconstruction and the Jim Crow Era, and the Modern Civil Rights Era.

Early Developments in Race Relations: The Emergence of Racism in Europe

Fredrickson (2002) offers an insightful overview of racism as it emerged in later Western Civilization. The rise of racist attitudes was part of the cultural trends that began in the European Middle Ages. One pattern was that of Christians in the 12th and 13th centuries persecuting Jews and showing intolerance toward anyone deviating from accepted standards of conduct and morality. This pattern was particularly true in Spain where, between the 15th and 16th centuries, Jews and Muslims were not only persecuted but were also regarded as being of different blood (Menocal, 2002).

Another development was a trend in medieval Spain and Portugal that led to an acceptance of black Africans as slaves. Prior to their expulsion from Spain in 1492, Muslims had practiced slavery for several hundred years (Sweet, 1997). Both blacks and whites were held as slaves; however, the more menial and undesirable tasks were often assigned to blacks. Over time, skin color became a significant symbol associating blackness with slave status.

Taken together, the persecution of Jews and Muslims, standards for ethnic purity, and the acceptance of blacks as slaves, these trends in the Middle Ages were important developments leading to the rise of modern racism. Although there were noted religious influences on racial attitudes in medieval Europe, Fredrickson (2002) argues that modern racism was not realized until its underpinnings developed apart from Christianity. Despite its previous association with persecution, Christian doctrine during the late medieval and early modern periods held that salvation was available to all who were baptized, thus there was a belief that people everywhere had a kind of equality in the eyes of God (Fredrickson, 2002; Smedley, 1993). The conflicting views on race within the Christian community suggest a divided and mitigated religious influence on racist ideology. Modern racist ideology apparently stemmed more from science and philosophy than from religion.

Roots of Modern Racism

Natural History in the Enlightenment

In his extensive analysis of the concept of race, Montagu (1997) explains how noted naturalists in the 18th century, including Buffon, Linnaeus, and Blumenbach, all contemplated the notion of race. Montagu notes that Buffon's connotation of race was that humans were a single species, but that geographically separate groups could be described as being of differing types. This reasoning derived from belief in monogenesis, the notion that all humans were of a common origin. Along with Buffon, Linnaeus did not establish rankings among human types, but he seems to have made qualitative distinctions. To Linnaeus (quoted in Eze, 1997, p. 13) Europeans are "gentle, acute, inventive and...governed by laws" whereas black Africans are "crafty, indolent, negligent...governed by caprice." Blumenbach (1865/ 1969) concludes that all humans are of one species, postulating that there were five original human types, including Caucasian, Mongolian, Ethiopian, American, and Malay. Blumenbach also states that the Caucasus region was the point of origin for humans, thereby hypothesizing that the earliest humans were white and that all other varieties then diverged from the Caucasians.

Enlightenment naturalists, as both Fredrickson (2002) and Montagu (1997) point out, did not use the concept of race in the sense of biologically unique groups of humans. In the mid- to late 18th century, a number of scholars maintained belief in the monogenesis thesis. It was thought that variations such as appearance and aptitude were not due to immutable traits but were rather attributable to other factors such as climate, soil, and vegetation.

During the 17th and 18th centuries, stories and records from European explorers stimulated interest in people from distant lands (Montagu, 1997). As naturalists and other scholars became interested in studying humankind in all its varieties, ethnic prejudices were clearly evident in their thinking. People from Asia, Africa, the Americas, and other distant places were regarded as unfamiliar, strange, and uncivilized (Eze, 1997). Europe was viewed as civilized and advanced, while natives from foreign lands were often viewed as savages.

In time, geographically oriented explanations for human differences fell out of favor. Naturalists became more intent on comparing anatomical differences among humans (Augstein, 1996), and by early 19th century some of the first biologically based concepts of race began to appear. However, in addition to insights from naturalists, the tenets of Enlightenment philosophy also influenced perspectives on race.

Enlightenment Philosophy

Two important topics in Enlightenment philosophy bear examination: personhood and human rights. Philosophers during the Enlightenment were drawn to fundamental issues concerning the state of nature and the state of man. Locke (1690/1960), Rousseau (1762/1950), and Kant (1784/1963) represent philosophers who considered humans to have originally existed in a state of nature—a condition without government, written laws, or organizations that extended much beyond the family or ethnic clans. In one sense, state of nature referred to the God-granted existence into which all humans are born (Locke, 1690/1960). In this natural state, humans are endowed with reason and are motivated to act, autonomously, on behalf of self-preservation. In the state of nature, all people are free, independent, and equal. When humans agree to form political entities that establish rules for a civil society, they then leave the state of nature and enter the state of man. Through individual consent those in the state of man may form a government and set forth laws that serve the common interests of life, liberty, and property. In a second sense, state of nature referred to humans living in an unspoiled, primitive condition, felt to be more authentic than European society. Those who populated the uncivilized world, although considered savages, nevertheless lived in a condition marked by purity and innocence.

A prominent current of Enlightenment thought, therefore, was that primitive peoples, even those who enjoyed an unspoiled life, were not civilized and were different from Europeans. From a Eurocentric point of view, the state of man encompassed civilization and its achievement of moral judgment and justice. Within this branch of Enlightenment philosophy, to enter society and acquire personhood meant leaving the state of nature, as had occurred in Europe.

Philosophical views on human and political rights were influenced by scholars such as Locke (1690/1960), whose writings affirm that humans by nature are free and independent. Only by his consent can man be subjected to the authority of a government. Thus, Locke was proposing that ordinary citizens could join together to form a civil society by means of a social contract that provided for individual rights. However, Locke's views on slavery and human rights are not clearly consistent. Locke argues against slavery in most forms including hereditary slavery, although he allows for slavery as the result of a just war. Locke also helped draft the constitution for the Carolina Colony in North America (Welchman, 1995), sections of which gave slaveowners extensive authority over Negro slaves. Inasmuch as Africans were taken against their will and then enslaved in North America, it is not clear how such enslavement could be viewed as the result of a just war (Mills, 1997).

Montesquieu (1748/1989), another Enlightenment philosopher, champions the democratic model of government that protects individuals' rights through a system of checks and balances among legislative, executive, and judicial branches. Montesquieu asserts that there are certain societies in which democracy is not viable; although clearly opposed to slavery in a democratic republic, he nevertheless notes there are places where a right to slavery exists.

There were diverse philosophical perspectives expressed throughout the Enlightenment and clear patterns can be difficult to summarize. However, several philosophical tenets from the Enlightenment influenced culture and politics in the United States and became fundamental to what Mills (1997) terms the racial contract. Under the social contract, individuals leave the state of nature and agree to live together in a civil society. Mills (1997) argues that the social contract actually encompasses three forms of contract: political, moral, and epistemological. The political contract leads to the formation of the state and the rights and liberties that exist within it. The moral contract leads to codes of ethical conduct in society. The epistemological contract leads to society's standards for what is accepted as knowledge. Mills' notion of the racial contract is a set of formal and informal agreements among members of one group of humans construed as "white" to categorize all others as "nonwhite" and of a different and inferior moral status. Mills (1997) notes:

> but in any case the general purpose of the Contract is always the differential privileging of the whites as a group with respect to the nonwhites as a group, the exploitation of their bodies, lands, and resources, and the denial of equal socioeconomic opportunities to them. All whites are *beneficiaries* of the Contract, though some whites are not *signatories* to it. (p. 11, italics in the original)

Mills further argues that the epistemological and moral components of the racial contract have helped determine what counts as factual knowledge (e.g., who is white, who is a person) and what counts as proper conduct in society (e.g., what is equitable, what is just). All told, according to Mills (1997), the racial contract has resulted in a durable system of white privilege that whites have constructed and yet not fully grasped:

> Thus, in effect, on matters related to race, the Racial Contract prescribes for its signatories an inverted epistemology, an epistemology of ignorance, a particular pattern of localized and global cognitive dysfunctions (which are psychologically and socially functional), producing the ironic outcome that whites will in general be unable to understand the world they themselves have made. (p. 18)

Mills' racial contract is a formal explanation of how major scientific, social, philosophical, and political outgrowths of the Enlightenment helped shape European cultural assumptions that became influential in the United States. Over time, societies in the colonies diverged from European cultural traditions, but regarding the rise of racism, several patterns persisted: the association of blacks with slavery, a system of white privilege, a low regard for the mental abilities of blacks, the viewpoint that Africans were uncivilized, and acceptance of slavery as a means to benefit European owners of property. Although chattel slavery was no longer practiced in England (Fredrickson, 1988), enslavement of Africans was allowed and sanctioned in the British colonies in North America, thus there was a predisposition toward racism present in the early days of European life in North America.

Race Relations in the United States

The generally accepted date for the first arrival of Africans in North America is 1619 when 20 blacks were brought to Jamestown by Dutch traders (Reiss, 1997). According to the law at the time, these Africans became indentured servants and, indeed, for the first 30 to 40 years blacks in Virginia were not generally enslaved. However, by the mid-17th century laws began appearing that enabled the enslavement of Africans (Kolchin, 1993).

The vast subject of race relations in the United States encompasses far more than the advent of slavery. However, the practice of slavery in the United States was of such overarching significance that race relations must be viewed from a perspective that fully incorporates the institution of slavery, the legacy of which was to be felt long after its demise. We turn first to the early years of slavery in the North American colonies.

The Colonial Era

In his comprehensive historical analysis of North American slavery, Berlin (1998) describes the appearance of Africans in the Americas as part of a large-scale trans-Atlantic system of trade. During the 15th and early 16th centuries, Europeans in West African trading centers bought and sold weapons, textiles, gold, and African slaves. As trade flourished, Europeans and Africans frequently interacted and learned parts of each other's languages and ways of doing business. Africans and Europeans intermarried to some extent, although these marriages were not widely accepted by either community. The offspring of these marriages have been referred to as Atlantic creoles (Berlin, 1998).

The Atlantic creoles did not hold a secure social position in their communities; however, they were skilled negotiators who assisted in procuring and selling slaves (Berlin, 1998). The West African slave trade also involved agents from the interior of Africa (Wright, 1990). Through the interactions among Africans, Europeans, and the Atlantic creoles, the early West African pidgin languages developed (Holm, 1988), from which certain linguistic and communication patterns emerged that would play a role in the subsequent evolution of African American Vernacular English.

During the 17th and 18th centuries, trade in and around the ports of West Africa grew substantially, accompanied by a steady rise in the number of slaves. During the 16th century, many slaves were bought and sold by the Portuguese, Spanish, and the Dutch; however, by the mid-17th century, slave traders from England accounted for a far greater proportion of the African slave trade than those from any other nation (Eltis, 2000). The English slave trade in the Caribbean and South America was most significant. The slaves sold to North Americans by all Europeans constituted only 6 percent of the total number of African slaves brought to the West (Fogel & Engerman, 1974). Nevertheless, by 1680 there were nearly 7,000 slaves in North America, and by 1700 there were over 28,900 (Berlin, 1998).

Although there were slaves in every North American British colony, in the northern colonies there were fewer slaves because the local agricultural economy did not lend itself to large-scale farming as in the Chesapeake (Maryland and Virginia) and the Lower South. Slaves in the North were more likely to live in or near cities and work as household servants, farmhands, and general laborers (Kolchin, 1993). It is noteworthy that in the northern regions slaves were more likely to gain their freedom. By 1790, 40 percent of the blacks in the North were free and by 1810, 74 percent were free (Berlin, 1998).

In the agricultural areas in the early to mid-17th century, it was common to find indentured servants of European origin; however, by the late 17th century, Africans became increasingly relied upon for agricultural labor. There were economic advantages to slave labor and Africans were considered suitable for manual labor. Reliance on slave labor was also facilitated by the slaveholders' ability to exert greater physical and psychological force in controlling their slave laborers (Fogel, 1989).

Colonial settlers enacted slave codes—laws that governed the status and treatment of slaves (Wright, 1990). Treatment of slaves and indentured servants included corporal punishments such as whipping and mutilation (Kolchin, 1993). In the early 17th century, Africans in the Chesapeake commonly became indentured servants, although some Atlantic creoles and other Africans enjoyed some rights available to white settlers including marriage, ownership of property, and rights to settle certain disputes in court (Berlin, 1998). During the 17th century, black laborers and European indentured servants often worked alongside the English planters in the Chesapeake, resulting in a particular influence on language in that region.

Harsh treatment of African slaves began with practices among the slave traders in Africa (Thomas, 1997). Slavery had been practiced in Africa for some time; however, the value and number of slaves rose with the emergence of the trans-Atlantic trade. Those who became slaves were often kidnapped or were victims of wars and were then taken to port settlements where they were held in confinement. Curtin (1969) states that

great numbers of slaves died while being taken to seaports, while wait-
ing to be transported and during the trans-Atlantic voyage. Considering
that the total number of slaves shipped to the Americas is estimated to be
between 10,000,000 and 12,000,000, and that anywhere from 10 to 20 percent of those died during the Atlantic crossing, the number of slaves who
died in the process of being captured, sold, and shipped to the West is
staggering (Behrendt, 1999; Curtin, 1969; Johnson & Campbell, 1981). The
trans-Atlantic slave trade constituted an enterprise of immense parame-
ters: "Over the course of four centuries it caused the greatest interconti-
nental migration in world history to that time, and it affected people and
the history of their offspring on all lands bordering the Atlantic" (Wright,
1990, p. 17).

During the Atlantic crossing many slaves died due to disease, malnu-
trition, beatings, and suicide. Once the slaves reached North America,
their severe treatment continued with physical force being used to pun-
ish as well as to demoralize slaves (Berlin, 1998). The treatment of slaves
and growth in the slave population began to affect the social and political
climate in the colonies.

As previously stated, by the mid-17th century, blacks in the Chesapeake were becoming regarded as slaves. Over the next 50 to 75 years,
the southern colonies evolved from societies with slaves into slave societies. In the North American colonial context, societies with slaves incorporated slaves into a general class of laborers and servants. However,
slavery was central neither to the primary economy nor to the social
structure as in a master-slave system. In slave societies, the use of slave
labor became integral to the economy and social structure. Slaveholders
gained control of their regional governments and through slave codes
extended their authority over the lives of the slaves. By the time of the
prerevolutionary period, the colonies in the Chesapeake and Lower
South had transformed themselves into slave societies, while the other
colonies gradually changed into societies with slaves (Berlin, 1998).

In the 1770s, a fluid political milieu existed in the colonies as some
people retained their loyalty to Britain, many fought for independence,
and more blacks began obtaining freedom. In 1777, slavery was abolished in Vermont and shortly thereafter in Massachusetts (Kolchin, 1993).
By the early 19th century, all northern states had either abolished or were
in the process of abolishing slavery. Free blacks were much less common
in the South where, by 1810, the free black population constituted 3.9
percent of all blacks (Kolchin, 1993).

Before steering our discussion away from the Colonial Era, one other significant subject must be addressed. As the colonial leaders met to draft the Constitution, slavery had become a major and divisive issue, especially regarding questions of taxation and states' wealth (Fehrenbacher, 2001). Taxing slaves as property and recognizing the personhood of slaves became critical issues. Furthermore, if slaves were considered persons, would they then be counted along with all others for the purposes of representation in the U.S. Congress?

The debates had a major effect on the content of the Constitution. But the debates also revealed how fundamental the practice of slavery had become in an array of issues concerning the new government, including congressional representation, taxation, voting, civil rights, interstate commerce, international trade, and foreign relations. In order to form a government that could assert federal powers as well as reserve certain powers for the states, the framers of the Constitution compromised on key points pertaining to slavery. Finkelman (2001) claims that the Constitution was a pro-slavery document in several important respects including: (a) prohibition of citizenship for nonwhites; (b) representation in Congress according to which a slave was counted in a state's population as three-fifths of a person; (c) a prohibition against ending the importation of slaves before 1808 (as opposed to an immediate ban); (d) a prohibition against a fugitive slave from a slave state obtaining freedom in a free state; and (e) provisions for fugitive slaves to be returned to their owners.

Finkelman (2001) points out that the three-fifths clause immediately gave slave states increased representation in Congress, and if new slave states were added to the union, this representational advantage would become greater still. Thus, slaves could not vote, but their presence augmented the congressional voting strength of slave states. Was the Constitution a pro-slavery document? Richards (2000) points out:

> In the sixty-two years between Washington's election and the Compromise of 1850, for example, slaveholders controlled the presidency for 50 years, the Speaker's chair for forty-one years, and the chairmanship of the House Ways and Means committee for forty-two years. The only men to be re-elected president—Washington, Jefferson, Madison, Monroe, and Jackson—were all slaveholders. The men who sat in the Speaker's chair the longest—Henry Clay, Andrew Stevenson, and Nathaniel Macon—were slaveholders. Eighteen out of thirty-one Supreme Court justices were slaveholders. (p. 9)

Clearly, the Constitution afforded the pro-slavery factions important opportunities to prolong the practice and influence of slavery. It is a bitter irony that after the American colonists set forth the Declaration of Independence, fought a war for independence, and then adopted the Constitution, in 1790 the 717,000 slaves in the United States (Berlin, 1998) were recognized as less than whole persons and were regarded as property, not to mention restrictions placed against them regarding citizenship, voting, due process, and other rights. In the case of the United States Constitution, one can easily see how Mills would conclude that the racial contract was in full force in the earliest days of the United States.

The Antebellum Era

The general theme of race relations during the pre-Civil War period was the emergence of an interracial interaction field that included free blacks in the North living in a social caste system, and slaves in the South who faced a pro-slavery ideological entrenchment.

The Antebellum North

It is significant that the first generations of slaves were given names by their masters (Berlin, 2003; Kolchin, 1993). Over time, slaves made their own choices in naming their children, although they often ended up using the names provided by their masters (Kolchin, 1993). By the early 19th century, however, free blacks in the North were taking English first names for themselves, and they also began claiming English surnames such as Johnson and Moore (Berlin, 1998). The symbolic significance of the name-changing process was that free blacks were determined to leave behind the vestiges of slavery and establish new identities for themselves. As a marker of a shift in identity formation, changes in naming patterns symbolized an emerging cultural orientation for blacks.

In the early 19th century, many blacks in the North were ex-slaves and freedom from a master was of extreme significance. Yet, blacks in many areas were able to obtain only marginal employment, often as day laborers (Berlin, 2003). Many blacks could afford to live only in modest housing, often in districts within or near cities and populated by other similarly affected blacks.

Most northern states restricted voting rights for blacks and even in 1840 there were virtually no voting rights for 93 percent of the free blacks in the North (Litwack, 1961). Northern blacks typically were excluded from serving on juries and there were no black judges (Litwack, 1961). Other restrictions imposed by states and localities included curfews, posting of bonds to insure good behavior, and limited rights to assemble (Klinkner & Smith, 1999). In other areas of social life, blacks faced laws and customs that segregated education and public facilities and banned interracial marriage.

During the Antebellum Era, there were efforts to demonstrate that blacks were an inferior species compared to whites. For example, in the late 1830s and 1840s in Philadelphia, Dr. Samuel G. Morton had assembled a collection of over 600 skulls from various parts of the world (Gould, 1996). Morton had painstakingly measured the cranial capacity of the skulls from five different ethnic groups: Mongolian, Caucasian, American, Malay, and Ethiopian. Morton's analysis determined that the largest mean cranial capacity belonged to Caucasians, while the smallest belonged to the Ethiopians (Morton, 1849). Morton argued that cranial capacity correlated with intellectual potential and, therefore, concluded that the Caucasians were most intelligent and the Ethiopians the least intelligent. Such reasoning supported the polygenesis thesis that humans originated in separate groups or races.

Gould (1996) has documented flaws in Morton's methods, and his reanalysis of Morton's data revealed no significant intergroup differences whatsoever in cranial capacities. Gould further observes that scientists are not immune to conducting data analyses that tend to reflect their own cultural values. In the 1840s and 1850s, there were efforts, as exemplified by Morton's work, to show that African Americans were inferior based on scientific evidence. Such efforts strengthened not only the belief that blacks were inferior, but also the assumption that blacks could never become full and equal members of society.

While white society placed limitations on black advancement, blacks in the North were striving to elevate their status through self-help efforts in four areas: the family, the school, the workplace, and the church. One important way blacks tried to help each other was by sharing in the formation of households (Wright, 1993). Black families housed relatives and took in boarders, thereby contributing to growth and stability in the family.

In education, there was a widespread pattern in the North of segregated schools and little support for publicly financed black schools (Litwack, 1961). Most blacks felt that ultimately they wanted their children to attend integrated schools. However, in the meantime blacks organized independent schools in Philadelphia, New York, Baltimore, and elsewhere. In New York and Massachusetts, these schools successfully raised funds from private donors and also secured some state appropriations.

Finding suitable employment presented great challenges to blacks in the North. As Berlin (2003) notes, fraternal and benevolent societies were formed by blacks to aid their compatriots in need of housing, jobs, social support, and other such assistance. Many down-trodden blacks were barely earning a living, and the aid societies offered a helping hand. Another important black cultural institution of this period was the church. From the early 18th century on, slaves in the North had been practicing Christianity, often in white-dominated churches (Wright, 1993). Blacks seemed more attracted to the evangelical denominations, and occasionally black preachers conducted the main service; however, black worshippers typically had separate seating areas, and other religious services (e.g., baptisms, weddings) were segregated. In the late 18th and early 19th centuries, northern blacks began forming their own churches. Among the most prominent of these was the African Methodist Episcopal Church organized by Richard Allen in Philadelphia in 1817 (Berlin, 2003).

The Antebellum South

In the Antebellum Chesapeake and the Lower South, the Constitution not only left slavery essentially intact but also, as noted, afforded the individual states various opportunities to strengthen the institution of slavery. This discussion will summarize three important developments: (1) new slave states; (2) slave migration; and (3) race relations in the master-slave system.

Leftover from the Constitutional debates were unresolved issues concerning the slave status of new states entering the Union. Slave states admitted to the Union in the early 19th century included Louisiana in 1812, Mississippi in 1817, and Alabama in 1819. However, heated debates occurred when it was proposed that Missouri, north of the other slave states, would enter the Union as a slave state in 1820 (Wright, 1993). The resolution to this issue was to admit two states, Maine as a free state and Missouri as a slave state, and to admit new states from the Louisiana Territory as free or slave, depending on location (Ransom, 1989). Virtually the same issue was revisited in 1850 and again in 1854, when other areas from the Louisiana Territory and regions in the West were considered for statehood.

Adding even more divisiveness to these issues was the 1857 Supreme Court decision in *Dred Scott v. Sanford* (Ransom, 1989). Scott was a slave whose owner had died in Minnesota. Scott sued for his freedom, claiming that he was living in a free state and, therefore, eligible for freedom. Scott's case eventually went to the U.S. Supreme Court where Chief Justice Roger Taney, himself a former slaveholder, wrote the majority opinion that ruled against Scott. The opinion concluded that blacks were not citizens and, therefore, had no legal rights. Taney wrote that blacks were a "subordinate and inferior class of beings, who had been subjugated by the dominant race, and whether emancipated or not, yet remained subject to their authority" (quoted in Fehrenbacher, 1978, p. 343). Thus, just prior to the Civil War, the nation's highest court had affirmed the inferiority of blacks, declaring that even freed blacks were subordinate to whites.

One significant outcome of new slave states entering the Union was the movement of slaves into these areas, a forced mass migration known as the Second Middle Passage (Berlin, 2003). By the early 19th century, cotton had become a profitable crop in many areas of the South including the new states. The cultivation of cotton required intensive human labor and slave gangs were productive workers. As cotton plantations prospered, the usage of slaves rapidly increased. Between 1790 and 1860, the slave population in the United States grew substantially from slightly under 720,000 to approximately 4 million (Johnson & Campbell, 1981). It is estimated that nearly 750,000 slaves were transported from the eastern states to new slave states in the Western Lower South, the Mississippi Valley, and later to Texas and Arkansas (Johnson & Campbell, 1981).

Amid a climate of harsh relations and extremely demanding work in the developing western lands, numerous slaves attempted to run away. In some cases, sympathetic whites assisted runaway slaves, although the number of runaways who successfully reached freedom was relatively small. However, tens of thousands of slaves attempted to run away (Kolchin, 1993). Interactions between blacks and whites along the border states were fraught with suspicion and mistrust. Although some whites were willing to assist runaways, most whites avoided interaction with blacks or reported such blacks to authorities. Fugitives were quite suspicious, never knowing for sure whom they could trust.

Another important aspect of race relations in the Antebellum South, the master-slave system, deserves special attention. Slave masters first established their authority in the Colonial Era when slave codes enabled them to exert extensive control over their slaves. The American-born slave master class was a most significant development in American slavery and American history (Kolchin, 1993). The master-slave relationship became the model for all human relations in the slave societies as the slave masters controlled not only their own families and plantations but also their communities, local government, courts, and state governments (Berlin, 2003).

In the Antebellum South, most farms were small and operated with few or no slaves. Yet, the economy was dominated by large plantations, many of which were highly profitable. Historians have estimated that with the gang-labor system, the large plantations in 1860 were 70 percent more productive than small farms with few slaves or non-slaveholding farms (Fogel, 2003). So successful was the agricultural economy in the Antebellum South that its most valuable crop, cotton, surged in production from 35 million pounds in 1800 to 2.3 billion pounds in 1860 and provided the bulk of all exports from the United States from 1815 to 1860 (Bailey, 1998).

With no legal standing of their own in society, no citizenship, no voting rights, and forced to work without wages, slaves were seemingly powerless against their white masters. Yet, slaves showed a determination to resist domination and found ways to exert leverage against their owners. Earlier in this chapter, the process of changing personal names was described as an important symbolic shift in African American identity formation. In reality, the naming process was more complex than might first appear. Berlin (2003) and others (e.g., Dillard, 1972; Kolchin, 1993) describe how African and African American slaves gave their children names deriving from African languages and customs. Slaves appeared to use the names given to them by their white masters in the presence of the master and other whites, while, in fact, blacks often maintained their African names and kept their usage hidden from whites (Berlin, 1998). This kind of secretive usage of language by slaves apparently relates to other usages of coded or indirect speech intended to prevent whites from understanding certain meanings being communicated among slaves (Smitherman, 1977). Dalby (2003) also notes that African Americans have traditionally used various speech codes to both conceal information from whites and to reinforce in-group identity.

In trying to assert a degree of independence and autonomy in the Antebellum South, slaves employed various tactics to resist the master's dominance. In addition to giving their own names to children and running away, slave resistance took other forms: verbal and physical confrontation, work stoppages, feigned sickness or injury, sabotage of equipment, theft, and occasionally, but rarely successfully, insurrection (Kolchin, 1993). Slaves thus exercised several forms of resistance, resulting in a negotiated set of rules. Masters knew there were limits to their power and slaves knew how hard their owners could reasonably push them. Accordingly, many masters offered rewards to slaves in the form of gardens or small plots of land for producing their own crops and raising animals (Berlin, 2003).

One final issue in master-slave relations is the paternalism to which historians of slavery frequently refer. The notion of slaveholder paternalism derives from the American-born masters and their growing numbers of American-born slaves, joined together in what masters thought of as an alliance or a kind of family (Kolchin (1993). Acting as protective fathers, slave owners took care of their slaves in the sense of providing clothing, food, health care, housing, and a structure for life and work. The masters extended their influence into slave family life as they often advised on child rearing and settled disputes (Berlin, 2003).

On many plantations, slaves grew accustomed to their owners and, in a sense, became accepting of their local condition. Great anxiety accompanied the sale of a plantation or the rumor of a sale because slaves did not know what to expect from a new owner (Wright, 1993). Plantation owners regularly reserved holidays such as Christmas and crop harvests for celebrations and gave slaves extra food and time off (Kolchin, 1993). In some instances, slaves expressed sympathy and affection for their masters.

Overall, however, slaveholder paternalism had pronounced negative effects, especially in the all-controlling tendencies of masters who influenced the South at two levels. On their own plantations and in their own locales, masters deliberately regulated their slaves' lives, thereby trying to make slaves dependent upon them. Work rules, housing, dress codes, religion, social behavior, and innumerable other activities were governed by the master (Kolchin, 1993).

Masters also intruded into the personal lives of slaves in a most damaging way: making sexual advances upon females. Referring to the period from the 1660s to the 1860s, Kennedy (2003) observes: "There was probably more black-white sex during this period than at any other time (thus far) in American history. Most of it was unwanted sex, stemming from white males' exploitation of black women" (p. 41). Fogel (1989) indicates that on smaller plantations in the Antebellum South, in one-sixth of families headed by a mother, the father was white. The trauma of rape was a tragedy in itself; however, adding further injury to the victims of sexual assault was the fact that the rape of a female slave by a white man was ordinarily not considered a crime (Kolchin, 1993).

Another negative characteristic of paternalism was the imposition of behavioral norms involving interpersonal and social rules. For example, before buying slaves, a prospective purchaser would be interested in their character and behavior, wanting to find out whether they were co-operative and obedient. Buyers were often suspicious of a slave's truth-fulness, due to a deep-seated code of honor that differentiated the master class from slaves. In his book on the culture of the Antebellum South, Greenberg (1996) describes a deeply respected code of honor among slaveholders, the gentlemen of the slave societies. Greenberg asserts that to question the honesty of a southern gentleman by calling him a liar was a serious offense and could result in a challenge to a duel.

Slaves, however, were not permitted to present a truthful persona. In the Antebellum South, the masters effectively instilled a stereotype of slaves as dishonest and deceitful. Slaves had no license to question a master's truthfulness, even when they knew their masters were lying. As Greenberg (1996) notes:

> The difference between masters and slaves arose not in the area of truthful-ness, but in the area of power. Power enabled masters forcefully and pub-licly to dishonor their slaves by unmasking them and calling them liars. Both masters and slaves dressed up for the masquerade ball of slavery, but it was only masters who felt strong enough to walk around the ballroom pull-ing off the masks of their slaves. Any slave who sought to unmask his mas-ter could expect immediate and deadly retaliation. (p. 33)

In a second sense, paternalistic slaveholders exerted great influence in a larger, regional pattern across the slave societies. Slave codes estab-lished at state and local levels forbade teaching slaves to read and write (King, 1995) and prohibited slaves' rights to own property or enter into contracts, rights to testify in court, rights to assemble, and rights to le-gally marry (Kolchin, 1993).

The master-slave system also served to reinforce a deepening racist ideology in the Antebellum South. An ideological racism was wide-spread all through the slave societies, not just on the large plantations. Most farmers and city dwellers had few, if any, slaves, yet whites every-where embraced what van den Berghe (1978) refers to as *Herrenvolk* de-mocracy—a rationalization for slavery and white supremacy that recognized democratic principles while depriving rights to blacks. In the Antebellum South, there was a strongly held and widespread belief that whites were a superior race, and that blacks were an inherently inferior race.

As the planters prospered and controlled their state governments, and with little effective opposition to the status quo, a widespread con-servatism characterized the South (Kolchin, 1993). White southerners at this time seemed attuned to a regional patriotism and sought to uphold their cultural traditions. With growing awareness of antislavery forces in the North, the promotion of slavery became intertwined with defending the southern way of life.

The Civil War, Reconstruction, and the Jim Crow Era

From the standpoint of race relations in the United States, the turbulent period from the start of the Civil War to the 1950s was one of far-reaching change, most of it occurring in an atmosphere of strife. The main theme in this discussion is that from the 1860s until the 1950s, racial segregation and resistance to racial equality became institutionalized in much of the United States.

Race Relations during the Civil War

In many ways, race relations seemed to change little during the war. At first, President Lincoln and other northern leaders justified the North's entry into the war with appeals to preserve the Union. Lincoln had never been wholeheartedly against slavery (Fredrickson, 1988), and ending slavery was not a primary goal behind the Union's initial wartime plans.

In Virginia in July 1861, the first full-scale battle in the Civil War resulted in a clear Confederate victory (McPherson, 1988). This defeat was stunning to the North and dispelled thoughts that the war might be short-lived. As the Union Army began increasing its enlistment efforts, some leaders called for recruiting blacks, although the official policy was not to enlist them. However, slaves began escaping to the Union Army, which had ruled that blacks in such instances could be put to work in non-combat roles and paid for their service (Hargrove, 1988).

By the spring of 1862, the war was not going well for the Union and there was little advancement by the Union Army (Paludan, 1988). Lincoln decided on a more aggressive stance in the war as he contemplated recruitment of blacks in the military and issuing a decree that would free slaves. In September, Lincoln informed his cabinet that he would officially free all slaves through an executive order that would take effect on January 1, 1863 (Ransom, 1989). The proclamation stated that slaves in states that had rebelled against the United States would be freed. Although parts of the South were occupied at this time by the Union Army, the order had little direct effect outside these areas. Yet, word of the proclamation spread quickly throughout the South and more slaves began fleeing to the Union Army.

After the Emancipation Proclamation, blacks served as armed soldiers in the Union Army and often served capably in combat (Ransom,

1989). There were at least three significant implications of blacks in the military during the Civil War (Klinkner & Smith, 1999). First, military duty was a symbolic move toward freedom, equality, and citizenship. Second, by their capable service during wartime, blacks offered images that countered negative stereotypes of blacks as undisciplined and lacking in confidence. Third, although at first a black in the Union Army effectively received only half the pay his white counterpart got, blacks and some whites objected, and finally, in 1864, Congress authorized equal pay for blacks and whites.

By 1864, the prospects for the North had improved and more areas in the South were under Union control. As noted, a growing number of freed slaves had moved to be near the occupying army. There was widespread confusion and disarray as blacks, now free of the paternalistic plantation structure, needed housing, clothing, and other elements of normal living (McPherson, 1982). Some free blacks took advantage of affordable leases that allowed them to farm confiscated plantations. Such policies toward freed slaves later became formally instated with congressional legislation in 1865 that established the Freedmen's Bureau. Support for this legislation was justified, in part, by the military service blacks had rendered during the war. In addition to making land leases available to freed blacks, the bureau also assisted in the formation of several predominantly black colleges (Foner, 1988).

On April 9, 1865, the war ended as the Confederate Army agreed to the terms of surrender (Paludan, 1988). During the four-year conflict, the slave societies failed in their attempt to claim their independence, and, finally, 200 years of slavery in North America drew to a close. Even though Lincoln's emancipation of slaves was a monumental event, Klinkner and Smith (1999) call attention to the 180,000 blacks who served in the Union Army and helped insure the military victory that permanently ended slavery.

Reconstruction

From 1865 to the 1880s, the United States underwent a "massive experiment in interracial democracy without precedence in the history of this or any other country that abolished slavery in the nineteenth century" (Foner, 1988, p. xxv). This discussion of race relations during Reconstruction will point out the increased assertion of states rights in the South and difficulties faced by blacks in their transition from slavery to freedom.

In March 1866, Congress passed a civil rights bill that extended citizenship to blacks and granted them rights to own property, enter into contracts, and testify in court (McPherson, 1982). Congress then pressed for a constitutional amendment that would effectively nullify the *Dred Scott* decision, guarantee citizenship to blacks, and provide due process and equal protection under the law for all citizens (Foner, 1988). This legislation passed in the form of the Fourteenth Amendment, although subsequent court rulings based on the amendment often disappointed civil rights advocates.

From a political standpoint, Reconstruction moved ahead unevenly as competing forces in Congress argued about goals and policies in the late 1860s. Radical Republicans, enjoying success in the congressional elections of 1866, fashioned the Reconstruction Act of 1867, which provided that the remaining states of the Confederacy would be divided into five military districts (Foner, 1988). Provisional state governments could operate under the supervision of the military and endeavor to adopt new constitutions that included voting rights for all men and also ratified the Fourteenth Amendment. Upon meeting these conditions, a state's representatives could be readmitted to the Congress (McPherson, 1982).

In response to the perceived threat of growing black and Republican political strength, former members of the Confederate Army and others in the South organized fraternal groups with white supremacist orientations, the best known of which was the Ku Klux Klan (Foner, 1988). By 1868, the Klan had become an armed terrorist group that threatened and murdered blacks, Freedmen Bureau workers, and Republican leaders in the South. Republicans carried few southern states in the 1868 general election as terrorist tactics kept many Republicans from voting. From April to November 1868, more than 2,000 persons, mostly black, were killed in Louisiana (McPherson, 1982).

There was progress in education for blacks during Reconstruction. Missionaries and others from the North moved to the South to establish schools and to serve as teachers. Census data indicate that in 1870 over 90 percent of blacks in the South were illiterate (Ransom, 1989), but blacks were eager to learn and as education became more available, blacks took advantage. Providing education for blacks was a great step forward in civil rights; however, most states in the South authorized little public funding for education, and even the primary education that was available to blacks was limited to only one-fifth of black school-age children during early Reconstruction (Irons, 2002). Learning was further hindered by the fact that most black parents were illiterate and could not help their children with homework.

The social caste environment in the North continued with blacks finding it difficult to obtain good jobs. In the northern labor markets, blacks were not sharing in the growth of well-paying industrial jobs as labor unions often excluded blacks (Bernstein, 2001). Blacks also received low wages as they found themselves increasingly competing with immigrants for jobs.

In some areas of the North, there were meaningful reforms that benefited blacks in education, voting, and other civil rights. During the 1870s, restrictions against blacks migrating to several northern states were removed, poll taxes were eliminated in some areas, discrimination in use of public transportation gradually receded, and blacks gained access to public schools (Foner, 1988).

One important development during Reconstruction was the continuing debate among African Americans regarding their cultural identity. The black nationalist movement had received attention in the Antebellum North, and after the war African American identity was of greater importance to blacks in many regions across the United States. One prominent black leader of this era, Booker T. Washington, became a successful educator and a proponent of self-help for blacks through manual labor (Adams & Sanders, 2003). As principal of Tuskegee Institute, Washington attracted national attention as he urged blacks to improve their lot in life through thrift and hard work and not be so concerned with issues of identity and segregation (Klinkner & Smith, 1999).

Washington advocated an accommodation by blacks to white society; however, others opposed Washington's views. W.E.B. Du Bois was one black leader who disagreed with Washington, arguing that bright and ambitious blacks should not be satisfied with vocational training and should be able to take advantage of the best educational opportunities, the same ones that whites were receiving (Klinkner & Smith, 1999). During the 1880s and the 1890s, as blacks became better educated and more conscious of their cultural identity, they sensed conflicting orientations — with some adhering to an assimilationist stance and others, a black nationalist stance.

In 1892, Democrats took control of the White House and both houses of Congress. Immediately, Congress repealed several acts that protected black voting rights. Soon, virtually every southern state passed laws restricting black suffrage (Adams & Sanders, 2003). By 1896, Louisiana's percentage of black male voters had plunged from 93 percent to 9 percent, and by 1906 in Alabama only 2 percent of black males were registered to vote (Thernstrom & Thernstrom, 1997).

During the 1890s, *Plessy v. Ferguson*, a landmark Supreme Court decision, seemed to symbolize the transition from Reconstruction to the Jim Crow Era. Homer Plessy was regarded as a black person even though his ethnic background was seven-eighths white. In 1892, Plessy boarded a train in New Orleans and sat in the white seating section (Adams & Sanders, 2003), after which he was arrested for violating a public accommodations law. Backed by a group of light-skinned men of color, Plessy took his case to a Louisiana district court that ruled against him.

The case eventually reached the U.S. Supreme Court. Plessy was challenging not only the Constitutional authority, under the Fourteenth Amendment, to deprive him of equal protection under the law, but also the authority of the State of Louisiana to designate his ethnicity (Kennedy, 2003). In 1896, the Supreme Court ruled seven-to-one against Plessy (Adams & Sanders, 2003). The majority opinion stated that laws providing segregated facilities had been widely recognized in the United States and as long as such facilities were equally available to both races, there was no deprivation of constitutional rights. Thus, the "separate but equal" precedent was established at the highest judicial level. In a manner reminiscent of the *Dred Scott* case, the Supreme Court affirmed, in effect, that blacks were relegated to an inferior status. At the turn of the century, the racial contract fully retained its viability.

The Jim Crow Era

From the 1890s to the 1950s, social life in the United States was largely segregated by race. Through laws and customs, white proponents of segregation were intent upon preventing social interaction between blacks and whites and treating blacks as second-class citizens. Summarizing some of the most notable developments during the Jim Crow Era, the following section will outline the painfully slow reforms that eventually overthrew legal segregation.

Two patterns of southern white resistance to Reconstruction manifested themselves in the Jim Crow Era. One was the widespread use of terrorism and brutality. As noted, groups such as the Ku Klux Klan intimidated blacks as well as whites who were in favor of civil rights for blacks (Foner, 1988). During the Jim Crow era, however, terrorist violence intensified. Klinkner and Smith (1999) note that blacks were lynched in increasing numbers from 1882 to 1901, reaching a peak of 161 in 1892 and remaining as high as 105 in 1901.

Legislation constituted the second pattern of southern white resistance to equality for blacks. Jim Crow provisions became institutionalized all across the South as states passed laws that not only segregated blacks and whites but also effectively restricted black access to voting, education, legal protection, and economic opportunities (Adams & Sanders, 2003).

In education, the pattern during the Jim Crow era in the South was to provide separate public schools for blacks and whites; however, the black schools were decidedly inadequate and blacks received limited educational opportunities (Irons, 2002). Furthermore, southern blacks at this time typically lived in rural areas and worked as sharecroppers. Although earning meager incomes, sharecroppers nevertheless worked hard and often required their children to stay home from school and work with them. Irons (2002) notes that even as late as the 1930s, black children of school age in the South attended school for just 15 or 20 weeks a year.

Two aspects of Jim Crow legislation must be appreciated. First, the laws on segregation applied to virtually all aspects of social life in the South. Racial segregation was mandated in public transportation, schools, workplaces, restaurants, hospitals, orphanages, public libraries, and at drinking fountains (Adams & Sanders, 2003). Woodward (1974) observes that across the South one found signs marked "Whites Only" or "Colored," denoting entrances to theaters, restaurants, toilets, and all other public places. Legal segregation applied to all forms of recreation such as use of sports fields, beaches, and swimming pools, as well as attendance at stadiums, circuses, theatres, and other such places.

A second important aspect of Jim Crow legislation was that the enforcement often took place at the interpersonal level of interaction. In *An American Dilemma* (1944), Gunnar Myrdal's massive study of race relations in the United States during the 1930s and the 1940s, it is noted that in the South, virtually all public officials were white, including police officers. Myrdal observes, "The Negro's most important public contact was with the policeman. He is the personification of white authority in the Negro community" (1944, p. 535). Violation of segregation laws, loitering, and other behaviors found to be suspect by police could easily lead to warnings or arrest (Myrdal, 1944). In charges of more serious crimes, beatings by police often led to forced confessions, the legality of which was rarely questioned in court.

To avoid untoward encounters with whites, blacks needed to observe the rules of Jim Crow social etiquette. Apart from following codes against integration, blacks needed to observe other rules of behavior such as "hand-shaking, hat lifting, use of titles, house entrances to be used, social norms when meeting on the street, and so forth" (Myrdal, 1944, p. 60). The Jim Crow rules of etiquette evinced a culture prescribing interaction rituals that both whites and blacks observed and conducted as co-participants:

> The code of etiquette governed every social situation from hunting to casual meetings on the street. For blacks encountering whites, the code demanded, among other things, "sir" and "ma'am," averted eyes, preferably a smile, never imparting bad news, and always exhibiting a demeanor that would make a white comfortable in believing that this deferential mien was not only right but the way things ought to be. The white, in turn, would almost always address the black by a first name or by generic terms such as "boy," "uncle," or "aunty," regardless of age. The tone would always be condescending. (Goldfield, 1990, pp. 2–3)

In response to the antagonistic climate of race relations, blacks in the South acted to resist and defend themselves against the Jim Crow system. One action was migration, the result of which was a large-scale movement of blacks from the South to the North and to the Lower Midwest. By the 1890s, blacks were migrating to Oklahoma and to several states in the North. Pennsylvania, New Jersey, New York, and Illinois received over 70,000 black migrants from the South (Johnson & Campbell, 1981). Even though in 1910 the South was still home to 89 percent of the 10 million blacks in the United States, blacks moving to the North became a prominent trend (Thernstrom & Thernstrom, 1997).

Blacks also pursued legal action to defend against the Jim Crow system. After a violent, race-related outburst in Illinois, activists formed the National Association for the Advancement of Colored People (NAACP) in New York in February 1909. Among the founders of the NAACP were prominent blacks such as W.E.B. Du Bois, Ida B. Wells, and Reverend Henry Brooks, and well-known whites such as Jane Addams and John Dewey (Klinkner & Smith, 1999). The NAACP supported legal teams who defended blacks in a variety of criminal and other cases.

Life in the North for many blacks was a struggle, but there was progress in many respects. Compared to blacks in the South, northern blacks were able to find more and better jobs. In the political realm, blacks were voting in the North, in distinct contrast to the Jim Crow South. An important trend in black voting patterns in the 1930s occurred as blacks began shifting their allegiance from the Republican to the Democratic Party.

During World War II, as in World War I, the military was segregated. At first blacks served as menial laborers, but eventually there were black troops serving in combat. Many blacks performed well in combat, and some significant attitude shifts occurred showing greater respect for blacks in the military (Klinkner & Smith, 1999). It was not until the Korean War that black and white soldiers fought side-by-side in integrated military units.

Blacks resisted joining the armed forces in World War II as many of them saw the army as a military version of the Jim Crow South. A campaign conducted by a black newspaper encouraged blacks to fight for a double victory: success in fighting the enemy overseas, and success in fighting discrimination in the United States (Sullivan, 1996). The "Double V" campaign helped draw attention to the fact that the United States was fighting for democracy and human rights abroad, yet African Americans were denied important rights in their own country.

Fredrickson (2002) states that there were three overtly racist regimes in the world in the 20th century: Nazi Germany, South Africa under its apartheid system, and the Jim Crow South. In all these regimes, Fredrickson argues, explicitly racist ideologies existed in these areas: concerns for racial purity, bans on intermarriage, laws mandating segregation, disenfranchisement of the out-group, and limitations on economic opportunities that left the stigmatized group in a perpetual state of poverty. During World War II, as atrocities in Nazi Germany became exposed, people began seeing what the horrible, logical extension of a racist regime could lead to. People in the United States started realizing that the existence of the Jim Crow system was undermining the moral authority of the United States in its quest to promote democratic ideals.

Important political events in the late 1940s hastened the downfall of the Jim Crow system. When Franklin Roosevelt died in office in April 1945, Harry S. Truman was sworn in as the new president. Truman demonstrated a remarkable commitment to civil rights, the first 20th-century president to do so. In 1946, Truman created a Civil Rights Committee to study race relations in the United States and to recommend corrective actions. The recommendations included creating a new Civil Rights Section in the Justice Department, enacting federal statutes against police brutality, abolishing poll taxes, and ending segregation in the armed forces (Gardner, 2002). President Truman also acted in symbolic ways to reach out to the African American community. In 1947, Truman became the first president to address the NAACP at its national convention (McCullough, 1992). Then, in his 1948 State of the Union Address to

Congress, Truman placed civil rights near the top of his priorities, pledging vigorous action along the lines recommended by the Civil Rights Committee.

The end of the Jim Crow system finally arrived in the 1960s when the passage of significant civil rights legislation began dismantling it. However, of all the events in the 1950s that marked the beginning of the end, none was more notable than the historic Supreme Court decision in *Brown v. the Board of Education*. In the early 1950s, civil rights cases increasingly came before the Supreme Court and Truman recognized the growing importance of education as a civil rights issue. Furthermore, with the formation of the United Nations, Truman realized that the United States would need credibility as it emphasized democratic ideals in relations with newly emerging nations (Gardner, 2002)

In 1952, Truman's last year in office, the Supreme Court was reviewing several cases pertaining to segregation in public schools. The court consolidated four of these into one case known as *Brown v. the Board of Education* (Gardner, 2002). The case for the plaintiffs was argued by several attorneys, one of whom was Thurgood Marshall, an African American working on behalf of the NAACP. Marshall, who would later serve as a Supreme Court Justice, argued that since the 1896 *Plessy* case, the Supreme Court had gradually ruled in favor of a broader interpretation of the Fourteenth Amendment, finding unconstitutional those state laws that segregate individuals on the basis of race.

By the spring of 1954, Chief Justice Earl Warren had managed to persuade all the justices to agree on a ruling in favor of desegregation, thus rendering the "separate but equal" principle unconstitutional. In March 1954, Warren read the court's unanimous opinion, stating these now-famous words (quoted in Klinkner & Smith, 1999, p. 238):

> [to separate black children] from others of similar age and qualifications solely because of their race generates a feeling of inferiority as to their status in the community that may affect their hearts and minds in a way unlikely ever to be undone . . . We conclude that in the field of public education the doctrine of 'separate but equal' has no place. Separate education facilities are inherently unequal.

Many newspaper editorials heralded the ruling as a sign that the United States was being true to its own democratic deals (Klinkner & Smith, 1999). Halberstam (1993) notes that the ruling completely undercut the remaining legitimacy of segregationists and also made civil rights issues more appropriate for coverage by the media. The public was now becoming accustomed to civil rights as an important current event. The

Brown decision also symbolized that the Jim Crow system's viability was seriously threatened, and that a new phase in the struggle for civil rights was beginning.

The Modern Civil Rights Era

The period from the early 1960s to the 21st century encompasses the most sweeping change in favor of civil rights and equality. At the same time, this period symbolizes ongoing frustration with the failure to attain equal rights and the fruits thereof for African Americans. This following section focuses on events that led to both fulfilled and unfulfilled goals in race relations and civil rights.

The Civil Rights Movement in the 1960s

During the late 1950s, there were growing tensions in race relations and, increasingly, civil rights activists were proclaiming that blacks had waited long enough for equal rights. There were also hostile confrontations, especially in the South where school integration was met with resistance.

In an extremely close contest, John F. Kennedy was elected president in 1960 and became the last Democratic president to carry the majority of southern states. Kennedy was in favor of gradually working toward federal civil rights legislation, but as he began his term as president he treaded lightly on the subject of racial issues. As in the 1940s and the 1950s, race relations in the United States took on international significance. A violent racial protest occurred in Birmingham, Alabama, in the spring of 1963, media coverage of which extended to many foreign countries. As Klinkner and Smith note, "So great was the perceived damage to America's global image that President Kennedy directed all U.S. ambassadors to work to counteract the 'extremely negative reactions' of foreigners to the Birmingham crisis" (1999, p. 256). Violent protests continued across the United States in the summer of 1963, 758 in all, during which 13,786 protesters were arrested in over 70 southern cities (White, 1965). President Kennedy began directly calling for strong civil rights legislation.

A massive civil rights demonstration was planned for August 28, 1963, in Washington, DC, although President Kennedy had tried to persuade its organizers to postpone it (Thernstrom & Thernstrom, 1997). Despite concerns that violence would erupt, the 200,000 marchers gathered peacefully in front of the Lincoln Memorial with the highlight being the "I Have a Dream" speech delivered by Martin Luther King, Jr. The memorable speech was covered live by major television networks and, along with the march, the entire demonstration was symbolically significant as it offered a nonviolent image of the civil rights movement. The violent struggle for civil rights quickly resumed, however, as four young black girls were killed by a bomb at a church in Birmingham on a Sunday morning in September (Goldfield, 1990).

In November 1963, John F. Kennedy was assassinated and Lyndon Johnson became president. Johnson decided that passing meaningful civil rights legislation was imperative and he urged Congress to pass a strong bill. Such a bill came before the Congress in the spring of 1964. Supporters of the bill argued that passing the bill was the morally right thing to do, that black soldiers who had served in Korea deserved equal rights, and that the United States' image in the world would receive a boost from passage of the bill (Klinkner & Smith, 1999). After lengthy debates and filibusters, the 1964 Civil Rights Act passed both houses of Congress and Johnson signed it. The bill abolished discrimination in public accommodations and employment, barred federal funds to institutions that discriminated on the basis of race, and strengthened federal powers of enforcement (Klinkner & Smith, 1999).

In 1965, President Johnson pressed Congress for legislation that would extend and protect voting rights. The result was a comprehensive law that brought federal scrutiny to all counties where less than half of the voting-age population had voted (Thernstrom & Thernstrom, 1997). Effects were swift and dramatic. In six of the southern states where in 1964 less than 46 percent of voting-age blacks were registered, registrations by 1969 had jumped to at least 55 percent and in four states to over 60 percent (Thernstrom & Thernstrom, 1997).

President Johnson acted in a number of ways to promote rights for blacks and other minorities. The so-called Great Society legislation in 1964 created programs in early childhood education for underprivileged children, expanded the food stamp program, and provided medical assistance for elderly persons (Blum, 1991). By executive order, Johnson initiated the first substantial affirmative action program. He also appointed more blacks to executive branch positions in the federal government than all previous administrations combined (Borstelmann, 2001). Despite these achievements and a sense of progress in civil rights, racial strife continued with race riots erupting in 257 cities between 1964 and 1968 (Thernstrom & Thernstrom, 1997).

Blacks in the 1960s often faced discrimination in search of residential property to rent or purchase. In particular, blacks entering the military encountered oppressive housing restrictions near military bases in the United States, especially in the South, and even veteran black soldiers were victims of discrimination in their search for housing after returning from the Vietnam War. It was a familiar refrain for African Americans: they were being asked to fight for the cause of freedom overseas, but their freedom was restricted in their own country.

Congress passed federal fair housing legislation which President Johnson signed in 1968. As was the case in the aftermath of previous wars, service in Vietnam was presented as a justification in support of antidiscrimination laws, this time in the area of housing (Klinkner & Smith, 1999). Together, bills on civil rights, voting rights, and fair housing were the crowning legislative achievements of the Modern Civil Rights Era. Moreover, there were solid gains for blacks in employment, income, education, and political involvement in the 1960s. Thernstrom and Thernstrom (1997) outline notable advancements for blacks in all these areas, leading to solid growth in the black middle class.

The political influence of black voters led to a clear trend toward electing more blacks to political offices at all levels. All across the United States, as voters and as candidates, blacks became more active and influential in elective politics. Among the many appointments of blacks in the federal government was Thurgood Marshall who became a Supreme Court justice in 1967, the first African American judge on the high court.

The 1970s and Reactions to the Civil Rights Movement

In the 1970s, race relations remained unsettled, with school desegregation preoccupying many school districts and courts in the United States (Irons, 2002). In numerous metropolitan regions, whites were moving out of inner cities, resulting in urban cores increasingly populated by blacks, and rings of white suburbs. The so-called "white flight" was due to many factors, but, clearly, one key reason was the desire of whites with young children to leave school districts that were becoming predominantly black and were perceived to be inferior.

Despite economic gains for blacks in the 1960s, there were disturbing signs present as well. In many areas, there was a rise in single-parent black households, mostly headed by females, and incomes were lower in single-parent households, as compared to two-parent households. Data indicate that in 1969, among black children in female-headed families, 68 percent lived in poverty (Thernstrom & Thernstrom, 1997). The overall poverty rate for black families in 1970 was 30 percent, compared to the 8 percent rate for white families.

Another factor working against gains in black incomes was a major socioeconomic trend identified by Wilson in his book *The Declining Significance of Race* (1978). Since the 1960s, structural changes in the American economy have led to fewer good jobs for unskilled workers. According to Wilson, those without advanced education or training have tended to become a socioeconomic underclass and are often limited to a life of underemployment in urban ghettos. According to Wilson, this phenomenon is due more to socioeconomic class dislocation than racial discrimination, thus it affects everyone without advanced education, regardless of ethnicity. As Thernstrom and Thernstrom (1997) observe, the socioeconomic progress for blacks in the 1960s coincided with an extended period of income growth for nearly everyone in the United States. Since the 1960s, however, average earnings have leveled off. In the 1970s and the 1980s, there were significant increases in earnings, but this was mainly due to rising incomes for educated workers. During the 1980s, high school graduates aged 25 to 34 saw their earnings increase by only 5 percent, whereas, the earnings for college graduates rose by 42 percent (Thernstrom & Thernstrom, 1997).

An important legal dispute related to race, education, and language took place in Michigan in 1977. In Ann Arbor, parents of black students in the public schools sued the school board because they concluded that their children were experiencing a form of discrimination (Baugh, 1998). The schools in Ann Arbor were racially integrated, but noticeable numbers of black students had experienced unsatisfactory treatment including being held back from advancement to higher grades, being placed into special education classes, and being tracked at lower levels of instruction (Labov, 1982). The central argument was that interactions between teachers and black students who spoke Black English Vernacular (BEV) had resulted in a language barrier in the classroom.

The lengthy proceedings involved testimony by linguists and educators, the result of which affirmed that BEV was a distinct variety of American English with pronunciation, vocabulary, and grammar that differed significantly from Standard American English. The judge ruled in favor of the plaintiffs, stating that in the classroom the problem was not due to a communication barrier between teachers and students. However, the judge concluded that a barrier did exist in the form of negative attitudes teachers held toward students who spoke BEV and the reactions of students to those attitudes (Labov, 1982). The Ann Arbor case brought linguistic and communication issues into the courtroom in a way that highlighted contemporary difficulties in interracial education.

Race Relations: The 1980s and into the 21st Century

Since the 1980s, three main themes have emerged from the analysis of race relations in the United States: (1) declining interest in civil rights issues; (2) current events highlighting racial divisions; and (3) a shift in public policy toward personal or local accountability and away from action by the federal government. The declining interest in civil rights can be seen first in the Reagan administration budget cuts in federal agencies and in claims of reverse discrimination. During President Ronald Reagan's first term, the budgets of federal agencies with civil rights interests were reduced, and the number of cases pursued by these agencies declined (Klinkner & Smith, 1999).

In the 1980s, under President Reagan, the federal government reduced enforcement of affirmative action, often referring to what were called abuses of preferential treatment. Reagan stated, "If you happen to belong to an ethnic group not recognized by the federal government as entitled to special treatment, you are a victim of reverse discrimination" (Reagan, 1983, p. 169). This was one of Reagan's themes that, as several authors have noted (e.g., Hochschild, 1995; Klinkner & Smith, 1999; O'Reilly, 1995), became part of a trend in the 1980s and the 1990s, using race to appeal to anxiety among white voters. While running for president, Ronald Reagan, George H. W. Bush, and, at times, William Clinton, all employed strategies that linked African Americans with crime, problems with public assistance programs, and undeserved benefits of affirmative action. In the 1980s and the 1990s, there were numerous examples of political communication using phrases such as "war on drugs," "welfare reform," "reverse discrimination," and "quotas," all arguably code words for appeals to uneasiness and anxieties among white voters (Klinkner & Smith, 1999). This kind of political discourse put civil rights advocates on the defensive, solidified support among white voters who were becoming less sympathetic to civil rights issues, and reinforced the trend of declining interest in civil rights.

Combining with decreasing interest in civil rights issues was a pattern in current events that called attention to a racial divide. One sensational event related to charges of police brutality in the Rodney King case in California in 1991 (Kennedy, 1997). While following King, a black man, police determined he was evading them. Police apprehended King, then subdued and beat him, scenes of which were recorded on video tape. The police officers were charged with assault and after a lengthy trial, the officers were acquitted of the most serious charges. Immediately after the trial, several days of violent riots occurred in Los Angeles, by the end of which 52 were dead, 2,382 injured, 16,291 arrested, and property worth a billion dollars damaged (Kennedy, 1997).

In examining the King case, Kennedy (1997), a professor of law, concludes that the legal issues and courtroom testimony were more complex than many realized. The proceedings resulted in a verdict that was not unreasonable. The more significant point, however, was that many believed there was police brutality in this case and that this symbolized the presence of an underlying element of racism within many law enforcement agencies.

Another controversial race-related event was the 1996 resolution passed by the Oakland, California, Board of Education on the use of Ebonics (a.k.a. African American Vernacular English; see Chapter 3) in the public schools. The school board passed a resolution on the implementation of a program helping students achieve competence in English while also showing respect for the linguistic integrity and usage of Ebonics (Kretzschmer, 1998). School board personnel recognized that most students entering the Oakland public schools spoke Ebonics and were not performing well, not unlike the students in the earlier cited example of language and communication difficulties in Ann Arbor in the 1970s.

Several professional associations offered statements that supported the central thrust of the resolution (Kretzschmar, 1998). However, news of the resolution appeared in the mass media with distorted reports of Ebonics being mandated in the schools, Ebonics being recognized as a foreign language, and the Oakland schools lowering their academic standards and not emphasizing Standard American English (Baugh, 2000). A controversy lingered for several years, with several commentators condemning the role of Ebonics in education as a trap that simply fosters inferior academic performance by black students. Others, mainly scholars and educators, noted that the resolution was calling for programs that ultimately could help students develop competence in SAE.

Affirmative action remained controversial. In 2003, the Supreme Court agreed to hear a case on affirmative action in university admissions (Crosby, 2004). The admissions policies of numerous universities were considered, but the court focused on the policies of the University of Michigan. The court found that there were important reasons for the university to maintain ethnic diversity in its student body, but that Michigan's undergraduate admissions procedures effectively incorporated a quota favoring minorities and, thus, were unconstitutional. Following the lead of several other states, in 2006, voters in Michigan approved an amendment to the Michigan Constitution that banned the use of affirmative action in admissions to the state's public universities (Schmidt, 2007).

Finally, as we examine race relations from 1980 to the present, another trend is apparent, one that might be called a shift toward local and personal accountability. Such a shift has resulted in policies that reduce institutional and governmental intervention in socioeconomic and educational programs and in measures that curtail these programs and/or shift responsibility to states and localities. For example, debates on affirmative action in college admissions raised the question of preferences based on membership in a group, as opposed to individual merit. To some researchers and commentators, receiving preferential treatment simply because one belongs to a historically disadvantaged group is wrong in at least two respects (D'Souza, 1995). First, some deserving white students may experience reverse discrimination as they are rejected in favor of someone from a preferred minority group. Second, those who benefit from preferences are harmed by a stigma that indicates that they are not academically well prepared for college and are, therefore, not expected to do well. One effect of court rulings against affirmative action in college admissions is to shift emphasis away from group-oriented preferences, and toward an emphasis on individual qualifications.

One issue in discussions of affirmative action is the idea of victims receiving preferential treatment. A group of black intellectuals has argued that blacks who seek to benefit from ill-conceived or undeserved preferences too easily assume the role of a victim. Steele (1990) asserts that one result of the civil rights movement of the 1960s was the emergence of a victimhood identity for blacks. In Steele's view, to the extent blacks expect preferential treatment because they are victims detracts from the emphasis on the time-honored goals of hard work, educational achievement, and individual initiative. Another viewpoint is expressed by McWhorter (2005), who refers to the "Cult of Victimology" as a debilitating mindset of many African Americans that leads to constant blaming of white society, while keeping blacks from putting in their best effort.

Another sense of victimhood often arises in discussions of a so-called racial achievement gap. Thernstrom and Thernstrom (1997) refer to a racial gap in academic achievement, pointing out that in 1976 the average composite SAT score for white students was 944, and for black students, 686, a gap of 258. By 1991, the gap had narrowed significantly to 191, but by 1996 the gap had increased slightly to 202. A more complete discussion of the achievement gap is presented in Chapter 4.

The victimhood explanation for the achievement gap is based on comparisons of the social and educational environments from which many black children come, as compared to most white students. Irons (2002) summarizes these environmental comparisons by noting that the incidence of poverty is strongly correlated with lower educational achievement. Impoverished environments can affect all families, regardless of ethnicity; however, it is the concentration of poverty that seems to present the greatest difficulty for black pupils as poverty is often concentrated in segregated, mostly black schools. In 1999, 45 years after the *Brown* decision, 70 percent of all black students attended public schools that were predominantly black (Irons, 2002; see also Chapter 4). It is argued that black students born into a low income environment are often victimized by a condition over which they have little or no control.

In the 1990s, several states tried to implement school voucher programs that would enable students from low income homes to enroll in schools outside their neighborhoods (Hochschild & Scovronick, 2003). In principle, the voucher programs would enable students to exercise greater choice in their pursuit of educational opportunities, thus shifting greater responsibility toward individuals and families, and away from state-designated school districts.

In another area of shifting responsibility, some of the federal government's public assistance programs underwent extensive change in the 1990s. The most important of these programs was Aid to Families with Dependent Children (AFDC), which was overhauled during the Clinton administration. Responding to claims that AFDC and related welfare programs diminish incentives to work and leave recipients too dependent on public assistance, President Clinton proposed substantial changes in AFDC (Blumenthal, 2003). Congress passed welfare reform legislation in 1995, main features of which were to limit recipients to five years' of AFDC assistance and to transfer the administration of the entire program to the states (Klinkner & Smith, 1999). Thus, responsibility for public assistance shifted from the federal government to the states, and a main goal of this program became helping recipients leave the program and enter the workforce.

The changes in the AFDC program obviously affect recipients regardless of ethnicity, but the discourse in welfare reform often invokes a racial stigma that links African Americans to poverty (Loury, 2002). Even though a decided majority of African Americans have middle-class incomes (Marger, 2009), there is a false impression that poverty among black families is far more widespread than it is (Gilens, 1999). Thus, there is a tendency for middle-class and upper-class whites to identify AFDC as something related to poverty and, therefore, part of a "black" problem (Loury, 2002). Discussions of changes in public assistance programs focused on limiting participation and shifting responsibility to individual states. However, from the standpoint of race relations, the policy debates were often racially tinged as the role of public assistance was implicitly considered to have racial dimensions.

Currently, in the 21st century, race relations are greatly affected by a public attitude that improved relations remain a worthwhile goal, that much improvement has taken place, and that most of the significant statutory forms of racial discrimination have been eliminated. Still, an uneasy "glass half-empty" sentiment exists that American society remains racially divided and that race relations remain problematic.

Conclusion

This chapter has attempted to describe the evolving nature of the way blacks and whites in American society have related to each other. While Chapter 1 describes the social construction of race, this chapter shows the influence of historical constructions of race. In a profound sense, the history of race relations in the United States is simply American history itself. There is no way to understand American history *or* American race relations without appreciating the role of the slave trade, the emergence of slave societies, the circumstances of the Civil War, the emancipation of slaves, and the course of civil rights since the Civil War. Thus, this chapter emphasizes how European Americans and African Americans have continually engaged in an interracial deliberation over roles, rights, and responsibilities in U.S. society.

Several trends have persisted throughout the history of race relations in the United States. First, long-standing, negative predispositions toward the status of black Africans existed in Western Europe, eventually exerting great influence on race relations in the British colonies in North America and in the United States. Second, there have been few, if any, periods in American history during which European Americans willingly acted to extend equal rights to blacks. Rights for African Americans have come mainly after confrontations and struggle, and even when rights have been granted to blacks, there has often been a negative reaction by whites followed by a decline in enforcement of civil rights. Third, military service and international events have often influenced race relations in the United States. Military service has often been given as a justification for greater civil rights for blacks, and international relations, especially from the 1930s to the 1960s, raised the visibility of race relations in the United States to a global level. Fourth, at key points in the history of race relations, court decisions have played a pivotal role in clarifying the legal basis for equal rights for blacks. As a kind of sociopolitical barometer, major court decisions have indicated how far society was willing or able to go in granting greater rights to blacks. Finally, throughout American history, African Americans have exhibited tendencies to both assimilate and not assimilate into white society. At times many blacks have formed identities with an assimilationist orientation, while at other times, assimilation has meant accommodating white society, a stance that was unacceptable to many blacks.

Mills (1997) contends that the racial contract has provided the sociopolitical template for race relations throughout modern Western European and American history and, even now, continues to prevail. Against the backdrop of the racial contract, political, legal, and cultural trends provide ample evidence that while the United States may be slowly evolving into a just and fair society, it has required long-term, concerted efforts to attain the civil rights and the degree of racial harmony we now enjoy.

CHAPTER 3

Language Issues in Interracial Communication

Among the many factors involved in interracial communication, none seems to be more influential than language. A number of important communication issues coalesce around language, including topics, settings, conversational patterns, identity, interaction rituals, and others. As Hymes (1974) stated, interlocutors develop identities and engage in oral communication through ways of speaking that are appropriate to their own speech communities. When we consider the use of African American Vernacular English (AAVE) and Standard American English (SAE) in the United States, we find that speakers of these two varieties often communicate through different ways of speaking and exhibit different intentions and practices.

The language variety used by many African Americans is variously referred to by terms such as AAVE, Black English, Black English Vernacular, and Ebonics. In following the preference of Wolfram and Thomas (2002) to use the term AAVE, it is understood that this label carries an ethnolinguistic orientation, which is consistent with the overall approach taken in this book. AAVE will be discussed as a nonstandard dialect of American English, in contrast with SAE.

The goal of this chapter is to outline some key comparisons between African American and European American communication patterns in the United States, with a focus on language and speech style. After discussing the origins of AAVE, we will examine some of the distinctive linguistic and stylistic features of AAVE. A final section compares AAVE to SAE, discusses code switching, and comments on sociolinguistic research methods.

The Origins and Nature of AAVE

Origins of AAVE

Wolfram and Schilling-Estes (2006) discuss four current theories on the origins of AAVE. The Anglicist hypothesis, the oldest theory, holds that AAVE emerged in a manner similar to other varieties of American English. As Chapter 2 notes, Africans destined for slavery came to North America speaking their own native languages as well as pidgin language varieties that originated in West Africa (Holm, 1988). Some slaves arrived from the Caribbean where pidgin languages were also in use (Rickford & Rickford, 2000). Over time, comparatively fewer slaves arrived from Africa and the slave population increased more due to births in North America. Children acquiring pidgin as their first language resulted in the development of a Creole language variety (Poplack, 2000), sometimes called Plantation Creole (Dillard, 1972). After several generations, the speakers of Plantation Creole began speaking more and more like the local white residents and vestiges of their Creole speech diminished. Commenting on phonology and grammar, McDavid and McDavid (1951) note that the speech of blacks exhibited borrowings from Southern white speech and their regional analyses show that in the same locales, blacks and whites were speaking mostly the same variety of English.

The creolist hypothesis (Wolfram & Schilling-Estes, 2006) maintains that the African slaves in the 17th and 18th centuries spoke Creole language varieties, one of the more noteworthy of which was Gullah, spoken in coastal South Carolina. As noted, Creole varieties from the Caribbean also may have influenced slave speech in the colonial South as some slaves came to the United States from Jamaica, Barbados, and elsewhere in the West. Living a segregated life in the Antebellum South, slaves continued speaking Creole varieties and tended to acquire language from each other and not from white residents (Rickford & Rickford, 2000). Thus, according to the Creolist hypothesis, for well over a century, early black speech exhibited a Creole influence that made it different from the English spoken by whites in the South.

A third and more recent theory is the neo-Anglicist hypothesis (Wolfram & Schilling-Estes, 2006). While following the Anglicist hypothesis in positing the similarities in speech of blacks and whites, the neo-Anglicist hypothesis argues that AAVE has evolved into a language variety that has diverged from other varieties of American English. Labov (1998) claims that African American (AA) speech and General English (GE) have been two of the main influences on AAVE, with GE also sharing characteristics with other American dialects (OAD). Labov (1998) notes, "The most distinctive feature of modern AAVE is the rich development of semantic possibilities in the AA system, possibilities that are unavailable and unknown to speakers of OAD" (p. 147). Labov and others believe that AAVE shows evidence of a unique development independent of earlier characteristics shared with Southern English. While influences of GE are clear, AAVE continues to evolve and display divergence from OAD and SAE.

Wolfram and Schilling-Estes (2006) make the case for a fourth explanation for the origins of AAVE: the substrate hypothesis. The notion of a substrate effect is that a language variety may show the residual influence of earlier language contact, even though the influence is not substantial. Wolfram and Schilling-Estes note that there is limited evidence of a widespread Plantation Creole in the Antebellum South, yet contact with Creole speakers during the early years of the slave trade could nevertheless have affected the development of AAVE.

To these four theories, one could add another perspective, that AAVE has been significantly influenced by African languages. Blackshire-Belay (1996), Morgan (1993), and Smitherman (2000) are among the scholars who have denoted the presence of African words, phonological patterns, and speech rituals now found in AAVE that can be traced to Africa. Rickford (1999) also summarizes research on African influences on several nonverbal patterns in speech found in the United States as well as in the Caribbean. Rickford comments that such nonverbal behaviors may be easily overlooked, and that greater attention from researchers would likely yield much more about African influences on language, speech, and communication in the United States and other areas in the West.

It is difficult to determine the extent of the African influence on AAVE. Two of the earlier mentioned theories implicate an African influence in the form of Creole varieties resulting from early contact between Europeans and Africans in the 17th century and early 18th century. McWhorter (1998) asserts that while one may identify African influences in speech style and rituals, there is only limited evidence of any significant African influence in sentence structure, aspect, and phonology. McWhorter concludes that AAVE has far more in common with nonstandard British speech varieties than with African languages.

Theories on the history of AAVE are important in the study of interracial communication in at least two respects. One, it is important to recognize that AAVE has a long history showing the elaborate nature of its linguistic and sociolinguistic development. Two, historical issues are relevant to the question of whether AAVE and SAE are becoming more or less similar to each other. As Wolfram and Thomas (2002) point out, even though consensus is lacking, there is solid support for the neo-Anglicist hypothesis. One argument that AAVE has diverged from SAE has been advanced through the intriguing analysis by Mufwene (2003). As noted in Chapter 2, Africans arriving in the Chesapeake area in the

17th century were not initially enslaved and regularly interacted with Europeans. These Africans formed the largest concentration of blacks in North America at the time, yet whites were in the majority and, gradually, the language spoken by blacks resembled that of whites (Mufwene, 2003). Furthermore, Africans in the Chesapeake in the early 17th century often became indentured servants who worked alongside European indentured servants. Later, especially in the coastal regions of South Carolina, Africans were in the majority and the Gullah variety emerged. A form of language divergence thus occurred: slaves on the coastal plantations spoke Gullah, whereas inland slaves spoke a variety of English resembling that of whites in the region—American White Southern English (AWSE). In Mufwene's analysis, contact between slaves and whites in the colonial era was an important factor in the early speech among slaves, and the influence of Gullah and other Creole dialects was more limited.

What theoretically led to the divergence between AAVE and AWSE or, later, SAE, according to Mufwene's (2003) reasoning, was the strict segregation enforced during the Jim Crow Era. Beginning with Reconstruction and continuing throughout the Jim Crow Era were the policies and laws that specified racial segregation in housing, education, and social interaction, among others, as discussed in Chapter 2. The spread of AAVE then occurred as blacks migrated from the South into many regions across the United States, especially into urban areas. As life for blacks continued to be segregated, AAVE then developed into a distinct dialect with notable innovation occurring during the 20th century. The migration of blacks to the North thus was a pivotal event in the evolution of AAVE.

Linguists who have argued in favor of divergence (e.g., Bailey & Maynor, 1989; Labov, 1998; Mufwene, 2003) theorize that modern AAVE has diverged from modern SAE or OAD and has also exhibited the typical pattern for dialects to diverge from their earlier forms. Although, as Labov (1998) has observed, there are many features of syntax shared by AAVE and OAD, when one considers the various stylistic, grammatical, and phonological elements together, there are important differences between AAVE and SAE, as well as OAD. In considering convergence and divergence, it is important to note that the issue is far from settled and research is ongoing (Rickford, 1997).

One issue complicating the question of divergence is the significant diversity, regional and demographic, displayed by speakers of AAVE. For example, Wolfram and Thomas (2002) describe AAVE in Hyde County, North Carolina, with data showing evidence of vernacular language norming. Younger AAVE speakers in Hyde County have shifted away from traditional, local patterns and toward contemporary urban AAVE. In rural Hyde County, Wolfram and Thomas also find younger European Americans accentuating their local dialect. Therefore, in this region one form of divergence has been observed as newer AAVE patterns show changes away from earlier AAVE. Divergence is also evident in the black/white comparisons, especially among younger speakers.

Linguistic and Stylistic Features of AAVE

There are varying estimates on the number of African Americans who use AAVE to some extent. Johnson (2000) mentions earlier estimates from the 1970s and the 1980s ranging from 60 percent to 80 percent. Smitherman (2000) states that 90 percent of African Americans use and identify with AAVE, at least some of the time. Estimating who speaks AAVE must be done within the context of code switching, to be discussed later in this chapter. It appears that a clear majority of African Americans speak AAVE to some degree, and even those who do not regularly speak it are familiar with it and can identify with it.

For our purposes, the nature of AAVE can be summarized in two respects: one linguistic, the other stylistic. In this discussion, references to linguistic structure and style follow the traditional distinction between language systems and language use. As numerous sociolinguists have commented (e.g., Labov, 1972a; Hymes, 1974; Milroy & Milroy, 1985), features such as syntax, phonology, and morphology are part of the linguistic structure of a language—the language system. The abstract knowledge of these features gives speakers the linguistic resources necessary for producing well-formed utterances. However, a prerequisite for competently performing these utterances in social interaction is an understanding of the rules for using the language. Such rules are shared by members of one's speech community (Hymes, 1974).

Linguistic Features of AAVE

Over the last 40 to 50 years, a growing body of research has examined the linguistic structure of AAVE. Building on the earlier work (e.g., Baugh, 1983; Dillard, 1972; Labov, 1972a; Wolfram, 1969; and others), several fine studies—including those by Green (2002); Mufwene, Rickford, Bailey, and Baugh (1998); Wolfram and Schilling-Estes (2006); and Wolfram and Thomas (2002)—discuss current research on the linguistic structure of AAVE. Johnson (2000) has developed a good summary of some of the key linguistic elements of AAVE. Presented here are the main points of

Johnson's summary in the areas of phonology, syntax, and morphology, all of which contrast with SAE. Table 1 lists the phonological elements noted by Johnson. To show how AAVE contrasts with SAE, the table provides examples of the AAVE form and its SAE equivalent.

Johnson (2000) further describes features of the morphology and syntax of AAVE, listed in Table 2. Again, in order to provide points of contrast, examples from AAVE are followed by their SAE equivalents.

Table 1. Phonological Features of AAVE and SAE Comparisons

Description	AAVE Example and SAE Comparison
L-lessness	*col'* instead of cold; *wil'* instead of wild
R-lessness	*mo'* instead of more; *sistuh* instead of sister
Weakening of final consonants	*tes'* instead of test; *fac'* instead of fact
Substitution of _th_ sounds	*dis* instead of this; *wif* instead of with
Ang and *ing* substitution	*thang* instead of thing; *sang* instead of sing
Construction of "going to"	She was *gon* go home, instead of, She was going to go home.
Initial syllabic stress	*PO-lice* instead of po-LICE
	PE-can instead of pe-CAN
Azxe	*ax* instead of ask
Summarized from Johnson, F. (2000, pp. 141–143).	

Table 2. Morphology and Syntax of AAVE

Feature	AAVE Example and SAE Comparison
Habitual aspect: be/bees	She *be late*, instead of, She is late.
Remote time "been"	*He been working at that company*, instead of, He has been working at that company for a long time.
Absence of "be"	*He a good teacher*, instead of, He is a good teacher.
"Done" construction	
a. Completive sense	*He done got married*, instead of, He got married.

Feature	AAVE Example and SAE Comparison
b. Future action	*We be done washed all the cars by the time JoJo gets back with the cigarettes* (Baugh, 1983), instead of, We will have washed all the cars by the time JoJo gets back with the cigarettes.
Semi-auxiliary "come"	*She come going into my room—she didn't knock or nothing* (Spears, 1982), instead of, She had the nerve to go into my room without knocking.
Unmarked plurality in noun phrases	*I walked three mile*, instead of I walked three miles.
Unmarked past tense	*He pass the salt*, instead of, He passed the salt.
Zero third-person singular verb	*He take the train*, instead of, He takes the train.
Multiple negation	*I don't have no way to help you*, instead of, I don't have any way to help you.
Note: Multiple negation is also found in other nonstandard American English dialects	
Dummy "it"	*It's someone at the door*, instead of, There's someone at the door.
Zero passive voice	*The head office cut the library budget*, instead of, The library budget was cut.
	Note: Attribution of agency is indicated.
Summarized from Johnson, F. (2000, pp. 144–148).	

   The set of linguistic components Johnson (2000) has described is very useful as a summary of some key linguistic features of AAVE. As such, it is not necessarily intended to be comprehensive or highly technical, and one must also realize that research on AAVE is ongoing with most usages being continually examined and further clarified. Furthermore, as earlier noted, there are important variables in how speakers use AAVE and how its speakers display diversity in the social and regional forms of this language variety. This summary of linguistic features shows the more distinctive characteristics of AAVE. Some of these features are not necessarily unique to AAVE; however, these linguistic elements, in combination, characterize essential features of AAVE and offer evidence that this variety has a structure that is notably different from SAE and other varieties of American English.

Stylistic Features of AAVE

Also important in discussing the nature of AAVE are the stylistic features that many AAVE speakers share and incorporate into their ways of speaking. As with the linguistic structure of AAVE, there are several recent discussions of stylistic aspects of AAVE including the work of Johnson (2000), Morgan (2002), Rickford and Rickford (2000), Smitherman (2000), and others. Hecht, Jackson, and Ribeau (2003, pp. 161–172) offer a useful summary of AAVE stylistics. The stylistic features are discussed here in a manner closely following the Hecht et al. analysis, especially in the development of these five core symbols that characterize African American communication style: sharing, uniqueness, positivity and emotionality, realism, and assertiveness.

Sharing

Hecht et al. (2003) note that African American communication style emphasizes a communal sense of experience that reinforces group identity. Through enactment of symbolic forms of sharing, African Americans exhibit a sense of affiliation found in several aspects of communication behavior such as touch and proxemics, relational intimacy, and speech rituals. Hecht et al. note that in the United States blacks engage in more touching, overall, than whites. While more touching occurs among blacks from lower socioeconomic groups, it is also true that more touching takes place within black/black dyads than black/white dyads. Accordingly, more touching among African Americans is associated with interpersonal interaction at closer distances, in comparison to European Americans.

Hecht et al. (2003) further note that the act of sharing results in African Americans developing generally closer and more intimate relationships compared to European Americans; however, such intimacy may not extend to relationship formation between blacks and whites. One example of a problematic issue in interracial relational communication is cited by Hecht et al. in reference to eye contact. These authors suggest that blacks interacting with whites may maintain eye contact with speakers to an extent less than whites are accustomed to. A typical eye contact pattern for European Americans is for listeners to look at speakers more than speakers look at listeners, just the reverse of the pattern for many African Americans (Majors, 1991; Ruscher, 2001). Thus, a kind of awkwardness may occur among interracial interactants as they may misinterpret patterns of eye contact for speakers and listeners. Another pattern may emerge in certain public contexts. Williams (2000) describes how blacks in public sometimes feel they are being ignored by whites through a deliberate lack of eye contact, even though both persons may be familiar with each other. Williams writes that blacks often feel whites do not want to interact with them in public, thus direct encounters are avoided by not establishing eye contact.

Regarding relational communication from an interracial perspective, it is interesting to speculate on the impact of growing numbers of black/white married couples. The U.S. Census Bureau (2003) reports that from 1980 to 2002, the number of black/white marriages more than doubled, from 167,000 to 395,000, equaling 6.8 percent of all marriages. This increase is dramatic given that as recently as the late 1960s black/white marriages were illegal in many states. More black/white couples in courtship and marriage represent greater interracial, intimate contact and are a sign that society is becoming more accepting of these relationships, with implications for trends in relational communication. Harris and Kalbfleisch (2004) report an exploratory study of black/white interracial dating preferences, finding that the race of a potential dating partner affects the choice of date initiation strategies. There is an indication that more direct verbal strategies are selected when trying to arrange a date with someone from the other race. One potentially problematic issue in interracial intimacy is the uneven ratio of males to females of both races. For many years, the number of black men married to white women has been more than double the number of black women married to white men. In 2002, for example, of the 395,000 black/white marriages in the United States, nearly 279,000 (over 70 percent) were comprised of black men and white women (U.S. Census Bureau, 2003). Graham (1995) writes that some black women feel rejected by black men who prefer to date and marry white women.

An important aspect of sharing is the practice of communication rituals, several of which are verbal insult games, boasting, and toasting (Hecht et al., 2003). The verbal insult game, *playing the dozens* (Garner, 1983), has been in existence for many years and may have originated during slavery or even earlier in Africa (Smitherman, 2000). As Garner (1983) notes, while *playing the dozens* speakers exchange insults, often disparagingly commenting on the other's mother or other relatives. Rickford and Rickford (2000, p. 68) recorded these insults heard at a playground in East Palo Alto, California:

Yo motha got a wooden eye, every time she blink she get a splinter.
Yo mama so fat, instead of usin a beeper, she uses a VCR.

To display skill in the game, speakers need to draw upon their verbal resources to deliver clever retorts and "keep their cool" so as to show strength and presence of mind. Reactions from an audience reveal a community-based sense of norms for judging success (Garner, 1983). In playing the game effectively, speakers show that they can compete without becoming unnerved, thereby engaging in character building. The common references to derogation of someone's mother may parallel usages found in other cultures including groups from Central Asia, Russia, and Africa (Jemie, 2003). It is important to note that *playing the dozens* typically occurs between those who are familiar with each other, understanding that their insults are part of a metacommunicative game (Smitherman, 2000). Insult rituals are understood as a form of play and not as a form of substantive conflict or genuine insult.

Boasting is ritualized in the sense that speakers understand this kind of speech as a form of play and amusement (Hecht et al., 2003). Kochman (1981) asserts that boasts are intended to be humorous and not claims of fact. As exaggerated praise of self or claims of prowess, boasting, like *the dozens*, often occurs before an audience and the speaker is receptive to audience reactions. Green (2002) refers to a braggadocio tone that is common in AAVE, especially rap music lyrics.

Toasting involves tales of heroism and daring deeds told in poetic form (Hecht et al., 2003). Rickford and Rickford (2000) note that a well-known toast such as *Stagolee* tells the story of a folklore character such as a trickster or a bad man who engages in courageous or dangerous acts. Gates and McKay (1997) discuss African American toasts as a form of balladry, with similarities to other ballads in American popular culture such as *John Henry* and *Frankie and Johnny*. A toast may also tell a story of sexual conquest; however, the admiration for the hero is not so much due to male sexual prowess as his ability to outsmart his foes. Hecht et al. state that the toast is an exclusively African American speech event and is conducted mainly by males.

Uniqueness

As a complement to sharing, uniqueness calls attention to the individual (Hecht et al., 2003). Uniqueness and sharing thus constitute the end points of a stylistic continuum of performance within the African American community. Whereas events such as *playing the dozens* and boasting illustrate the core symbol of sharing, one may see elements of uniqueness in colorful speech acts as well as in appearance and movement. White and White (1998) describe a traditional appreciation for an expressive style in clothing, hair, dress, and dance within African American culture dating back to the Antebellum Era. Gray (1995) discusses contemporary black youth culture as expressed distinctively through hair styles, dance, dress, and language. The importance of uniqueness is underscored by Johnson (2000, p. 125): "This aspect of African American culture places the individual within a community where it is expected and accepted that personal distinctiveness should define the individual."

A well-known component of many African American speech events is *call and response* (Daniel & Smitherman, 1976), a speech ritual that is not only an aspect of sharing but also displays uniqueness. In *call and response*, as often occurs in black worship services, a speaker-audience interaction occurs during which a speaker initiates a stirring invocation, a request for audience involvement and participation (Holt, 1977). Responses from the audience further motivate the speaker to summon her or his speaking skills and call on the audience to again join in the shared speech activity. Wharry (2003) notes that in black worship services the preacher's call may rely on phonological qualities of performance, and Tarone (2003) finds that such phonological qualities often include level or rising final pitch contours. Although *call and response* is truly a shared activity, the speaker draws upon his or her own verbal resources to utter appealing phrases that motivate the audience. Thus, the speaker displays originality and strives for uniqueness in an effort to help conduct an interaction characterized by sharing.

Positivity and Emotionality

Hecht et al. (2003) discuss this symbol as a general sense of spontaneity and an upbeat feeling. These authors refer to an "aliveness" that is deep-rooted in African American culture and orients blacks to being open to feelings of the moment. Looking beyond hardship to a better future, using humor to counter setbacks, and adopting a positive attitude to manage stress are all part of this core symbol. Positivity and emotionality also include an awareness of one's inner sentiments and impulses, realizing that being open to one's emotions can be cathartic.

Realism

Hecht. et al. (2003) note that African American culture values a sense of personal honesty and expressions of authentic selfhood. Being "real" or "keeping it real" refers to one's ways of speaking that are accepted within one's own speech community, and not acting in a way that is false to one's culturally grounded sense of self. Smitherman (2006, p. 36) defines "keeping it real" as "being true to the Black experience; also true to oneself and one's roots." Hecht et al. also note that realism means acknowledging facts and not pretending a situation or condition is something other than what it is. Part of being "real" is to confront the realities of racism and discrimination, while maintaining a positive outlook and a belief that one can overcome adversity.

Assertiveness

Embracing an assertive speech style means claiming one's due rights without denying others' rights (Hecht et al., 2003). As opposed to aggressiveness, which is a more combative, selfish stance that overlooks the rights of others, assertiveness refers to standing up for oneself. One theme in Chapter 2 is that blacks often had to fight for civil rights in the face of an oppressive society that was usually not willing to extend rights to them. Assertiveness has, therefore, developed as a strategic orientation to situations in which one needed to act out of self-interest. Hecht et al. note that several elements of African American speech style reflect assertiveness. *Woofing*, for example, is a speech act intended to excite or intimidate another (Green, 2002). Especially in athletic contests, *woofing* can be a strategy to distract and unnerve an opponent. Others may mistake the intensity expressed in *woofing* as an escalation leading to physical confrontation, and assertiveness thus may be misinterpreted as aggressiveness. Rawls (2000) also discusses an aspect of assertiveness in an analysis of talk among co-workers in an office. Rawls examines data showing how a black worker who is already working hard may be asked to complete some extra work by an employer. When the black worker responds by saying "no," white co-workers and supervisors may interpret the response as a brash refusal with accompanying connotations of complaining and being unwilling to do one's share of the work. Again, the assertiveness of the speaker may be interpreted incorrectly, as the motivations of being assertive may orient to an unrecognized or misunderstood speech style.

One other important feature of AAVE stylistics is embedded in several of the core symbols noted by Hecht et al. (2003). Forms of indirect speech are common in a variety of speech events, the main feature of which is to imply an unstated meaning. As noted in Chapter 2, forms of indirect or coded speech among blacks may have originated over 250 years ago in the American slave societies. One of the most prominent forms of indirect speech is *signifying*, which has at least two connotations. In one sense, in a conversational setting, *signifying* means hinting at some information of interest to the speaker, but not directly asking about it (Green, 2002; Rawls, 2000). Rawls (2000, p. 253) notes how persons who self-identify as black display *signifying* in conversation:

22 T: You in the class?
23 R: Mm.
24 T: Oh, ok.
25 R: Well, this is my first year at schoo-, at school.
26 T: Really?
27 R: Mm.
28 T: You just graduated high school?
29 R: No please, girl, I'm 29. [I'm almost 29]
30 T: [Oh, I was about to say]

Rawls asserts—as can be seen in the above conversation between two female speakers talking casually—there is an aversion to asking directly for information. T seems interested in finding out R's age, but instead of directly asking for this information, she expresses interest in a way that invites R to respond if she chooses. In this instance, T is *signifying*, thus avoiding a direct question about age, but letting it be known she is nonetheless interested in this information.

In a second sense, *signifying* means a verbal act of disrespect toward another (Smitherman, 2000). This second connotation, also known as *joanin'*, *cappin'*, *soundin'*, or *dissin'* (Smitherman, 2000, p. 255), involves subtle but unmistakable derogation of another. One famous example of this type of *signifying* in public occurred during the U.S. Senate hearings on the nomination of Clarence Thomas to the United States Supreme Court in 1991. Thomas had been accused of sexual harassment and interpreted the charge as racially based, reminiscent of the way black men during the Jim Crow Era were accused of sexual assault based on false evidence. Amid the allegations presented before the Senate Judiciary Committee, Thomas stated: "I am a victim of this process . . . I will not provide the rope for my own lynching" (Thomas, 2007, p. 264). By *signifying on* the committee, Thomas showed his contempt for the members who took the accusations seriously (Smitherman, 2000). Commenting on the sociolinguistic function of signifying, Mitchell-Kernan (1972) notes, "The apparent meaning of the sentence 'signifies' its actual meaning" (p. 326). *Signifying* commonly occurs in verbal insults and some authors refer to it nearly synonymously with *the dozens* and other insult sequences (Rickford & Rickford, 2000; Smitherman, 2000).

A complete examination of *signifying* is beyond the scope of this discussion. *Signifying* encompasses several dimensions of social life and verbal expression within African American culture. Implicit in the use of *signifying* are understandings of metaphorical and ironic meanings in language. This usage of language is not only highly valued among African Americans but also constitutes a verbal resource demonstrating a facile ability to play with words, connotations, and clever analogies. Lee (1993) considers *signifying* an underappreciated verbal art, insights from which ought to be incorporated into multiethnic curricula in secondary schools and methods for teaching the interpretation of literature.

The foregoing discussion of the linguistic and stylistic features of AAVE outlines some of the more noteworthy aspects of AAVE. As the linguistic and stylistic patterns are combined in situated speech, we get a sense of how this variety of language is used in everyday life. By considering the origins as well as the linguistic and stylistic features of AAVE, we can appreciate the distinctiveness of this variety of American English. When SAE and AAVE speakers interact, they are not only using different dialects, but their speech styles and orientations to communication are different as well.

One of the main points in the foregoing discussion is to show the existence of an AAVE-based orientation to language and communication. We need to realize that when blacks and whites interact, they often come with knowledge, assumptions, and expectations about communication but fail to recognize that the other may come from a different orientation. Consider three examples of speech style and problematic communication. Kochman's (1981) extensive ethnographic research based on interracial communication in the classroom identified a clash of black and white communication styles that was capable of producing conflict. The clashes were often due more to communication style than disagreement over substantive issues.

Secondly, recall that in the spring of 2008, the pastor at a Chicago church became the focus of national media attention, especially because then-candidate Barack Obama was a member of the congregation (Sullivan, 2008). Media and Internet reports showed short video clips of the pastor preaching in a fiery style seemingly filled with anger and, to some, an anti-American sentiment. A former professor of Wright noted that those regularly listening to Wright's sermons over the years would confirm that his were traditional Christian messages with an emphasis on the needs of the disadvantaged (National Public Radio, 2008). Many of those who negatively judged Wright based only on short video clips were not accustomed to black styles of preaching, mistook the animated, passionate delivery as hateful, and did not fairly judge the content of his sermons.

A third example comes from the context of law enforcement and the problematic communication arising during interactions between police and drivers (Dixon, Schell, Giles, & Drogos, 2008). Data gathered in Cincinnati, Ohio, indicate that police officers' interracial interactions with drivers tend to show less approachability, less respect and politeness, and less overall listening on the part of the police (Dixon et al., 2008), which may result in drivers feeling antagonistic. In all these cases, we can see the clear potential for differences in language usage to contribute to problematic communication. These kinds of dilemmas result as much or more from misinterpreting the intentions and emotions of the interactants, as misunderstanding the meaning of verbal utterances.

Contemporary Speech in the United States: SAE and AAVE

Standard American English

From a sociolinguistic point of view, language exists only in the form of its varieties. That is, speakers acquire and use language in a localized manner that reflects their own speech communities. English, for example, exists in diverse forms as one finds from comparisons among speakers from across the United States and Canada, throughout the United Kingdom, Nigeria, India, and other countries where it is spoken. There is no one pure form of English, but rather there are only the many "Englishes" that are found in regional, demographic, and socioeconomic variations. Such varieties are examples of dialect, defined by Tracy (2002) as "an identifiable and characteristic way of speaking a language" (p. 93). Dialects combine vocabulary, grammar, and pronunciation in a manner shared by a community of speakers.

As Green (2002) and others note, dialect can be an imprecise and emotionally loaded term, as it is not always clear what constitutes a language and what constitutes a dialect, nor is it clear what constitutes a significant difference between two dialects. Moreover, dialect has evaluative connotations when, as it commonly occurs, people attach judgments of quality and preference. McWhorter (1998) asserts that languages do not have default varieties that constitute their essential or pure forms, yet there are those who seem to believe such default versions exist. The notion of a default variety is consistent with the concept of a standard dialect, a variety of a language that is "devoid of both general and local socially stigmatized features, as well as regionally obtrusive phonological and grammatical features" (Wolfram & Schilling-Estes, 1998, p. 283). A standard dialect is also associated with usage in education, government, publishing and the media, business, and other prominent institutions in society. Preference for a standard is maintained through prescriptions that are reinforced in education, publishing, and employment practices in large organizations (Milroy & Milroy, 1985). Occasionally, as seen in the Ebonics controversy in the late 1990s, public commentary reflects preferences for a standard dialect. It must be noted, however, that there is nothing inherently superior about a standard dialect or, for that matter, inherently inferior about a nonstandard dialect, at least from a linguistic perspective. All dialects are functionally equivalent in the linguistic sense. Of course, from a socioeconomic or political perspective, all dialects are not functionally equivalent—a particularly salient point when considering AAVE in the United States.

SAE is the preferred dialect in the United States, and its speakers reinforce its prominence through its use in education at all levels, in most employment selection processes, in employment in information-based occupations, and in advancing through organizational hierarchies. Although not all speakers of SAE enjoy equal advantages, SAE functions with the status that a standard variety confers. Furthermore, speakers of nonstandard dialects are at a disadvantage due to negative attitudes held toward them and their speech. Recent reviews of research literature (e.g., Cargile and Bradac, 2002; Ray, 2004) show a general pattern of AAVE being judged negatively in comparison to SAE, especially by European American listeners. Exceptions to the general pattern have been noted in some studies, one of which was conducted by Tucker and Lambert (1969). This research finds that white and black listeners from the northern United States judge AAVE (termed Educated Negro Southern) lower on various traits than SAE (termed Network Standard), but higher than the Southern Educated White variety. In another investigation, Johnson and Buttny (1982) report that speakers who sound black are judged similarly to speakers who sound white. However, when speakers who sound black address topics of an abstract nature, their speech is judged less positively.

In employment contexts, two studies from the 1970s examined the function of language attitudes and speakers of AAVE. Hopper and Williams (1973) report that compared to candidates who speak AAVE, those who speak SAE are significantly favored for white collar positions. However, Hopper's (1977) investigation of race and dialect in simulated interviews finds that candidates, black or white, speaking nonstandard dialects received low ratings across all job categories. Hopper (1977) notes, surprisingly, that blacks speaking SAE fared better than or as well as whites in ratings of employability. Research on speech and employability is further discussed in Chapter 4.

Related research from the 1970s was reported by Giles and Bourhis (1976) in their study of black speakers in Wales. One main finding is that West Indian blacks are able to speak effectively with a Cardiff accent and that listeners expect blacks to accommodate to the locally accented speech of Whites from a similar socioeconomic background. Giles and Bourhis comment that blacks in Wales seemed to accommodate to a white speech style to a greater extent than blacks in the United States. At that time, apparently, blacks in Wales felt more encouraged to speak in a white speech style. Interactant race and regional settings interplay in unique ways, thus adding complexity to language attitudes.

Garner and Rubin (1986), in their examination of language attitudes among black attorneys in the southern United States, found that most of the respondents regarded AAVE positively. As noted by the authors: "BE (Black English) had the greater potential for communication accuracy than did other dialects, and was used in casual settings around blacks and whites" (Garner & Rubin, 1986, p. 46). However, the black attorneys also note that in professional contexts they use SAE. In another study, Koch and Gross (1997) find that younger black listeners, 13 to 15 years old, respond more favorably to AAVE than SAE in judgments of likability and competence. Although the extensive literature on language attitudes provides findings that are complex and not easily summarized, Cargile and Bradac (2002) conclude that nonstandard speakers are judged favorably on overt status when the groups they represent are "perceived to be competitive with, and not entirely subordinate to, the dominant group" (p. 351). Thus, we may find exceptions to the general pattern of AAVE being judged unfavorably.

Notwithstanding the exceptions, the findings from much of the research literature show that SAE is often judged more favorably than AAVE, especially on judgments of competence (e.g., educated, confident) reached by European American listeners. As Wolfram and Schilling-Estes (1998) note, social evaluation of a language variety may reflect overt prestige as well as covert prestige. Overt prestige refers to a widespread recognition of power and influence, whereas, social evaluation may reflect covert prestige, a locally oriented recognition of social identification and solidarity.

There are at least two reasons for the overt prestige accorded to SAE in the United States. First, as already noted, SAE enjoys an elevated status within the United States due to its acceptance as the preferred dialect in education, business, government, and other prominent sectors of society. Indeed, the status of SAE has arguably spread even beyond the United States, as Bayard, Weatherall, Gallois, and Pittam (2001) claim. Based on language attitude data collected in the United States, New Zealand, and Australia, these authors report that people speaking SAE are generally evaluated favorably on competence and likability. Moreover, SAE is rated higher than British Received Pronunciation or, in many cases, higher than the variety of English spoken by the respondents from Australia and New Zealand. The findings of Bayard et al. are attributed to the presence of SAE in materials produced in the mass media and widely distributed within and outside the United States.

Second, although the overt prestige associated with SAE is noteworthy in and of itself, the comparative disadvantage of AAVE in overt prestige is also due to the long-standing presence of negative judgments toward African American culture in the United States. Nonstandard dialects, in general, are judged lower in overt prestige than standard varieties, thus AAVE is just one element of the dynamics involved in various standard/nonstandard comparisons. However, the legacy of slavery and racial discrimination has affected attitudes toward African American culture in ways that are distinctive and enduring. As discussed in Chapter 2, even as far back as the colonial period in North America, the vast majority of Africans and African Americans were recognized as unworthy of full personhood, and the tendency to withhold respect for the status and rights of African Americans has continued throughout American history. As Wolfram and Schilling-Estes (1998) assert, "It is no accident that standard varieties of a language typically are associated with socially favored and dominant classes and that nonstandard dialects are associated with socially disfavored, low-status groups" (pp. 157–158).

SAE Compared to AAVE

As noted, when the linguistic and stylistic characteristics of AAVE are taken together, the main features of AAVE make it distinctive and noticeably different from SAE. To more specifically contrast SAE and AAVE, let us note first that the linguistic elements of AAVE summarized earlier were shown in a manner that compared and contrasted their nonstandard characteristics with the standard elements of SAE. Similarly, we may discuss stylistic features of SAE and AAVE, indicating points of contrast and comparison. While speech styles do not completely coincide with dialect, the stylistic and linguistic features are intertwined in the usage of AAVE as well as SAE. The five core symbols of African American communication developed by Hecht et al. (2003) are used as the frames of reference for this discussion.

Sharing

In AAVE, sharing orients to a communal sense of experience. As an element in European American culture, sharing operates differently, especially in the sense of sharing opinions (Martin, Hecht, & Larkey, 1994). Williams (2000), an African American, offers an illuminating personal viewpoint on sharing and opinions, noting patterns of interaction at social parties. Williams comments that at a white-oriented party, people arrive "on time," appetizers and not main courses are served, there is background music, talk is extensive, and guests may stay only for a couple hours. Talk at such parties consists of opinion-sharing conversations about common employment experiences ("shop talk"), child care, summer plans, and other such areas; conversation as such is one of the main activities. Williams contrasts this with a black-oriented party in which guests tend not to arrive "on time," substantial food is served, there is dancing and loud music, guests stay for a long while, and talk is not necessarily the main form of interaction. Williams' point is that the focal experience at a black-oriented party is sharing in the sense of eating, enjoying music, and dancing, not the exchange of information and opinions. Williams' evidence is anecdotal; however, her observations are consistent with conclusions reached by various scholars (e.g., Martin, et al., 1994; Hecht et al., 2003; Johnson, 2000; and others).

Uniqueness

As aspects of uniqueness, individuality and personal expressiveness are prominent within African American culture (Hecht et al., 2003). While this may seem to overlap with the individualism so strongly felt in European American culture, there are differences between the two senses of uniqueness. First, uniqueness for blacks means wanting to call attention to one's self through speech that is energetic and lively. As noted by several scholars (e.g., Abrahams, 1989; Majors & Billson, 1992), personal expressiveness is an important feature of black speech style and may take the form of animated gestures, varied vocal inflection, emphatic speech, a display of emotion, and content that is based on one's personal convictions. Kochman (1981) has noted, based on his extensive ethnographic analyses, that in comparison to European American speech, "black style is more self-conscious, more expressive, more expansive, more colorful, more intense, more assertive, more aggressive, and more focused on the individual than is the style of the larger society of which blacks are a part" (p. 130). Hecht et al. (2003) further assert that in the black speech style, speakers emphasize a personal role that takes precedence over status or hierarchically established positions. One experimental study (Rogan & Hammer, 1998) finds that African American mean language intensity scores are exceeded by those of European American participants. Note, however, that these scores were obtained from written samples of language and thus were not observed in the context of situated speech, nor were there any measures of nonverbal dimensions of communication.

In a second sense of uniqueness, that concerning individuality, black communication patterns also contrast with those of European Americans. In mainstream European American culture, emphasis on the individual takes the form of self-expression through the communication of one's personal opinions that others are obliged to respect, but not necessarily agree with (Carbaugh, 1988). Philipsen (1992) and Carbaugh (1988) discuss a mainstream American communication code affirming the essential worth or dignity of the self that is realized through interpersonal communication. In the self-affirming sense, communication "refers to *close, supportive,* and *open* speech between two or more people" (Philipsen, 1992, p. 74; italics in the original). This kind of communication, when successful, occurs between individuals who mutually contribute to the ratification of each other's sense of self, and the interactants' selfhoods are grounded in relational communication. Philipsen and Carbaugh assert that the code of dignity is prominent in mainstream American culture.

In African American culture, personal expression orients to a sense of selfhood that is grounded within one's community. One assumes a sense of self prescribed by the community rather than forged through one's interpersonal communication. As Rawls (2000) points out, in African American culture a "set of expectations for self demands the presentation of an orientation toward the community" (p. 256). Thus, it is not individual dignity that is necessarily valued most highly, but the attainment and expression of an authentic self that is recognized and confirmed by the community.

Positivity and Emotionality

As Hecht et al. (2003) note, African American communication style shows a spontaneity and optimism related to overcoming feelings of adversity, a key component of which is a sense of "aliveness." In relation to positivity and emotionality, it is not precisely clear how European American speakers may display different patterns of communication, but two points are relevant. One, as illustrated through one of the primary themes in Chapter 2, throughout much of American history, African Americans have faced a dominant society that was oppressive and only reluctantly extended equal rights. As the dominant group in the United States, European Americans have developed a sense of whiteness (Frankenburg, 1993; Hale, 1998; Nakayama & Martin, 1999), an identity marked by privilege and an implicit perspective on how to think of and conduct oneself. As a social construct, whiteness is integral to the racial contract articulated by Mills (1997) and clearly parallels the discussion of white and black notions of identity in the double consciousness hypothesis of Du Bois (1903). As Mills notes, white people live in a society with built-in self preferences, yet whites do not fully recognize or appreciate what they themselves have constructed. When whites communicate the kind of optimism and vitality associated with positivity and emotionality, they are not responding to negative or oppressive forces that confront them. On the other hand, for blacks, being upbeat and exhibiting a sense of "aliveness" can assist in coping with discrimination, something whites encounter much less frequently, at least in a racial sense.

Secondly, the positivity and emotionality described by Hecht et al. (2003) have roots in African culture. Daniel and Smitherman (1976) summarize the key elements in a traditional African worldview, explaining how a regenerative spirituality and an intuitive notion of active participation in social events are common in African cultures. In its modern American manifestation, black speech features spontaneity and "a lively, conversational tone, and with an ever-present quality of immediacy. All emphasis is on process, movement, and creativity of the moment" (Smitherman, 2000, p. 65). Such energy and liveliness are less typical of the speech style of most whites in the United States, whose cultural heritage is European American.

Realism

As discussed by Hecht et al. (2003), realism in black communication style reflects personal authenticity and honesty. "Keeping it real" and grounding one's self in African American culture are essential features of realism. As noted in the discussion of uniqueness, authenticity in selfhood for European Americans is more likely to be co-constructed through interpersonal communication. Moreover, most whites in the United States belong to a mainstream culture that dominates the society in which they and African Americans live. As Du Bois (1903) argues, blacks in the United States have been forced to live with a "double consciousness," with one identity oriented toward African American society and, at the same time, another identity oriented toward the dominant society. Furthermore, the white identity includes a perspective on African American culture, thus blacks are made to view themselves through a white-oriented psychological framework, a concept depicted so evocatively through Du Bois' metaphor of the veil. Identity for African Americans is often "raced" (Rawls, 2000), part of which means that blacks are accountable to their own culture as well as European American culture, while whites are accountable only to their own culture and are not bound to respect African American culture. In the context of mainstream American society, the "raced" self is, for many African Americans, a significant feature of identity that results in an incomplete sense of self.

In examining authenticity in selfhood, black and white, aspects of realism are difficult to directly compare and contrast. Primary organizing principles of a white or mainstream European American speech style are a type of personal honesty, a code of dignity (Philipsen, 1992), and an assumed sense of whiteness. However, realism for blacks is oriented toward acknowledging one's African American heritage.

Assertiveness

As noted in the black speech style, assertiveness means upholding one's self interests. In one respect, assertiveness means the same thing for blacks and whites: standing up for oneself. Many of us in the field of communication have studied or taught interpersonal communication, one aspect of which includes understanding what assertiveness means and the importance of asserting oneself in various situations.

However, among African Americans assertiveness is influenced by a more deeply felt imperative. Barnes (2000) discusses an occurrence common to many black employees in organizations, namely, the feeling that one is being "passed over" for a promotion or that an employment opportunity is available but only certain, select individuals are informed of the opportunity. Blacks often feel that they are not given full consideration for promotion or that they are not informed of new employment opportunities, all due to forms of institutional racism (see Chapter 4). One of the goals of affirmative action is to standardize employment practices so that positions are publicly posted, application procedures are strictly followed, and evaluation of applicants proceeds according to established criteria. Yet, within 20 years of its inception at the federal level (see

Chapter 2), affirmative action came under attack, and now there has been a retreat from affirmative action in various states.

Due to the sense of privilege associated with whiteness, many whites may feel secure in trusting procedural reviews that, for them, work in fair and predictable ways. For blacks, however, the feeling may exist that procedures and bureaucratic structures cannot be fully trusted to operate on behalf of their interests. Kennedy (2002) discusses several legal cases of employment discrimination, some of which were not finally resolved in favor of black employees until the cases reached the level of federal courts of appeal. There is the sense that blacks sometimes must assert themselves with greater urgency in order to get the consideration they feel they deserve. Employment is only one example of a context in which assertiveness may be enacted differently for blacks and whites; however, the same principles would apply in other contexts such as education and financial negotiations.

Summary of Discussion of Black/White Stylistics

The goal of this discussion of stylistic contrasts has been to highlight some essential differences between what may be called white styles and black styles of communication. It should be stressed that AAVE and SAE are dialects, which, although quite important, are in and of themselves only one aspect of how people use language in specific instances. When linguistic features of dialect are combined with communication style, one can attain a more complete understanding of interracial communication dynamics. Variations in dialect and style may occur due to region, gender, socioeconomic class, and other such factors; therefore, this discussion has tried to present some of the general findings that have emerged from extant research.

Code Switching

Another important issue concerning AAVE and SAE is the notion of code switching, defined by Milroy and Muysken (1995) as "the alternative use by bilinguals of two or more languages in the same conversation" (p. 7). These authors note that code switching includes alternatives among languages, dialects, styles, or other significant forms of spoken communication; thus the sociolinguistic environment for code switching does not necessarily require speakers of two different languages. Code switching is commonly discussed in reference to blacks in the United States alternating between AAVE and SAE or other varieties of American English. Hecht et al. (2003), McWhorter (1998), Morgan (2002), Smitherman

(2000), Seymour and Roeper (1999), and many others refer to African Americans who regularly speak AAVE as well as SAE, their choice of dialect being related to linguistic resources available for use in a particular context. Traditional approaches to code switching have identified two main types of switching: situational and metaphorical (Blom & Gumperz, 1972). Situational switching refers to a code change related to a clear relationship between language variety and social situation. An informal speech event may call for a nonstandard dialect according to community norms and, therefore, the selection of a preferred code. Such switching involves rule-governed choices according to mutual understanding of the roles and obligations of the interlocutors (Gumperz, 1982). For example, Ogbu (2003) observes how black high school students may speak SAE in the classroom and then switch to AAVE outside of class, thereby acknowledging a different social situation.

Metaphorical switching means using a code that corresponds to a topic and the emotional tone that is appropriate for communicating about the topic. In metaphorical switching, sometimes referred to as conversational switching, one's code indicates how one wants his or her message to be understood (Gumperz, 1982). In one example of metaphorical switching, Scott (2000) examines how black females switch between SAE and AAVE, using the words "look" and "girl" to indicate a sense of both solidarity and shared understanding. Scott notes in her data that these discourse markers always occur with a noted change in prosody that displays noticeable stress placement and intonation patterns, especially for "girl." In another study of code switching among black females, Nelson (1990) finds the use of AAVE necessary for expressing her sentiments toward aspects of the black cultural experience.

It is common to find references to black speakers who code switch between AAVE and SAE in the presence of whites or others speaking SAE. In employment interviews (Hopper & Williams, 1973; Akinnaso & Ajirotutu, 1982), formal education in a range of settings (Smitherman, 2000), legal discourse (Garner & Rubin, 1986), and various other contexts, it is advantageous for blacks to have code-switching competence. For a black person who can switch from AAVE to SAE in the presence of others who are speaking SAE, code switching is a skill that holds benefits in relation to the way success is often measured in institutional and professional settings. However, there are more dimensions to code switching than the black/white patterns in institutional settings.

As Sachdev and Bourhis (2001) observe, situational and metaphorical models are but two of the numerous approaches to the study of code switching in bilingual and multilingual environments. Even within the context of blacks speaking AAVE and SAE in the presence of other blacks, there are various forms of code switching. For example, Morgan (2002) is impressed with one such form of code switching: reading. To read is to enact direct forms of disrespect in the presence of another. One who gets read is negatively criticized for doing something inappropriate as in presenting a false sense of who one is or what one values. As a form of code switching, reading is characterized by inventive grammatical structures and vocabulary often associated with urban, hip-hop culture. In most cases, a word or phrase that has a certain meaning in SAE is used in a different way, giving a new sense to the expression. This form of code switching highlights another point of contrast between AAVE and SAE, thus a reader exploits the incongruity arising out of juxtaposing the two dialects. Usages such as *sick, ill, wack, Do you want to floss with us?* and a multitude of other expressions have been the improvisational result of reading (Morgan, 2002). Although the usage of codes such as reading adheres to rules, these forms have an improvisational quality as they continually change and new expressions are invented due to the semantic innovation commonly found in AAVE.

What has complicated the study of code switching among speakers of AAVE in the United States is a lack of agreement on what actually constitutes a change in language code. Use of individual words, changes in prosody and stress, and variations in the aforementioned linguistic and stylistic features of AAVE have all been referred to in discussions of code switching. Furthermore, several researchers have commented on speakers who demonstrate varying degrees of AAVE in their speech (Johnson, 2000; McWhorter, 1998; Smitherman, 2000), and Hecht et al. (2003) also refer to standard and nonstandard forms of AAVE. Thus, in a given context, the use of a few words or phrases or even certain nonverbal patterns in vocalics or gesture may indicate some form of code switching. Although, as Labov (1998) observes, OAD and AAVE share many features of syntax, slight alterations in phonology or the insertion of a select few words or expressions may be considered a form of code switching.

Research Methods

Before concluding this chapter, a brief comment on research methods is appropriate. As with any research endeavor in language, the study of AAVE in relation to SAE is constrained by certain limitations. Smitherman (2000) and Morgan (2002) have called attention to a gender bias in research in AAVE, resulting in data that have traditionally been oriented more to the speech and language of black men, causing at least two deficiencies. As Smitherman and Morgan both observe, the male-oriented data have focused too much on male adult/adolescent street culture and the problematic issues in urban life. This kind of research, while examining mainly one segment of black culture, marginalizes the role and speech of black women in the black community. Secondly, in some cases Morgan (2002, p. 86) notes that researchers "suggest that signifying and snapping function as a way for adolescent males to cope with overbearing black women." Such suggestions call attention to research that dismisses or overly simplifies the prominence of black females in African American culture. As various observers have noted, there has been too little appreciation for the roles and identities of black females, especially from feminist research perspectives (Collins, 1998; St. Jean & Feagin, 1998). A related concern motivated Smitherman (1995) to edit a compilation of essays on the Clarence Thomas hearings. All essays in the Smitherman volume are written by black females whose analyses and viewpoints reveal the diversity of experience, values, and goals among African American women.

A second limitation is the traditional dilemma posed by the Observer's Paradox (Labov, 1972b). The paradox is that language researchers are interested in studying how people speak in a natural setting, yet the presence of an observer may alter the natural context for language and speech. Present in many studies of language-in-use, this paradox seems especially evident when someone who is white wants to observe the speech of black persons. Turner (1949) reports a severe problem in collecting data from Gullah speakers in the Sea Islands area of Georgia. Turner once invited a white dialectologist to accompany him; however, the speech and presence of the dialectologist resulted in informants refusing to speak. Turner also notes that when talking to strangers, in general, the Gullah speakers were less likely to use many of the African words Turner was most interested in studying. Similarly, Cukor-Avila and Bailey (2001) have examined some potential methodological problems in conducting fieldwork in sociolinguistics, especially when the race of an interviewer could affect the kind of data elicited from black informants. These authors suggest that race, along with other characteristics of interviewers such as gender, could be a limitation in sociolinguistic field research and needs to be accounted for in determining the quality of data obtained from field research.

Conclusion

The primary goal of this chapter has been to examine some essential elements of AAVE and SAE, showing how these two varieties compare and contrast. As noted, these two varieties share many features, and in many ways the similarities between AAVE and SAE are greater than their differences. However, even though it is insightful to analyze the characteristics of AAVE and SAE separately, in order to understand a truer nature of interracial communication one must appreciate the sociolinguistic dynamics occurring during black/white interaction. Thus, this chapter has attempted to explicate some prominent features of interracial communication with an emphasis on language and speech style.

The evolution of AAVE is marked by particular periods of contact between African Americans and European Americans, as well as patterns of African American migration and segregation within the United States. That African American culture and language have existed and developed over such a lengthy period of time tells much about the nature of race relations in the United States and the conditions under which the dominant society acted to restrict contact. We also see that questioning whether AAVE and SAE are converging (or diverging) raises important issues within the larger discussion of integration and multiculturalism in the United States.

It is a testament to the vitality of African American culture that AAVE has endured and thrived for over 300 years and continues to evolve. Many sectors of social life in the United States remain somewhat segregated or only superficially integrated. Yet, increasing interracial contact has led to an ever-expanding arena for face-to-face interracial communication, and we can expect this trend to continue. Numerous social, cultural, economic, and political factors affect the complexities of interracial communication. However, no influence is greater than that of language, nor can we reach a deep understanding of interracial communication without appreciating the pivotal role played by language.

Chapter 4

Patterns of Interracial Communication: Educational and Workplace Contexts

Socioeconomic trends affecting African Americans in the United States since the 1950s have led to mixed results. The median black household income in 2006 was 61 percent that of the median white household income (U.S. Census Bureau, 2007). Although the income ratio may appear as a striking reminder that income disparities remain, there has been solid growth in the black middle class. Furthermore, overall data obscure the gains attained by blacks who are succeeding in a range of sales, technical, managerial, and professional fields. Socioeconomic gains for blacks have meant greater access to educational opportunities and greater overall integration in the American workforce, both of which have resulted in constantly expanding arenas for interracial communication.

Through analysis of some prominent patterns of black/white interaction, the chapter charts the course of interracial communication as it occurs in two central domains of contemporary American life: education and employment. The main theme in Chapter 4 is that as blacks and whites interact in face-to-face settings, language and communication play key roles and influence important judgments about an individual's knowledge, experiences, and abilities.

Interracial Communication in Education

Considering the school as an interaction field, one finds a rich context for examining interracial communication in two respects: the classroom learning environment, and the racial discourse in educational settings. First, we consider how communication and race directly affect the way learning occurs in the classroom. The section on racial discourse includes a brief discussion of discourse in higher education.

Communication and Learning in the Classroom

In considering interracial communication in the classroom, one key issue is the backdrop of academic performance, against which many educational objectives and methods of instruction are viewed. Early childhood studies have shown that black and white children enter lower school with roughly equivalent verbal abilities, but differences are apparent in certain comparisons. Walker (2000) observes that middle and upper income African American children are comfortable using SAE, while Stockman and Vaughn-Cooke (1986) note that lower income children, black and white, are more likely to use nonstandard dialects. A body of research has examined various features of language acquisition by black children, including cognitive style (Hale, 1994), semantic development (Craig & Washington, 1995), syntax (Jackson & Roberts, 2001) and phonology (Cole & Taylor, 1990). In some cases, research has focused on children from urban, lower income backgrounds, with results indicating more dialect-specific and/or more limited language competence when compared to middle income children, black or white, who mainly use SAE. In other cases, such as early childhood tests of vocabulary development, lower income black children have received lower than average scores.

In their research on word acquisition, Washington and Craig (1992) utilized the Peabody Picture Vocabulary Test (PPVT), a method of identifying a word by pointing to a visual image that corresponds to a word presented orally by the test administrator. Wolfram and Schilling-Estes (2006) note that depending on the precise utterances used and how they are heard and interpreted by the respondent, administering this test actually encompasses several morphological, phonological, syntactic, and stylistic constraints. When Washington and Craig (1992) incorporated a standardized version of the PPVT that included more dialect-sensitive words, the results were not statistically different from the nonstandardized version, yet questions remain about the validity of this test. One critical concern is whether the lexical items in vocabulary development tests such as the PPVT actually tap into a meaningful sample of words used by those speaking a nonstandard variety.

Stockman (1999) notes that tests of vocabulary using spontaneous speech may yield a more accurate measure of early childhood semantic development than tests such as the PPVT. In a study using spontaneous speech (Hart & Risley, 1995), comparisons of vocabulary development were analyzed for children from households of varying income and ethnicity, thus finding that socioeconomic class accounts for significant differences. For the working-class children, both whites and blacks show comparable vocabulary growth. When comparing lower, middle, and upper income groups, the predictable correlation emerges between higher income and greater vocabulary growth over time. The authors conclude that parenting and caregiving behavior are important factors in vocabulary development. Practices such as frequent interactions, gentle corrections of verbal behavior, and extensive positive feedback contribute more to a child's vocabulary expansion than the material advantages and learning resources often found in middle and upper income homes.

Other researchers have examined grammatical development (see Seymour & Roeper, 1999, for a review), noting that up to age three, speakers of AAVE and SAE show similar patterns of development. The age-graded differences in grammatical development are the focus of ongoing research, but it appears that after age three, differences between SAE and AAVE become more noteworthy in the areas of syntax, morphology, negativity, and aspect (Seymour & Roeper, 1999). One conclusion that often emerges from the research on early childhood verbal abilities is that a learning gap exists between blacks and whites, a difference that may also correlate with income.

The keen interest in black/white comparisons has often been shaped by what is known as the deficit hypothesis (Stockman, 1999). According to the deficit hypothesis, a retardation of language development and overall learning aptitude exists among lower income African American children as well as other children from lower income groups. In response to the deficit hypothesis, one common research agenda has been to examine the nature, causes, and effects of the retardation, one result of which has been the description of cultural pathologies (D'Sousa, 1995). Implicit in the deficit hypothesis is the assumption that all children acquire and develop language competence in the same way, therefore, attention is called to any group performing at levels below national norms. Unfortunately, as Stockman (1999) notes, national norms are not only typically drawn from middle income white populations, but, furthermore, by focusing on so-called language deficits, research into dialect-specific patterns in language abilities has received insufficient attention. Although there has been a recent growth in research on verbal learning that is sensitive to dialect, the current national emphasis on assessment and proficiency testing tends to highlight disparities and gaps, thus underscoring the deficit hypothesis.

Notwithstanding methodological concerns over conducting valid assessments of verbal abilities for African American children, the dominant perspective of many educators, educational researchers, and educational policy personnel is that a learning gap exists. Reading performance has been a critical issue for many policy planners and educators, their attention being drawn to national, state, and local reading assessments. Green (2002) summarizes data reported by the National Center for Education Statistics, National Assessment of Educational Progress (NAEP) from 1992 to 2000, showing that at grades four, eight, and twelve, African American pupils, on average, achieve lower reading scores than whites. Green notes that in most cases, among white fourth graders, no more than 29 percent are reading below the designated basic level, whereas among black fourth graders, at least 63 percent are reading below the basic level. More recent assessments (U.S. Department of Education, 2005) show the racial gap in scores remains, although reading scores have increased for both groups, with 42 percent of black fourth graders reading at the basic level, versus 76 percent of white fourth graders. For eighth grade students, 52 percent of blacks and 82 percent of whites are reading at the basic level, and at the twelfth grade level, 79 percent of white students and 54 percent of black students are reading at the basic level (U.S. Department of Education, 2005).

Upon examining the reading scores, three points stand out. First, when over two-fifths of younger black students are reading below the basic level, advancement in reading in successive grades is limited. Second, the NAEP data indicate that only 54 percent of black twelfth graders are reading at the basic level and are thus at a distinct disadvantage in pursuit of higher education or various careers. A third point is that even though the average scores of the white students are higher, there should also be concern over the number of white students who are not reading at the basic level. Again, it must be noted that the reading test methods and the use of comparative data, however questionable to some, are critical aspects of performance measures. Gaps, deficits, and basic reading levels are all judged in relation to performance data.

Green (2002) notes that classroom teachers encounter communication dilemmas when teaching language and verbal skills in an interracial setting, resulting in two particular difficulties. What constitutes an interracial setting is not only a combination of black students (AAVE speakers) and white students (SAE speakers) instructed by a white teacher who uses SAE, but also predominantly black classes in which the students are speaking AAVE, while the dialect of instruction is SAE, regardless of the teacher's ethnicity. One difficulty is the cumulative effect of frequently correcting an AAVE speaker with injunctions to change an utterance into

SAE. The correcting behavior may be counterproductive when it becomes ongoing and a sense of positive reinforcement is lacking. Green also asserts that negative learning outcomes may occur due to frequent interruptions in the natural diction of the student, who then may become anxious or reluctant to participate in class. At issue in both of these teaching behaviors is the potential for the communication of negative attitudes toward students who speak AAVE, as was shown to occur in the Ann Arbor schools (see Chapter 2).

A second difficulty associated with teaching behavior relates to curricular issues in helping students who speak AAVE learn how to speak and write effectively in SAE. Wolfram and Schilling-Estes (2006) describe three approaches to teaching Standard English to speakers of nonstandard dialects or languages other than English. One approach, sometimes referred to as eradicationism, is that SAE should be taught as a replacement for the dialects of nonstandard speakers. With connotations of teaching the "proper" form of English, the dialect replacement strategy considers nonstandard speech undesirable and/or inferior and, therefore, nonstandard dialects should not be retained. Another justification for this approach is the belief that nonstandard speech will hinder the student in her or his future education and career development due to social stigmatization. A second approach, known as bidialectalism, takes the position that nonstandard speakers need both their own vernacular and SAE and, therefore, considers SAE as an additional resource in students' sociolinguistic repertoire. Wolfram and Schilling-Estes (2006) state that if the use of SAE as well as nonstandard dialects (or another language) is encouraged, students can select the language variety that seems most appropriate in certain situations. Bidialectalism thus reinforces forms of code switching.

A third approach, known as the dialect rights position, affirms the functional linguistic equivalence of various dialects and, therefore, advocates that students be taught in their own vernacular. By respecting students' rights to speak their own dialect, this approach attempts to break away from an accommodation to a standard dialect, which the other two approaches explicitly or implicitly require. According to Wolfram and Schilling-Estes (2006), a principal value upheld in the dialect rights position is the acceptance of language diversity in societies that espouse multiculturalism. This position strikes many as too idealistic. As Wolfram and Schilling-Estes assert, given that the United States has a standard dialect, it must be acknowledged that whether it seems fair or not, SAE is the preferred dialect in education, business, government, and other major areas of social/professional interaction. The prominence of SAE and negative language attitudes toward AAVE were the likely reasons that in the late 1990s five states—Georgia, South Carolina, Oklahoma, Florida, and California—proposed or passed legislation aimed at prohibiting the teaching of AAVE in public schools (Richardson, 1998).

Knowledge and practice in writing and speaking are significant areas of learning, in and of themselves. However, when a student's nonstandard speech is judged negatively, student-teacher interaction can become a problem-oriented form of communication. Students may then experience a lack of positive reinforcement and thus proceed much less confidently in primary education. The quality of teacher-student communication is, therefore, of critical importance.

The difficulty facing classroom teachers is that approaches to teaching a standard dialect are directed by curricular mandates. Some predictable problems have arisen as a result of teachers trained in certain methods of teaching reading and language arts being thrust into a classroom where a curriculum specifies new or different approaches. Morgan (2002) describes one attempt in the 1970s by various school districts to incorporate a bidialectalism approach: Standard English as a Second Dialect (SESD). Motivated by the goal of fostering equality and social justice through language education, educators developed SESD curricula to help nonstandard variety speakers integrate SAE into their speech.

Unfortunately, as Morgan (2002) observes, most of the educators who introduced the new curricula failed to adequately explain their features to parents, did not develop valid assessments to indicate which students would likely benefit from the curricula, and did not train teachers to cast language instruction within a framework that gave attention to stereotypes, language attitudes, and other critical issues involving language and culture. Parents became dissatisfied and most of the SESD programs were discontinued. One series of dialect readers in the 1970s contained passages written in SAE and AAVE, and Wolfram and Schilling-Estes (2006) note that use of the readers seemed to result in reading improvement. Yet, they were controversial because parents and some educators argued that the materials were promoting socially stigmatized speech and that they seemed to encourage a language variety that ultimately would not benefit students in secondary and higher education. This viewpoint was also loudly expressed in the discourse surrounding the Ebonics controversy in Oakland, CA, as discussed in Chapter 2.

These two difficulties for teachers, interactions with students in the classroom and conforming to language arts curricular designs, are key issues in interracial communication in education. They also combine with one other significant activity in the schools: diagnostic testing. As stated earlier, a key issue in considering interracial communication in the classroom is performance, usually measured through standardized tests. Such tests of verbal abilities are problematic when it comes to evaluation of students who speak nonstandard varieties. However, the problems associated with the deficit hypothesis become even more damaging when students' participation in mainstream classes is interrupted by placement in special education classes. As Labov (1982) notes, in discussing the Ann Arbor School Board case, a number of African American students had been placed or threatened with placement in classes for the mentally handicapped and programs for the learning disabled, tracked at lower levels of instruction, or retained in grade. More recently, Patton (1998) and others have reported similar findings for black students due to diagnostic testing. Even though, as Smitherman (1977) has claimed, the validity of various diagnostic tests may be suspect, such tests continue to be used, the results of which can fully disrupt educational progress for blacks and others who speak nonstandard English.

Within an atmosphere of public education in which assessments show learning gaps existing between white and black students, diagnostic testing may too readily and unfairly identify black students as learning disabled or otherwise in need of special education. As negative attitudes exist toward AAVE and its speakers, one can see how black students may feel a lack of confidence in educational settings, leading to self-fulfilling prophecies. Stangor (2000) refers to self-fulfilling prophecy as stereotyping toward a group that results in the group behaving in a way that reinforces the stereotype. A particular kind of self-fulfilling prophecy, stereotype threat, has been proposed by Steele and Aronson (1995) in the context of minority students in testing situations.

In their 1995 study, Steele and Aronson hypothesized the presence of an anxiety due to a self-evaluative tendency that leads members of a stigmatized group to become aware of negative stereotypes of themselves. Stereotype threat is the term Steele and Aronson (1995) apply to this form of anxiety. It is hypothesized that in situations wherein members of a stigmatized group are asked to perform in a way relevant to negative stereotypes about them, a reminder of the stereotype may trigger an anxiety that impedes performance. Such anxiety thus results in behavior that lends support for the stereotype. In a series of experiments, Steele and Aronson (1995) demonstrate how black college students participating in intellectual ability tests perform worse when they are reminded of their ethnic identity. In the experiment in which some of the black participants were asked to indicate their ethnic identity (the "race priming condition") and some were not, the performance of students who had to divulge their ethnicity was significantly lower than that of the other group. In the "no race priming condition," black student performance was comparable to that of white students. The greatest effect of the stereotype threat occurred when the black students thought they were undergoing an actual test of their intellectual abilities.

If simply being asked to indicate one's ethnicity can trigger a stereotype threat, it seems clear that expectations from teachers and educators can also trigger such threats or similar effects. One aspect of a self-fulfilling prophecy may be found in the curricular feature of many schools in the United States, a practice known as leveling (Ogbu, 2003). Also known as tracking, this practice places students in classes according to past achievement and level of difficulty. Students with high grades and test scores are recommended for placement into more advanced classes, whereas others are recommended for less advanced classes. In some regions, students for entire schools are selected through the same process. There are variations in leveling as some schools allow students to self-select; some adhere strictly to test scores and grades; some group students according to counselors' recommendations, and some offer three or more levels of difficulty. What often happens in racially integrated schools is that the majority of the students in the most advanced classes are white and the majority of the students in the least advanced classes are black. Furthermore, Mickelson (2005) reports that students in advanced classes tend to receive more challenging instruction, and in many cases classroom assignments to less advanced classes are given to less effective teachers. Expectations and attitudes of teachers have been shown to influence student behavior in the classroom (Leacock, 1985; Tatum, 2007; Thernstrom & Thernstrom, 2003), thus, depending on the students and the local school culture, teachers may expect greater academic achievement from students in their advanced classes. With higher expectations students may feel encouraged to try harder, with the opposite pattern occurring in lower-level classes.

Thernstrom and Thernstrom (1997) agree that teachers' low expectations can lead to poorer performance by students, but in their analysis, one of the main reasons for this is a particular effect of racism. These authors conclude that racism can make it difficult for academic standards to be raised too high by white teachers and educators who fear they may be judged as engaging in racial discrimination. Black students also are affected as they may feel unwilling to risk failure and find it easier to blame white racism for their lower performance. The deficit hypothesis, achievement gaps, instructional communication dilemmas, problems with diagnostic testing, and self-fulfilling prophecies are all part of the classroom scene for interracial communication in U.S. schools. However, regardless of how one analyzes classroom communication and academic performance, issues in education arise within a larger social context in which a racial discourse prevails.

Discourse and Interaction in Educational Settings

When the Little Rock school desegregation case came before the Supreme Court in 1958, Thurgood Marshall asserted that in addition to providing a basic academic education, schools should also help students learn to live together with their fellow citizens (Irons, 2002). In the context of the 1950s, Marshall was arguing that even though academic achievement was the main product of formal education, an important by-product was the social knowledge, attitudes, and skills that would gradually help all children learn to live and work together. It is not clear whether most people agreed with Marshall at the time, nor, as we consider race relations today, can we conclude that blacks and whites going to school together have actually learned to live together or necessarily show a desire to do so. What seems to have emerged is a negotiated set of rules that affect how blacks and whites relate to each other while engaged in their educational pursuits.

Let us consider two common patterns of interaction. First, there is a pattern wherein discussion of race-related issues, race talk, is to be avoided. In his ethnographic study of a racially integrated school in the Midwest, Ogbu (2003) observes that a code of silence may operate, with most students and members of the community stating publicly that race relations are mostly harmonious in the school and in the community. Ogbu notes that in classroom discussions of race relations, black students may be reluctant to state their views that may contradict the public image. Ogbu (2003, p. 65) quotes one black student who, in private, stated his own interpretation of race relations in the community:

> Like on a surface kind of level it's supposed to be all peaceful, like you know, "We have no problems and you know everything's fine; and you know, Blacks and Whites are equal and whatever." But I think there is, there is a part of the White community of Shaker who does look at Blacks as being you know, inferior. And whether they, I mean obviously they don't like openly act out on these personal beliefs [because] that's illegal. But you know it does seem that there is that feeling. There's not really like we have a

race riot going on here or anything [to show that we have race relations problems] but like I think the community as a whole, it is segregated. And, like you know, the White community, they don't really care that much about the Black community. They don't care to, they don't want to deal with it.

The notion that race talk is subdued is related to several issues in interracial communication in educational settings. Bolgatz (2005) has described the difficulty she finds when she tries to initiate discussions of race in an interracial classroom. Tatum (1997) explains how white students and parents often avoid directly discussing racism because it is an uncomfortable subject for them. Tatum also comments that although blacks are more accustomed to talk about race with other blacks, they may hesitate to discuss race in the presence of whites because there is a feeling that they may upset whites who prefer a more passive or neutral orientation to the issue. Buttny (1997) notes how white university students may downplay racism or claim its impact is exaggerated in campus incidents, whereas black students feel racism is an ongoing occurrence in their lives.

One reason race talk is avoided by whites is a fear that one may say something that sounds racist; thus some sense of political correctness may be present (see Chapter 5). In primary education, Schofield (1986) reports that teachers often claim they adopt a color-blind attitude and are not prejudiced, both tendencies that may lead to the failure to address issues in intergroup conflict of a racial nature. At the college level, in their lengthy analysis of current attitudes on racism among American college students, Bonilla-Silva and Forman (2000) have studied written surveys and then conducted in-depth interviews, finding that students expressed more tolerant attitudes in the surveys. During interviews, the students' talk about race showed that through the use of various rhetorical strategies, the students maintained a color-blind form of racism, a prominent feature of race talk in the post-civil rights era. By stating a color-blind position, speaking in qualified terms, and by disclaiming prejudice, the students in the Bonilla-Silva and Forman study (2000) seek to avoid the appearance of engaging in racism. We will return to a discussion of color-blind discourse in Chapter 5.

Disavowing racism and stating claims that "I'm not a racist" operate with an important rhetorical force in contemporary discourse. Wood and Pearce (1980) show not only that the one being accused of racism is the target of negative aspersions, but also that he/she finds the charge of racism very difficult to refute. In defending against the charge of being racist, one finds it nearly impossible to avoid language that indicates that the speaker thinks in race-related terms. Thus, one who defensively claims, "I am not a racist because . . ." often speaks in a way that indicates a heightened awareness of race and, therefore, may lend support for the accusation. Studies of race talk (e.g., Barnes, Palmary, & Durrheim, 2001; Billig, 1988; van Dijk, 1987) have analyzed several discursive strategies (e.g., disclaimers, justifications, humor) employed by speakers who wish to be viewed as non-prejudiced, even though they are engaging in expressions of racism.

Fear of being labeled a racist also enters into a pattern that Pollock (2004) found in her ethnographic study of a school system in California. Pollock asserts that members of the local community and school personnel often avoid race talk and, therefore, become color mute, the verbal counterpart to color-blind. Pollock (2004) describes how various racially oriented labels are both applied and not applied in given situations, both patterns causing confusion and avoidance of issues related to ethnicity. While acknowledging the need to provide education for "all students," school personnel also use terms such as "disadvantaged," "low-income minority," and "students of color," all in an effort to describe various programs at the school at particular times (Pollock, 2004). Also noted is the avoidance of race talk due to political correctness:

> With race a hidden subject "at the outer limit of every actual discourse" about achievement, in schools and districts racial patterns in achievement appear to be secrets that at once must and must not be discovered. (Pollock, 2004, p. 170)

In general, then, a common pattern in educational discourse is for race talk to be avoided, not directly engaged in or discussed in terms that may suggest racial concerns, thus distancing speakers from talk that may be labeled racist. One unproductive outcome of avoiding race talk is that even when educational issues have racial dimensions, they may be avoided or never discussed in meaningful ways, at least in public.

A second pattern concerns student roles observed in contemporary schools. Barack Obama, then a U.S. senator from Illinois, refers to one such role as "acting white" (Barkley, 2005). With a black father from Kenya and a white mother from Kansas, Obama felt he grew up with a mixed ethnic identity. In high school, Obama started identifying more with his black heritage:

> Then, when I was in high school, I fell into all the stereotypes. I was trying to figure out what it means to be a black man. My father was not in the house, which is true for a lot of black men, so I didn't have someone in the house saying, "Ah, that's not what I'm talking about." I'm playing basketball, getting high, and I'm not taking my work seriously at all. And part of it was because that was what everybody else was doing. If you acted like you

were too serious about it, folks would think you were a punk. (quoted in Barkley, 2005, p. 23)

One paragraph later, during the same interview, Obama states:

> That's a big part of the reason it is so important to have black teachers, especially black male teachers. I'm not saying exclusively, but in many situations you need someone who can call you on stuff and say exactly what Charles has been talking about, that it's not "acting white" to read a book. This whole attitude of anti-intellectualism in our communities is one of the most damaging things we can do to our young people. (quoted in Barkley, 2005, p. 24)

What Obama is referring to is an apparently widely noticed but also controversial notion. Obama uses the phrase "acting white" in the Barkley interview; he had used it earlier in his address at the 2004 Democratic National Convention (*Washington Post*, 2004). Ogbu (2003) describes "acting white" among black students in the Midwestern high school he studied in the 1990s, and Fordham and Ogbu (1986) also discuss "acting white" in their study conducted in a high school in Washington, DC. Other authors have also noted the phenomenon of "acting white," as Wells and Crain (1997) observe in one focus group with black teenagers in St. Louis who had been bussed to county schools outside of their urban neighborhoods:

> For instance, the eleventh-grade transfer students participating in the focus group described how they "hate it" when African American students talk and act "all white" when they are at their county schools and then get on the bus and start talking "black" again. According to one transfer student, "There's some . . . black people that, in our school, they try to act white. I mean, I don't understand how they can dress like that." (p. 240)

These references to "acting white" are taken to mean that some black students feel peer pressure to affirm their identification with the African American community by not trying to excel in academic performance in a way that conforms to a perceived "white" cultural norm.

The concept of black students "acting white" is controversial in that some scholars question its validity. Dyson (2005) is an outspoken critic of the concept of "acting white," claiming that, in effect, there is no such thing among African American youth. In addition to asserting that an anti-intellectual element in U.S. American culture has long been present, Dyson cites contemporary research that contradicts notions of "acting white." Dyson notes, for example, the large-scale research project completed by Cook and Ludwig (1997), who have analyzed data based on attitudes of 25,000 high school students. This study concludes that there is little evidence for the notion of an oppositional peer culture among black youths.

Dyson also cites other research showing that when comparing white and black high school students in the United States and their motivations for academic achievement, there is no significant difference between the two groups. Ainsworth-Darnell and Downey (1998) conclude that, if anything, African American peer groups promote high-achievement values to a greater degree than European American students. Lundy (2003) has also criticized the notion of a black oppositional peer culture as a myth based on assumptions of a culture of poverty among African Americans.

One of the more recent studies finds that, overall, there is little evidence of "acting white" among black students (Tyson, Darity, & Castellino, 2005). This research examines survey data from 866 elementary and middle school students, and 231 high school students in North Carolina, collected during 2000–2001. Data were analyzed in relation to students participating in gifted classes and advanced placement (AP) classes and included black and white students. Although the study finds some evidence of "acting white," the pattern is not pervasive among black students and more often takes the form of nonracialized teasing. Also noted is a burden of high achievement experienced by white students, particularly when the high achieving group is seen as socioeconomically advantaged. The authors further note that black students who avoid taking AP classes tend to do so out of fear of failure and for self-concept preservation (Tyson, Darity, & Castellino, 2005).

To the extent that "acting white" is controversial, it may be due to a question of degree, and it may be true for only certain students, such as adolescent males (Tatum, 1997). McWhorter (2005) claims that "acting white" is a relatively recent phenomenon that apparently began appearing around 40 years ago. McWhorter finds it odd that in the pre-1960s era of segregated schools, there was little if any incidence of "acting white," and there were black students achieving academic success even though their schools typically had fewer resources than white schools. Therefore, according to McWhorter, "acting white" seems to have emerged with the advent of integrated schools. Along with Tyson et al., (2005) McWhorter suggests that "acting white" may be a psychological mechanism that offers protection in the face of a challenging educational environment. Perhaps "acting white" is a noticeable feature of the behavior of some black students, but mainly in integrated schools where tracking occurs, and it appears not to apply to the majority of students.

Research has also examined a phenomenon that could be termed "acting black." Perry (2002) completed ethnographic studies in two California high schools, noting that in one integrated but mostly white school, students showed an interest in acting "cool." When Perry asked students about hip-hop music, many used terms such as "cool," "tough," and "gangster." At this school, there was a sense that being "cool" was associated with black culture, and students dressed and spoke in a way that suggested a desire to associate with black culture, albeit as perceived stereotypically. Perry (2002) also writes that at this high school the white students felt that blacks looked down on them because the whites were perceived to be racist, although students did not explicitly discuss this. To the extent that "acting white" may be viewed as an aspect of oppositional peer culture, Perry's description of "acting black" is not clearly related to academic achievement and, therefore, not a true parallel to "acting white." Nevertheless, and as discussed in Chapter 5, "acting black" may be an aspect of a well established pattern of non-black persons attempting to imitate and appropriate aspects of black culture.

Summary of Interracial Communication in Education

This discussion has highlighted two patterns of interracial communication in education: interaction in the classroom and racial discourse in schools. It was shown that in the first few years of primary education, differences emerge in verbal abilities for African Americans and European Americans. With increasing emphasis on reading assessments, attention has been drawn to achievement gaps between African Americans and European Americans. Performance on assessment tests seems directly related to differences in socioeconomic status as well as competence in speaking SAE. Racial discourse was discussed in two areas: the avoidance of race talk and notions of "acting white." In both of these areas of discourse, interracial communication is often unproductive in terms actually addressing critical issues.

Although, by definition, patterns of interracial communication in schools occur in racially integrated settings, in contemporary U.S. American society, integration must be viewed within its contemporary context. According to the Harvard Civil Rights Project (Orfield & Lee, 2005), in the United States during the academic year 2003–2004, the typical white student attended a public school that was 78 percent white, while the typical black student attended a public school that was 91 percent non-white. Latino, Asian, Native American, and other ethnic groups are included in the non-white category. Thus, it is not accurate to conclude that the typical black student attends a school that is 91 percent black, and this is particularly true for black students in the American West and parts of the South. As noted in Chapter 1, growing diversity is changing the ethnic composition of American society, and notions of racial integration are different from the patterns of 25 years ago and earlier. Therefore, while examining black-white patterns of interaction, it is acknowledged that there are regions of the United States where the black-white patterns are only one aspect of ethnic dynamics, and one finds more of a multicultural atmosphere. In other regions, particularly in the Midwest and the Northeast, integration remains more of a black-white issue (Kozol, 2005).

Ongoing attention to interracial issues in education was highlighted by a Supreme Court ruling in June 2007 (Greenhouse, 2007). Having reviewed plans that took race into account in assigning students to public schools in Seattle and Louisville, a court majority ruled, five-to-four, that use of race in such assignments violates the equal protection clause of the Fourteenth Amendment. One justice wrote a separate opinion stating that a limited use of race was permissible in order to achieve diversity and to limit resegregation (Greenhouse, 2007). Thus, in one noteworthy respect, the court ruling was a four-one-four split decision. In its central thrust, however, the ruling took a color-blind perspective. Those who favored the court's ruling felt that the decision would not make a significant difference in the racial composition of schools, whereas those who were disappointed felt that the ruling would result in greater resegregation (Greenhouse, 2007). The fact that the case came before the high court is evidence that important, unresolved issues remain in the area of race and education.

If one wanted to select an interaction field displaying some of the most common and instructive examples of interracial communication, the schools offer one of the richest settings in the United States. Cultural values, social customs, student motivation, parental expectations, classroom environments, teaching methods, settings for interaction outside the classroom, and other variables, all come together to shape the way blacks and whites interact while at school. In an increasingly knowledge-based society, the value of a solid education cannot be overemphasized. Yet, schools offer opportunities for failure as well as success. Interracial communication in education directly influences learning. Moreover, interracial communication is an important factor in judgments of a student's academic abilities and also affects students' future endeavors. More than an artifact of or an ancillary activity within education, interracial communication constitutes an integral component of the learning process itself.

Interracial Patterns in the Workplace

Interracial communication in various organizations displays a sense of true progress in race relations, even as difficulties remain. Most agencies of government at all levels employ a racially diverse workforce. Especially considering the armed forces, other branches of the federal government, state and local government, and the numerous public educational institutions, one finds meaningful examples of organizations within the public sector that are operating effectively with a racially diverse workforce. Although corporate and nonprofit organizations vary widely in their levels of racial integration, there has been progress in the private sector as well. This discussion will feature several prominent patterns of interracial communication in workplaces. Two common patterns will be discussed: communication within a climate of diversity and interracial communication in personnel decisions.

Communication within a Climate of Diversity

As noted in Chapter 2, racial integration was limited throughout much of American history. Affirmative action, initiated in the 1960s, resulted in some advancement toward meaningful integration in employment, yet by the 1980s, there was political pressure to reduce affirmative action. Despite the uneven enforcement of affirmative action, since the 1970s there has been a gradual increase in racial integration in various places of work in the United States.

Let us note several characteristics of interracial communication in organizational settings. First, what is known about race and communication in organizations has been constrained by a lack of attention to racial issues. In their thoughtful analysis of race in organizational communication research, Ashcraft and Allen (2003) have found a paucity of research and writing on racial issues. For example, leading textbooks on organizational communication, even those including discussions of diversity, have often failed to call attention to race as a significant variable (Ashcraft & Allen, 2003). Although race is addressed, researchers have tended to examine other aspects of diversity such as gender, age, or ethnic identity. Furthermore, as Allen (1995) has observed, most discussions of race and diversity within organizational communication have considered diversity-related issues in the context of predominantly white organizations. With references to global and international communication networks, communication scholars have stressed that modern organizations have become increasingly diverse (see Stohl, 2001). Yet, treating race as just one aspect of diversity dilutes the importance and distinctiveness of race and racial identities within organizations.

Occasionally, however, we are reminded of the enduring presence of race and racial discrimination in organizations. Conrad and Poole (2002) describe two major examples of racial discrimination at large corporations in the 1990s: Coca-Cola and Texaco. Black employees at both of these corporations sued for damages based on systematic discrimination in hiring and promoting. Verdicts in these cases resulted in Coca-Cola being fined $192.5 million and Texaco being fined $176 million (Conrad & Poole, 2002). These high-profile legal cases call attention to discrimination based on race, and one may conclude that at least the victims eventually benefited from legal remedies. However, it should be noted that internal procedures for redressing discrimination in these organizations apparently were not effective, and the victims were forced to turn to legal action. These organizations failed, in a legally acceptable manner, to account for race as a critical variable in evaluating employee performance and providing opportunities for advancement.

Another aspect of diversity in organizations today is the question of how much, or how little, diversity is valued. Organizations differ greatly in the level of diversity within their workforces. May we assume that the greater the diversity within an organization, the higher the value placed on diversity? Can an organization truly value diversity, even though it does not have a very diverse workforce? Data from the U.S. Equal Employment Opportunity Commission (2000) show that in 2000, private industry in the United States had a total workforce of 43,995,543. Of this total, 6,177,400 (14 percent) were classified as minority, and 4,547,834 (10.3 percent) were classified as black. Given that in the year 2000 the black population within the United States was 12.31 percent (U.S. Census Bureau, 2000), it would appear that in the private sector blacks were employed at a level that was slightly less than their proportion of the overall population. Thus, by this broad index, one may conclude that there are reasonable levels of minority and racial diversity within the private sector, although blacks are somewhat underrepresented. Despite the appearance of ethnic diversity in the private sector, racial stratification in the labor market has resulted in uneven levels of racial diversity throughout organizations in the United States.

Uneven levels of racial diversity were found in the analysis of employment data from the 1970s to the 1990s conducted by Kim and Tamborini (2006). These authors note that although racial discrimination has receded in various types of jobs, it has not been entirely eradicated. In the course of examining claims of the declining impact of racial discrimination, Kim and Tamborini (2006) analyze several aspects of black and white employment data, including type of employment. In this study, employment data are grouped into two broad categories: technique-oriented occupations and service-oriented occupations. The technique-oriented occupations include professional specialties, technical areas, precision production, clerical work, general labor, and work in farming, fishing, and forestry. The service-oriented occupations include accounting, social science, teaching, religious work, management, sales, and various other services (Kim & Tamborini, 2006).

Over the period of the 1970s to the 1990s, it is concluded that although the negative effect of race has generally declined, race has continued to have a significant negative impact on workers in the service-oriented occupations, especially in the 1990s. These authors affirm conclusions from earlier research (e.g., Moss & Tilly, 1996), specifically noting that the nature and evaluation of social skills (e.g., effective interpersonal communication, effective interracial communication) may disadvantage blacks due to racial stereotyping, perceptions of cultural differences, and being viewed as deficient in social skills. Thus, one finds that even when racial diversity is present in a workforce or in certain occupations, diversity may be distributed unevenly.

The climate of diversity in the 21st century seems to reflect trends due to immigration as well as rates of reproduction among minorities. As noted earlier, the powerful trend toward increasing diversity in the United States has become self-evident as projected demographic data indicate that by mid-century, those of European American descent will no longer constitute the majority. Many organizations seeking to achieve diversity within their workforces are motivated by several goals and expected benefits. Allen (2008) notes that businesses are increasingly finding that diversity can serve as a resource that can positively affect financial performance. Cox (2001) has closely examined both the challenges and the benefits of employing a diverse workforce, noting these five advantages: (1) improved problem solving leading to greater revenues; (2) greater creativity and innovation; (3) enhanced organizational flexibility; (4) competitive advantage by attracting workers from a variety of backgrounds; and (5) employing workers from diverse backgrounds to help understand new markets and to assist in relations with diverse customers.

Cox (2001) also describes three reasons why organizations have often not succeeded in achieving goals of effectively employing a diverse workforce. First, there may be a pressure to conform to organizational norms. Thus, even when workers from diverse backgrounds join an organization, they may feel the need or are made to feel the need to adapt to the organizational culture. A second factor is the failure to adjust various subsystems within an organization in order to help the whole system function more effectively. An organization, for example, may hire more minorities and yet may not change other areas of the organization such as employee development or mentoring. In this manner, the potential benefits from greater diversity become limited. A third reason is an unrealistic perspective on how long it takes for an organization to effectively integrate and realize benefits from a more diverse workforce. Managers may expect results too quickly but then become disappointed and lose faith in the organization's ability to successfully reach the goals of diversity. Cox (2001) states that large organizations may need several years, at least, to implement an effective diversity program.

Let us note that diversity, even when acknowledged as a worthwhile goal, remains a problematic concept. In one sense, diversity has come to mean ethnic, religious, and/or cultural variety among individuals. An organization may believe it has diversity when its workers come from different backgrounds—ethnic, religious, and other such identity-forming aspects. This sense of diversity is problematic in that one may self-identify as belonging to one or another cultural group, yet that does not necessarily mean the same thing as true diversity. As Michaels (2006) observes, in the United States diversity may be attributed to skin color, cultural character, religious identity, nationality, or even language. Yet, one who claims a non-European American identity may come from a background that is socioeconomically no different from that of many European Americans and, therefore, may represent relatively minor aspects of diversity. Furthermore, and in keeping with one of the main themes of this book, what passes for diversity in an organizational sense may actually avoid or otherwise not address issues of racial diversity. This may not matter much to certain organizations and their managers, customers, or owners, but it contributes to a sense that African Americans may be overlooked in the contemporary diversity equation.

Interracial Communication in Personnel Decisions

Before discussing communication in employment interviews, let us note some aspects of identifying employment opportunities. One of the primary goals of affirmative action is to standardize the procedures for describing, advertising, and evaluating applicants for positions of employment. Despite a decline in affirmative action in many regions, public advertising for employment positions is still widespread, especially in higher-level administrative posts in the public and private sectors. However, informal social networks are often used to inform others of new positions. As Doob (1999) notes, one's social network has important implications for making professional contacts related to employment opportunities. In businesses dominated by white executives, social and professional networks may be less available to African Americans.

Location of employers is also related to networking in that where potential workers live determines not only proximity to jobs but also the kind of social contacts made in neighborhoods, at schools, and at religious activities. Another issue related to location of employment was the subject of an investigation by the Equal Employment Opportunity Commission in Ohio (Sloat, 2006). The Japanese automaker Honda operates an assembly plant in a small town in central Ohio and is currently building another plant in another small town in Indiana. Critics claim that Honda has located these plants in nonurban areas, far away from locations where African Americans tend to live, and also in areas where labor unions have little strength. The Ohio plant's senior manager for diversity and ethics was terminated, in her opinion, after she urged the company to hire more black employees (Sloat, 2006).

A first step in gaining employment in many organizations is the completion of a job interview. Buzzanell (1999) explains how many organizations reflect a dominant group orientation that leads to disadvantages for nondominant group applicants. Many organizations set out to recruit applicants and conduct interviews through procedures that are fair and offer equal opportunities. Yet, such procedures are understood according to the norms and customs within the organization and, therefore, may use a logic that is not understood or appreciated by applicants (Buzzanell, 1999).

Language use is one significant skill to which employers pay close attention in rating applicants. Earlier research (Hopper & Williams, 1973; Hopper, 1977) identified disadvantages during employment interviews for those speaking nonstandard English. Based on data collected at West Virginia University, Atkins (1993) finds that 93 percent of candidates speaking AAVE received negative ratings from employment recruiters. Doob (1999) observes that employers often use telephone conversations in initial evaluations of applicants. During telephone screening interviews, nonstandard English may be used as a basis for eliminating an applicant, a pattern similar to cases of linguistic profiling (Purnell, Idsardi, & Baugh, 1999). Braddock and McPartland (1987) report that for lower-level positions, dependability, attitude toward work, and ability to work in teams are highly valued traits. These authors also note that for upper-level positions, important traits are specialized knowledge, more advanced language competence, good judgment, leadership, and ability to deal with complex situations. Jablin (2001) reports that during selection interviews, communication skills (e.g., fluency, appropriate content, ideas presented in an organized manner) are critical factors in the evaluation of candidates. In all these cases, we see that language and communication skills are of fundamental importance during interviewing. Furthermore, how a candidate speaks may affect judgments of other traits and abilities.

In addition to dialect, speech style is a significant factor in the evaluation of an interviewee. The intentions of organizations to maintain policies of fair and equal treatment extend to interviews, guidelines for which are often structured by upper-level management. As noted by Buzzanell (1999, p. 146):

> In sum, procedural justice may be served via standardized practices, such as consistency in job-related questions and administration of interview schedules, but may not be sufficient for fair employment interviewing processes. Equal treatment assumptions make applicant "difference" invisible and, presumably, irrelevant to interviewing outcomes and processes. While all else may appear equal, non-dominant applicants' nontraditional rules, styles, communicative strategies, values, and approaches may hamper job attainment and/or comfort in interviews and organizational cultures.

Candidates' speech style and communication competence thus become critically important during interviews. Akinnaso and Ajirotutu (1982) explain how effective use of narrative forms in interviews is important, especially regarding appropriately responding to questions. When asked about previous work experience, how candidates respond can give insights into their personalities, judgment, and overall verbal abilities. In data analyzed by Akinnaso and Ajirotutu (1982), African Americans were more effective in their interviews when they could speak in a problem-solving mode and narrate in a manner that clearly responded to a question, as opposed to a narrative that was told for its own sake.

Baugh (1983) asserts that African Americans who speak AAVE are at a disadvantage when evaluated by employers who are looking for people who are competent in SAE. Negative evaluations of candidates who speak AAVE are due, at least to some degree, to language attitudes toward AAVE, as discussed in Chapter 3. Beyond language competence is the issue of appropriate speech style and judgments of how well a candidate matches the model of an ideal candidate. As Buzzanell (1999) has noted, organizational notions of ideal candidates are typically based on a set of unstated norms. For candidates from nondominant groups, it can be difficult to understand organizational cultural norms and learn how to perform effectively during an interview.

Once hired, employees face performance appraisals and opportunities for promotion. At its peak during the 1970s, affirmative action resulted in significantly more employment opportunities for minorities; however, there was a difficult adjustment period for blacks and whites who were often working together in a new employment environment. Shipler (1997, p. 524) describes this incident:

> When John was a rookie cop in Baltimore, fresh out of the academy in the early 1980s, he was the only black on a squad of experienced whites, and none of them would speak to him. "None of them. Nobody. They wouldn't even say 'Good evening,'" he remembered acidly. That was the code: You didn't talk to a rookie, white or black. A white might escape the rule by having a cousin or a classmate or a friend on the force, and that connection would open a way out of the cell of silence. In those years, a black had no one. And so he would be imprisoned in muteness until he proved himself.

Shipler is referring to an uneasiness about rules and customs resulting in special difficulties for African Americans in a previously all-white work unit. Although much has changed for the better since the 1980s, uneasiness still exists in the workplace. Part of the uneasiness is based on expectations and evaluations of workers who may face qualitative assessments of their work. Moss and Tilly (1996) describe the nature of performance appraisals in service-oriented businesses where an emphasis is placed on communication skills. Evaluation of such skills is often subjective, and stereotypes influence assessments that negatively impact many black employees. The earlier cited research by Kim and Tamborini (2006) finds evidence to support similar conclusions on evaluations of social skills and the presence of racial stereotyping. Performance appraisals enter into promotion decisions in a way that seems to disadvantage minorities. James (2000) finds that in financial service organizations, rates of promotion for whites and blacks are uneven as black managers experience slower rates of promotion.

Pettigrew and Martin (1987) identify a three-part dilemma facing blacks in many organizations: racial stereotyping, the solo role, and the token role. In addition to evaluations that are affected by stereotypes, being the only black in an organization (the solo role) can mean that others in the organization are unfamiliar with blacks and have unrealistic and/or prejudiced attitudes. The token role refers to a perception of black employees that they are in their positions because of affirmative action and not because they are fully qualified. Thus, one who is perceived as a token may enter a position with an assumption that he or she is incompetent. As will be discussed in Chapter 5, a pattern of negative stereotyping is usually not altered by one or even a few cases that run counter to the stereotypes.

One remarkable program that has been of great assistance in career development for minorities is the scholarship program A Better Chance, more commonly referred to as ABC (Zweigenhaft & Domhoff, 2003). Since its inception in the 1960s, ABC has enabled over 10,000 children from low-income backgrounds to attend selective private high schools in the United States. These students then matriculate at elite universities and colleges, and from there most of them have embarked upon successful careers. Most of the students are black. ABC has operated because it has been able to raise tens of millions of dollars to support its mission. Zweigenhaft and Domhoff (2003) discuss the successes and challenges of ABC in their book *Blacks in the White Elite: Will the Progress Continue?* This book describes the cultural adjustment that the students have to make in order to succeed in secondary and higher education. The success of the program is due to careful planning including summer orientation programs where students not only receive academic instruction but also engage in travel and athletics as well as in social and cultural events, all in a tightly scheduled regimen. In an important sense, the success of the program can also be attributed to extensive interracial contact (discussed in Chapter 6).

As noted earlier in this chapter, many organizations have unstated norms that are opaque to outsiders. Learning how to navigate the social and cultural pathways into and through organizations is a challenge to many minorities. Indeed, many of us, regardless of ethnicity, find organizational cultural norms difficult to understand. However, those from a background of socioeconomic privilege grow up with academic and social experiences that give them advantages in higher education and career development.

Zweigenhaft and Domhoff (2003) simply state the goal of ABC: "These students are brought to live and study with students who come from the very top of the social structure, the rich and the super-rich. They are being prepped for possible entry into the upper class and the corporate elite" (p. 6). By extending the "prepping" to low-income minorities, ABC is not only making otherwise unobtainable opportunities available to its students, but it is also showing that minorities can overcome negative stereotypes and demonstrate their talents when given such opportunities.

Summary of Interracial Patterns in the Workplace

This section has discussed communication and the contemporary context of diversity within organizations, and communication in personnel decisions. It was noted that little research in organizational communication has addressed issues of a racial nature. In a broader sense, whenever diversity within organizations has been studied, an emerging theme has been that organizations are becoming increasingly diverse, although uneven levels of diversity have been found. In personnel decisions, information about position openings in organizations may be learned through social networks, a situation that can limit awareness for African Americans. Blacks who apply for positions and are granted an interview are at a disadvantage when they do not demonstrate competence in SAE. Black applicants, as well as other non-dominant groups, are also disadvantaged when interviewing for positions with organizations whose local culture is not understood by outsiders. It was also noted that performance appraisals of minority employees can be negatively affected by subjective evaluations of social and communication skills. In the last section of the chapter we also examined a scholarship program that has achieved success in placing black students into exclusive private high schools and elite universities.

Conclusion

This chapter has examined interracial communication in two of the most common and important settings: the school and the workplace. Racial integration in the United States has been marked by triumphs, reversals, missteps, and uneven degrees of success, as we clearly see in schools and organizations. One theme of this chapter is that language plays a crucial role in education and employment. In early childhood development of verbal skills and knowledge, in secondary school performance, in interviews, and in career advancement, verbal abilities are taken as an indication of the learning that has occurred as well as of the potential for future achievement.

In education, language has a dual function as it is part of the knowledge students are expected to acquire, while it is also a principal medium of instruction. As measured by reading assessments, verbal abilities have been regarded as leading indicators of educational achievement. It is also well known that students learn more effectively when teachers communicate expectations of success. Thus, it is important to recognize the basis for differences in levels of achievement, while also acknowledging the presence of important factors in the classroom learning environment, as students interact with each other and their teachers.

In employment, it would appear that there is much to learn about interracial communication and its effects on organizational climate, hiring procedures, and performance appraisals. As pointed out in Chapter 2, effective racial integration in the workplace has occurred only in the last 50 to 60 years. Furthermore, the levels of racial integration now seen have been one result of affirmative action, enforcement of which has either declined or been eliminated in many regions of the United States. One can see progress in the realization of equal opportunities in employment. However, it appears that it will take considerably longer for the negative effects of racial stereotypes to significantly diminish.

CHAPTER 5

Stereotyping: Media Images, Social Cognition, and Discourse

The main focus of this book is on face-to-face interaction between blacks and whites. By reviewing historical developments in race relations, by analyzing how language and speech style affect interaction, and by examining communication in educational and organizational settings, we have reached a more complete understanding of interracial communication. However, another significant influence on interracial communication exists in the form of stereotyping.

This chapter discusses the influence of media images, social cognition, and discourse in the process of racial stereotyping, beginning with an explanation of the basic process of stereotyping. As will be shown, media images play a significant role in individuals' construction of social categories, formation and maintenance of which are affected by social cognitive processes. A discussion of cultural origins of stereotypes extends upon some of the themes developed in Chapter 2 and shows how trends in popular culture coincided with historical events in the United States.

The final section of the chapter examines how talk about race and race relations functions discursively to influence interpersonal and social communication, as well as public discussions of race. A main goal of Chapter 5 is to show how stereotypes are affected by cultural values, social customs, psychological processes, and materials in popular culture.

Stereotyping

There are at least two ways in which stereotyping and media images are involved in interracial communication. First, media images often reinforce stereotypes that may enter into interpersonal encounters between/ among blacks and whites. Second, from a mass societal perspective, media images of race and race-related issues provide information that enters into awareness of current events and affects how people talk about race. Let us turn our attention first to a discussion of the essential elements in the process of stereotyping.

Features of Stereotyping

The basic definition of stereotype is a belief one holds about particular qualities of others who are perceived to belong to a group (Stangor, 2000). Two principal cognitive functions are involved in stereotyping: social categorization and information processing.

Social Categorization

Social categorization is widespread and common. Humans are perfectly willing to group others in all sorts of ways: older people, police officers, persons whose office desks are messy, you name it! As noted by Tajfel and Forgas (1981), a critical aspect of social categorization is the differential valuation in the formation and preservation of the groupings with which others are associated. One's values toward a group influence how others are observed and then mentally associated with a group. Furthermore, one's values influence how individuals are judged, such that one's stereotypic judgments tend to confirm one's values toward the group (Stangor & Schaller, 1996). Thus, due to differential valuation, we may notice and react favorably toward individuals we categorize as members of a group we respect. The opposite pattern may occur as well, with negative valuations predisposing us to reach unfavorable judgments.

An important aspect of social categories is that we feel a need to belong to and be accepted in social groups, membership in which gives us a desirable social identity (Hogg & Abrams, 2001). The groups to which we belong are termed in-groups, as opposed to the groups to which others belong, the out-groups (Stangor, 2000). More specifically, belonging to one's in-group is based on feelings of an emotional bond and shared values, whereas individuals belonging to out-groups are thought to be unfamiliar and share values that make them different (Ting-Toomey, 2005a). When referring to one's in-group, references are often made to "we" and "us," unlike references to out-groups such as "they" and "them." Ruscher (2001) further notes a tendency for people to perceive out-group members as more homogeneous than members of their own in-group. Accordingly, we usually consider our fellow in-group members to be more diverse and varied, whereas we typically regard out-group members as mostly the same.

Information Processing

A second cognitive function involved in stereotyping is information processing. When we observe unfamiliar others, we may seek out, attend to, and evaluate information that is deemed useful in forming impressions. Along with categorization, information processing can lead us to judge characteristics of people and determine how they may or may not fit preexisting mental frameworks. Our frameworks often consist of schemas, or knowledge structures, that guide us in processing information about others through several stages including (1) attention, (2) labeling and interpretation, (3) memory, and (4) inferences (Schneider, 2004).

Stereotypes affect our thoughts and behaviors through processes that are complex and dynamic. Among the various components of stereotyping, we will consider three of particular importance: (1) activation and inhibition, (2) priming, and (3) shifting standards of judgment. One of the trends in the voluminous research on stereotyping over the last 30 years has been examining whether and how, in a given context, an individual will engage in stereotyping. Bodenhausen and Macrae (1998) offer a model of the stereotyping process that includes factors with both activating and inhibiting characteristics. For a stereotype to be activated one must, obviously, invoke a social category that is thought to be relevant. However, the occasion often arises when one considers not a single category but multiple categories based on demographics (e.g., ethnicity, gender, age), personal characteristics (e.g., appearance, speech mannerisms, gestures), institutional ranks (e.g., role occupants in various organizations), and other perceived identifiers. One or more stereotypes may be activated, while others are simultaneously inhibited (Bodenhausen & Macrae, 1998). Other variables affecting activation and inhibition are social environment (e.g., a lone teenager may be judged differently compared to a teenager who is among a group of older persons), recent or chronic usage of a stereotype (e.g., in a neighborhood where burglaries have been occurring, a resident may look at someone as a suspicious stranger), and immediate goals (e.g., one who is soliciting donations in public may be quick to approach a well-dressed person). In cases such as these, rapid and intricate cognitive processes occur during which one stereotype may become dominant as potentially competing stereotypes are inhibited (Bodenhausen & Macrae, 1998).

A second aspect of stereotyping is priming, described by Hamilton (2005) as "a concept or structure being 'activated' when some stimulus (a person, an experience, a conversation, etc.) brings that concept to mind" (p. 148). The stimulus thus primes a relevant concept (a stereotype), and thus knowledge pertaining to the stereotype becomes more accessible. In an influential experimental study of priming, Higgins, Rholes, and Jones (1977) find that previous exposure to favorable trait adjectives results in participants subsequently rating ambiguous behavior more positively. As Schneider (2004) concludes, numerous studies have confirmed the main findings of Higgins et al. (1977), with some studies demonstrating priming effects among those who are unaware of the primes. Priming is directly related to stereotype activation, as reports from the media or personal conversations may make us more receptive to stereotype-related information.

Priming, as well as other forms of stereotyping, may result in (1) assimilation effects in which stereotypic judgments orient to the meaning of the prime (Rothbart & John, 1985) or (2) contrast effects in which judgments orient away from the meaning of the prime (Glaser & Banaji, 1999). It can be difficult to explain why at times assimilation occurs and why at other times contrast occurs. Schneider (2004) notes that when individuals have low awareness of a prime that is closely related to its target, assimilation is more likely to occur. However, the more someone is aware of a prime, the more there may be a specific comparison drawn between the prime and a potential stereotype, and the additional cognitive processing may lead to a contrast.

Assimilation and contrast effects appeared in the 1988 presidential campaign, as televised advertisements showed a convicted criminal along with statements that Michael Dukakis was not tough on crime (Jamieson, 1992). It has been argued that after the appearance of political advertisements on television showing that William "Willie" Horton was black, voter attitudes related to race became more influential in the 1988 presidential campaign (Kinder & Sanders, 1996). When the advertisements were seen by viewers who harbored anti-black attitudes, the face and nickname of Horton seemed to be subtle reminders of racial stereotypes, thus the response was one of assimilation. Alternatively, for individuals who did not hold anti-black attitudes and/or were motivated to critically examine the prime, their additional cognitive effort was more likely to lead to contrast effects.

The shifting standards model of stereotyping (Biernat, 2003) adds complexity to assimilation-contrast effects by considering the form of judgment in a given context. As Biernat explains, patterns of stereotyping and related effects may vary according to the application of different kinds of assessments such as subjective versus objective judgments or varying standards of evidence. When activated stereotypes involve different forms of assessment, the results may show a contrast with or assimilation to the stimulus.

Consider, for example, results of several studies reviewed by Biernat (2003). Research findings show a pattern of differing stereotypical judgments in instances of low-status individuals (experimentally introduced using labels or clear indicators that applicants are female or black) in situations favoring white males, such as an executive position of employment. One pattern is for white males to be favored when a position has equally qualified applicants who are black and/or female. This pattern often occurs when evaluations are conducted using objective ratings. In this example, the stereotyping results from assimilation as the white male is implicitly favored for an executive position. At the same time, using subjective measures, a lower-status individual may be held to a lower standard and judged more favorably, due to a contrast effect. What affects the form of stereotyping is a shift in standards: a white male is objectively considered the best, but subjectively, a black or a female may receive favorable evaluations and be judged as "pretty good" for a female (or a black) (Biernat, 2003). Biernat also points out that even when a minority is considered relatively qualified, assessors may then require more objective evidence to rate the candidate as fully qualified. The assessment procedure makes a difference.

Summary of Features of Stereotyping

When we observe someone unfamiliar to us and believed to belong to a particular group, our values, past experience, and cognitive apparatus often lead us to stereotype the other. Stereotypes influence what we notice, how we react to, and how we evaluate information about others. This means that when we meet unfamiliar others we are not forming an impression of or interacting with them as individuals per se, but, rather, we are predisposed to perceive others as members of a social category. As a result, our stereotypes mediate our experiences with others, a factor of particular importance when considering in-group and out-group contexts.

As discussed in Chapter 4, there are various situations in classroom and employment settings in which interracial communication involves impressions, judgments, and stereotypes. Since racial integration has been limited during much of American history, blacks and whites often have relatively little direct experience in developing interpersonal familiarity with each other (Orbe & Harris, 2008). Thus, a common pattern is to substitute racial stereotypes for psychological-level information about others as individuals. Stereotypes are often present during interracial communication, and with stereotyping come the intricacies of such processes as activation, inhibition, priming, and shifting standards of judgment.

Origins of Racial Stereotypes

Understanding some key characteristics of stereotyping does not address the issue of how stereotypes come into being. Schneider (2004) states that there are two principal sources of stereotypes: cultural and social cognitive. The cultural origins of racial stereotypes within the United States have roots in the history and culture of Western Europe and the American Colonial Era, as discussed in Chapter 2. We will briefly review some basic developments in the origins of culturally based racial stereotypes and then examine several social cognitive processes that also give rise to and help maintain racial stereotypes.

Cultural Origins

Racial stereotypes have been so widespread that some may consider them part of a general, undifferentiated component of American culture. However, racial stereotypes of a cultural nature have emerged in different forms and from different sources during American history. To help frame our discussion of cultural forms of stereotyping, we will briefly examine some primary influences during three historical periods: the Antebellum Era, Reconstruction and the Jim Crow Era, and the Modern Civil Rights Era.

Antebellum Era

The racist ideology during the Antebellum Era helped maintain various stereotypes that had existed in earlier periods and strengthened beliefs that blacks were lacking in intelligence, exhibited low moral standards, and were unsuitable for assimilation into mainstream society. Over time, beliefs about blacks became more complex and multidimensional, but those promoting slavery sought to instill anti-black sentiments that blacks did not possess the temperament or intelligence to independently exist in the United States (Kolchin, 1993). It was in the interest of slavery to perpetuate beliefs that slaveholders needed to provide a necessary social structure and foundation for blacks, without which they would ultimately revert to savagery.

Reconstruction and the Jim Crow Era

For nearly 100 years after the Civil War, legal restrictions and customs affirmed a "second class" status for blacks. Also influencing attitudes toward the status of blacks were popular cultural products from advertising, minstrelsy, and film.

Advertising

Kern-Foxworth (1994) discusses how advertising symbols became well known in the 19th century, noting how widely distributed advertisements incorporated several existing stereotypic social roles that were applied to African Americans. Mammy (associated with Aunt Jemima Pancake Flour) and Uncle Tom (associated with Uncle Ben's Rice) were two of the most common roles. Along with the Sambo image, associated with various consumer products such as soap, coffee, cereal, and toys (Boskin, 1986), these characterizations appealed to popular tastes based on an acceptance of these symbols from the era of slavery.

Such symbols became well known and accepted, even though they were unrealistic, one-dimensional, and highly offensive, especially to blacks. Although the Sambo character had a long and complex folk history behind it, during the later 19th century caricatures emerged of a loud-laughing, carefree jokester who was given to laziness, song, and dance (Boskin, 1986). Similarly, the Mammy role was based on a simplistic image of an asexual, unattractive, loyal household servant, devoted to caring for the white master's family (Manring, 1998). Uncle Tom became known as a kind and cheerful servant who was accommodating toward whites (Boskin, 1986). After the Civil War and throughout much of the 20th century, these images in advertising circulated to the point that they attained iconic status in American popular culture (Kern-Foxworth, 1994).

Minstrelsy

Minstrel stage shows were another important medium that presented stereotypic characterizations of blacks in the 19th century (Toll, 1974). The minstrel style of live entertainment became popular before the Civil War, with minstrel troupes regularly performing in major cities in the South and North. Minstrel shows were based on comedy skits, dancing, and singing, using a standard format that suited the tastes of mass audiences. Stock characters (e.g., Sambo, Uncle Tom) were portrayed by whites who blackened their faces, often by means of burnt cork. As far back as the 17th century, blackface in various forms had existed in England and seemed tied to a fascination with representing and vicariously experiencing the lives of others who were thought to be completely different (Rogin, 1996). In 19th-century America, blackface performances took place in an intercultural interaction field where imaging the Other (Frankenburg, 1993) was common, especially in scenes staged at minstrel shows.

Rogin (1996) asserts that as a kind of racial cross-dressing, blackface portrayals appealed to working-class and middle-class white audiences who were intrigued with interracial impulses and who experienced a kind of pleasurable anxiety from the performances. Minstrel entertainers portrayed blacks in exaggerated, animated characterizations that reinforced prevailing stereotypes, adding to the effects of advertising. Enjoying unparalleled popularity, minstrel shows became the dominant form of mass entertainment in the United States in the 19th century.

Film

In his book *Blackface, White Noise: Jewish Immigrants in the Hollywood Melting Pot* (1996), Michael Rogin provocatively writes that performance modes following the minstrel tradition included vaudeville, recorded music, radio, and motion pictures. In each instance, Rogin argues that minstrel-style portrayals were not replaced but rather maintained and extended. In the case of film, *Uncle Tom's Cabin*, *The Birth of a Nation*, *The Jazz Singer*, and *Gone with the Wind*, four of the most important early motion pictures, all dealt extensively with images of race and, for the most part, maintained stereotypic characterizations and themes that had already been established in minstrelsy (Rogin, 1996).

In addition to roles from the minstrel era, Bogle (1996) identifies two stereotypic black roles in early movies: the tragic mulatto and the black buck. The mulatto role was that of a light-skinned female, often young and attractive, whose identity was marred by her interracial ethnicity and her difficulty in being accepted as a white person in mainstream society. The black buck, notoriously featured in *The Birth of a Nation*, was a savage-like black man associated with brutality and lust.

As Bogle (1996) describes trends occurring throughout the 20th century, he notes that in the 1930s there were films with blacks as servants in the traditional stereotypic sense. During the 1930s, there appeared independent films made by white producers for black audiences, and *Imitation of Life* (1934), a movie that directly dealt with interracial themes (Cripps, 1993a). The movies that targeted black audiences were popular and became a source of pride to black moviegoers at a time when theaters were segregated. *Imitation of Life*, in a rather daring effort to treat interracial issues, brought to black and white audiences the story of a black woman and her interracial daughter (Bogle, 1996).

In films of the 1940s and the 1950s, blacks appeared as musical performers and dancers and, increasingly, were cast in non-stereotypic roles (Bogle, 1996). Some films of this era, for example, *Pinky* and *Intruder in the Dust*, dealt with themes of racism and racial identity and invited audiences to accept greater complexity in roles for blacks. Such roles showed movement away from traditional stereotypic characterizations and settings (Cripps, 1993b).

The Modern Civil Rights Era

From the 1960s to the present, several important aspects of racial stereotyping may be found in film, television, and recorded music.

Film

A gradual trend in film has been for blacks to perform roles that have become more like the parts usually played by white actors. However, with the emergence of the blaxploitation genre (Cripps, 1993b), there seemed to be a revival of the black buck stereotype. *Sweet Sweetback's Baadasssss Song* (1971), the first film in this genre, focused on the life of a young black man who uses violent means in response to white police brutality, thereby taking on the persona of a folk hero. After widespread urban and race-related violence in the 1960s, the blaxploitation films seemed to strengthen, for suburban whites, stereotypes of a violent element in black culture. Viewed from a black perspective, one appeal of the blaxploitation films was the display of resistance to injustices present in inner city environments (Massood, 2003).

In the last 30 years, while unflattering stereotypes of blacks have not disappeared from film, the trend has been for black actors to be increasingly cast in roles based on individual talent and mass audience appeal, rather than racial identity (Bryant & Thompson, 2002). Moreover, younger black filmmakers such as Spike Lee, Julie Dash, and John Singleton have brought greater sensitivity to portrayals of black culture (Bogle, 1996).

Television

Commercial television in the United States began in the late 1940s and African American performers have been present from the start; however, their roles have often been limited and problematic. In the 1950s, various black performers as well as athletes and quiz show contestants often appeared on television; however, in many cases, appearances were limited and blacks were still seen in stereotyped roles (MacDonald, 1983).

From the 1960s to the 1990s, there was a gradual increase in black roles on television. In network television series, blacks played 6 percent of the roles in the 1960s, 8 percent in the 1970s, 12 percent in the 1990s, and 14 percent in the early 1990s (Greenberg & Collette, 1997). Bill Cosby was one of the first black actors to regularly appear in a non-stereotypic role in a successful, prime-time series: *I Spy* (1965–1968). Cosby co-starred with a white actor, Robert Culp, in this relatively popular series in which Cosby's race was somewhat incidental (MacDonald, 1983). After *I Spy*, there was a growing number of leading roles for blacks in prime-time television.

The overall trend in television has been an expansion in the number and variety of roles for black performers, leading to a gradual diminution in the presence of racial stereotyping. Other patterns in television can also be detected. One popular program airing in 1971 was the situation comedy *All in the Family* starring a white male head of the family who openly voiced his prejudices toward African Americans and other minorities. The lead male character, Archie Bunker, was portrayed humorously, thus suggesting a mockery of his old-fashioned prejudices. While, in a positive sense, the program raised awareness of racial issues in the United States, in a negative sense, it was viewed as a vehicle that put racism on display and made racial prejudice seem more acceptable (MacDonald, 1983). In the 1970s, several comedy spin-offs from *All in the Family* featured black actors whose characters seemed not far removed from some of the stereotypes of the minstrel stage (Doob, 1999).

In 1977, the eight-part series *Roots* became a television phenomenon, attracting over 130 million viewers (Tuttle, 1999). Based on a book by black author Alex Haley, *Roots* traced Haley's ancestry back to the days of the slave trade in Africa. The series was praised for the dramatic performances of its cast; however, critics claimed that *Roots* focused on the progress of blacks in resisting and overcoming the condition of slavery, rather than on an appreciation of the ideological basis of racism and the mistreatment of blacks (MacDonald, 1983). *The Cosby Show*, an extremely popular prime-time program in the 1980s, was not based on traditional racial stereotypes (Bogle, 2001). With an all-black cast, this series featured an upper-middle-class family whose members cared for each other and presented positive images of African American family life.

It is important to note one other area of television content with racial aspects: local news reporting. In summarizing research findings from the

1990s, Greenberg, Mastro, and Brand (2002) conclude that whites appear only half as often as blacks in news stories on crime, with blacks more commonly shown as perpetrators. This pattern, with clear implications for stereotyping, will be discussed in greater detail later in this chapter.

Recorded Music

Although various aspects of African American musical traditions are relevant to the issue of stereotyping, rap music is one particular genre that is relevant to this discussion. Rap music originated in New York in the 1970s, although it draws upon oral traditions such as toasting, jive talk, and gospel music from earlier periods (Bennett, 1999). In the 1970s, rap artists used portable sound-mixing equipment to speak in rhythmic, rhyming schemes heard over instrumental music, and the style was well received at live outdoor performances. Commercial audio recordings of rap music followed and artists enjoyed financial and artistic success (Cobb, 2007).

In the 1980s, "gangsta rap," a style of rap music, appeared with lyrics frequently oriented to themes of violence, misogyny, and self-destructive behaviors (Rose, 1994). Although only one subgenre of rap music, "gangsta rap" received sensational media attention and became associated with the perception of a violent African American youth culture that was attracting and influencing young white fans. Public concerns rose, as noted by Van DeBurg (2004), "During the 1980s and '90s, no cultural trend more tellingly influenced public opinion on African American villainy than the valorization of rap music and its creators by mainstream youth" (p. 196). Commentators called attention to the lyrics and content of rap music, offering negative criticism and focusing on political and social critique. However, as Kelley (1997) notes, critics overlook rap music as an expressive performance style in which content is subordinate to form. References to violence and antisocial behaviors in rap music lyrics are reflections of life in urban ghettoes and, in an important sense, may be understood as legitimate expressions of resistance to racism and oppression (Rose, 1994).

Summary of Cultural Origins of Stereotypes

The cultural origins of racial stereotypes reveal the effects of popular culture on preexisting stereotypic beliefs about blacks and black culture. This discussion has summarized some of the more prevalent trends in marketing, mass entertainment, and mass media. Stereotypic images from the past and present are also found in other forms of mass-distributed materials in the form of newspapers, magazines, postcards and greeting cards, toys, radio, cartoons, and the Internet, as well as in the forms of live entertainment such as traveling shows, concerts, and sporting events. In discussing advertising, minstrel shows, film, television, and recorded music, this section has highlighted some of the more influential sources of racial stereotypes in the last 175 years. As important as these influences have been, there remains another significant source of racial stereotyping in the form of social cognition.

Social Cognitive Origins

The social cognitive framework considers that stereotypes are the result of human interaction and experiences with people from different groups (Schneider, 2004). To begin, we need to clarify the nature of prejudice and discrimination. The previous discussion of stereotypes stated that social categorization is associated with values toward in-groups and out-groups. Holding negative attitudes toward a group is defined as prejudice, whereas treating someone unfairly due to membership in an out-group is discrimination (Ruscher, 2001). The nature of prejudice and discrimination is directly related to group behavior, as individuals ordinarily become socialized within their own groups and gradually learn to share their in-group's stereotypes and prejudices. Here we will attempt to summarize some of the more influential social cognitive processes that give rise to stereotypes and prejudices. In turn we will examine (1) socialization, (2) consensus, and (3) social identity.

Socialization

The process of learning values and beliefs that are shared by members of groups with which one affiliates is referred to as socialization. Although an umbrella term for human development that includes biological components (Bugental & Grusec, 2006), socialization incorporates cognitive and sociocultural processes. Learning can take place through various groups and group-related environments such as the family, peers, students, and numerous other social and political groups. In early childhood, for example, acquisition of ethnic categories has been observed in the tendencies to label others according to ethnicity by the age of eight (Aboud, 1984). Skin color has been found to be a salient stimulus when young children are asked to observe differences and similarities among others (Hirschfeld, 1996). The development of racial categorization among children is due, in part, to psychological patterns occurring at various stages of human development. Parental and peer effects may also exist, although the strength of these effects is uncertain. In their study of racial attitudes among eight-year-old children, Aboud and Doyle (1996) note that perceived similarity between parents' racial attitudes and those of their children is usually greater than their actual similarity. A similar pattern is reported for racial attitudes among friends. Further parental influence exists in the form of parents' selection of schools and activities for their children.

One important form of parental influence has been defined as racial socialization (O'Connor, Brooks-Gunn, & Graber, 2000). Racial socialization refers to black parenting behavior that prepares children to cope with effects of racism and discrimination (Hughes & Chen, 1997). Racial socialization includes knowledge of and attitudes toward achievement, ethnic pride, racial history, and other aspects of race (O'Connor et al., 2000) and, therefore, takes racial stereotyping into account. Socialization in the family, for blacks and whites, also results from a child observing how his/her parents discuss race and how they act in interracial situations.

Peer influences contributing to stereotyping may be found in several forms of socialization. O'Connor et al. (2000) report that among black and white girls (aged 8–9) the effects of same-race peer influences are greater than out-race influences. The peer influences, measured in terms of preferences for music and television programs, show that both black and white girls are interested in materials oriented to the other race. A preference for interracial friendships is present among 29 percent of the black girls and 15 percent of the white girls. Another interesting finding in this study is that black girls report more in-group peer preferences when their mothers maintain greater cultural distance socialization.

Among teenagers, peer effects from socialization are often linked to experiences in school. In his earlier-cited study of a suburban interracial school system, Ogbu (2003) refers to the high school building as being, in effect, the site of two schools: one white and one black. As Ogbu (2003) observes, "On several occasions senior high school students reported that peer groups and peer activities were organized along racial lines." (p. 63). In response to a question about black and white attitudes in the community, one black student at the high school offers this insight into the local peer culture, "Um, I don't necessarily think that they want us here and they [don't] like us here [in high school]. I just don't think that they do; [but] I don't know. Sometimes I just feel like I don't belong" (p. 66).

In the school setting studied by Ogbu, one aspect of adolescent identity development seems similar to a pattern described by Tatum (1997). In interracial educational settings in which neither black nor white students are in a clear majority, elementary school pupils commonly interact without distinct regard for race, whereas by middle school years, students usually segregate by race. In social activities, students may further segregate by gender, thus a clear race-and-gender distribution develops affecting friendship and dating patterns. At the middle school level and continuing into high school, there may be an increased presence of tracking, the results of which often lead to another form of racial segregation (Tatum, 1997). During this period, some aspects of "acting white" (discussed in Chapter 3) may occur with white students sometimes referring to this phenomenon in terms of stereotyping, and black students feeling unsure about their abilities and identities, especially when facing lowered expectations from teachers (Tatum, 2007).

As development reaches late adolescence and adulthood, racial stereotype formation due to socialization continues with influences from social, educational, political, religious, occupational, and many other groups. Another pattern of racial stereotyping indicates the presence of demographic characteristics that are based, at least in part, on socialization. Hurwitz and Peffley (1998) note that level of education, age, and gender are variables in the way whites stereotype blacks. Older, less educated, white males are more likely to subscribe to negative stereotypes of blacks, particularly in regard to work ethic and hostility.

Consensus

The source of racial stereotypes known as consensus refers to beliefs that are shared. Although a single individual may hold a stereotype, important aspects of racial stereotypes are revealed through the extent to which they are shared, particularly by a large number of people. Several issues confound our understanding of consensual stereotypes. Does awareness of a stereotype mean the same thing as personally endorsing it? Even if one consciously denounces a widely held and negative stereotype, could such a stereotype nevertheless have some sort of impact on one? How much sharing constitutes a form of consensus?

In their review of the shared nature of social cognitions, Hardin and Higgins (1996) note several aspects of verification. According to these authors, the process of achieving consensus is multifunctional, socially constructed, and anticipates future social interaction. Among the functions of shared stereotypes is a social regulatory characteristic that leads to ease of activation and greater likelihood of behavior being influenced (Sechrist & Stangor, 2001). The socially constructed nature of stereotypes means that people engage others in discourse that establishes, shapes, and maintains stereotypes. Interaction context, social roles, expectations of listeners, and audience preferences all influence how messages are exchanged and meanings are construed (Hardin & Higgins, 1996). The anticipatory feature explains how individuals may share varying interpretations or levels of consensus, depending on the audience (Fleming, Darling, Hilton, & Kojetin, 1990). In these respects, we see that consensus has socially dynamic characteristics that can make the content of stereotypes multifaceted, depending on social circumstances.

In-group identity is an important factor in consensus, especially in the context of in-group and out-group comparisons. That context can affect stereotypes is part of what Schneider (2004) calls the self-categorization model of stereotyping. This model considers that stereotyping occurs in situations in which individuals are directly comparing themselves to others from a different group. Self-categorization reflects a dependence upon context, and only when specific comparisons are being made are stereotypes activated. Consensus is affected, as the research by Haslam, Oakes, Reynolds, and Turner (1999) shows, when one's in-group identity is important. During in-group and out-group comparisons, in-group identity may become more salient, resulting in greater agreement on in-group traits. The consensus effects are attributed to the motivation among in-group members to develop shared perceptions of their group orientation.

Beyond the group interaction setting, consensus effects in racial stereotyping may be found in other contexts such as media consumption. In local news reports on television, for example, Gorham (2006) observes that people who watch television extensively may hold a view of social reality that corresponds to the information and the images they receive from television. Given the body of evidence for the existence of stereotypes of African Americans as perpetrators of crime (see Entman & Rojecki, 2000, for a review), and given that local television news often presents stories about crime, we might expect consensus effects for racial stereotypes among white viewers. A study by Oliver, Jackson, Moses, and Dangerfield (2004) examines readers' tendencies to identify facial features associated with various news reports. These authors find that participants identify Afrocentric facial features more than Eurocentic facial features when the news story pertains to violent crime. Dixon (2006) affirms that after exposure to news content with black suspects, heavy viewers of television news, more than light viewers, tend to perceive their social reality as more dangerous.

More recently, Dixon and Azocar (2007) have noted that "exposure to racialized crime news shapes perceptions of Blacks and race relations and leads viewers to see criminal activity as a Black activity" (p. 245). Entman (1992) also finds that in televised news segments about crime, white suspects are more often featured making statements in their own defense, compared to black suspects who are usually featured without such statements. In general, viewing stories on crime linked to black suspects may not only reinforce racial stereotypes but can also lead to a shared viewpoint that crime is widespread in the real world. Consensus effects are also implicated in the research of Armstrong, Neuendorf, and Brentar (1992), who report that white college students with higher exposure to television news tend to overstate the extent of poverty among African Americans. Viewing news stories on television clearly reflects cultural stereotypes. However, it is argued that through conversation, personal stories, and various forms of interpersonal and social communication, individuals develop a consensual reality that helps maintain shared stereotypes (Ruscher, 2001).

One other important issue should be noted regarding consensus. Hamilton and Gifford (1976) describe a kind of stereotyping resulting from observation of infrequent but distinctive events. Behavior by group members in a certain situation, although not necessarily common, is noticeable when the observer does not have extensive experience interacting with the group. The observation may lead to the inference that there is a meaningful co-occurrence of a situation and a certain behavior, thus drawing attention to this relationship. Hamilton and Gifford (1976) discuss how white observers who are aware of negative characteristics associated with blacks may want to avoid interaction with blacks. When undesirable behavior by blacks is observed, there can be a tendency to think that this behavior is representative of all blacks, even though it has not been commonly experienced. We may also note that the same pattern can occur when blacks observe behaviors by whites. The result is an illusory correlation (Hamilton & Gifford, 1976) that makes the co-occurrence seem more widespread than it is in reality. Moreover, Ruscher (2001) notes that when in-group members hold negative stereotypes of an out-group, observations of a few positive behaviors tend not to change the overall negative valuation of the out-group.

In a similar vein, experimental research by Jackson, Sullivan, and Hodge (1993) examines patterns of white participants' ratings of academic achievement of white and black student targets. An in-group bias emerges, resulting in poor performance by the white students being judged as due to lack of effort, whereas successful performance by blacks is seen as due to luck. Success for the white students is judged to be the result of effort. In general, then, although illusory correlations may lack factual verification, they may nevertheless take on a degree of perceived validity that can help maintain stereotypes.

Issues of consensus are hard to separate from the question of whether and to what extent stereotypes are accurate. Although one might assume that stereotypes, more often than not, are inaccurate, judging accuracy is inextricably interwoven with perceived homogeneity of in-group and out-group members. Even when we suspect a stereotype is mostly inaccurate, we may still find that it contains an element of truth (see discussion below) and, therefore, such a stereotype can nevertheless affect us. Furthermore, consensus is important because perceived accuracy can carry as much or more weight than actual accuracy. Schneider (2004) offers three reasons why stereotype consensus is a significant issue. First, we tend to believe stereotypes when there is widespread support for them. Second, we are more likely to activate stereotypes when we believe they are subscribed to by others. And third, stereotypes that receive consensual support are more likely to remain firmly implanted and more resistant to change.

Social Identity

Tajfel (1978) defines social identity as "that part of an individual's self-concept which derives from his knowledge of a social group (or groups) together with the value and emotional significance attached to that membership" (p. 63). One important function of membership in groups is that such membership helps us maintain a positive social identity (Hogg & Abrams, 2001; Simon & Brown, 1987). Regarding stereotyping, two aspects of social identity are significant. First, individuals establish group membership through beliefs that are shared by the group. Shared beliefs are important because they not only reinforce positive values toward one's own group but may also lead to reinforcement of negative values toward out-groups (Schneider, 2004). As noted by Schneider, in-group values do not necessarily emphasize negative judgments of out-groups. However, in-group membership often carries with it a motivation to think highly of one's own group and accentuate differences between one's own group and various out-groups.

Secondly, behaviors by one's group may be a means to demonstrate group identity and differentiation. Just as clothing and mannerisms can contribute to in-group identity, language and slang, Giles and Johnson (1987) explain, may also be factors in group identity. In another investigation related to language and social identity, Maass, Salvi, Arcuri, and Semin (1989) discovered a stereotypic pattern in the way language is used to describe in-group and out-group behaviors. This study finds that desirable in-group behaviors and undesirable out-group behaviors are described in more abstract language, whereas undesirable in-group behaviors and desirable out-group behaviors are described in more concrete language. It is hypothesized that in-group and out-group stereotypes may predispose one to use abstract language that more easily lends itself to generalizations. The authors also note that abstractions are less verifiable, thus when such abstractions conform to preexisting stereotypes they may be more resistant to change. The work of Maass et al. (1989) demonstrates a linguistic intergroup bias and is consistent with later research by Schnake and Ruscher (1998). By including participants' level of racial prejudice as a variable, Schnake and Ruscher find that more racially prejudiced European American participants tend to use more abstract language to describe stereotypic behaviors of African Americans.

Two important aspects of stereotyping and the maintenance of social identity are (1) minimal group effects and (2) self-affirmation. The influential work of Henri Tajfel (1978) and associates (Tajfel, Billig, Bundy, & Flament, 1971) has established support for the idea that even in informal laboratory groups to which persons have been arbitrarily assigned, those in newly formed groups begin showing feelings of belonging to their group and discriminate in favor of their group. Known as the minimal group paradigm, Hogg and Abrams (2001) note that findings from these types of studies are robust and have been replicated many times. By extension, in life outside the laboratory, persons who identify with a social group engage in activities and emphasize shared beliefs in an effort to enhance their group distinctiveness. Schneider (2004), for example, suggests that black students who "act white" may be displaying social identity effects. Moreover, individuals draw upon stereotyping that enables them to affirm a positive image of themselves through the negative evaluation of others (Fein & Spencer, 1997). Viewing it as an extension of social identity processes, Fein and Spencer argue that when one's self-image is threatened, one may be motivated to restore his or her self-esteem by invoking negative perceptions of others, especially when others are part of a group that is already negatively stereotyped.

Racial profiling is an additional activity relevant to race and stereotyping. Racial profiling may not be a clear case of any one form of stereotyping but may combine features of all three aforementioned forms of social cognition. Chriss (2007) describes the basis for racial profiling by noting how law enforcement officers typically have extended periods of "down time" when they routinely patrol areas. During such times, police personnel may operate with an awareness of symbolic assailants (Skolnick, 1966), a category of people who, by their appearance and behavior in certain contexts, seem somehow suspicious and, therefore, justify closer inspection. To the extent minorities are targeted and questioned on the basis of ethnicity, this process may be termed racial profiling. For example, one study of racial profiling in Boston was conducted by Antonovics and Knight (2004). Over a period of 21 months during 2001–2003, these researchers documented that over 43 percent of all searches conducted by the Boston Police Department were of vehicles driven by African Americans. This was despite the fact that vehicles driven by African Americans constituted less than 33 percent of the vehicles that were stopped. The authors conclude that police officers were more likely to conduct a search if the motorist's race was different from that of the officer, and that preference-based discrimination plays a significant role in this behavior. Research mentioned in Chapter 3 (Dixon et al., 2008), although not directly studying racial profiling, also referred to problematic interactions when drivers and police officers were not of the same race.

The profiling paradigm has also been extended to language. Purnell, Idsardi, and Baugh (1999), for example, have experimented with phone calls placed by speakers of SAE, AAVE, and Chicano English. When calls are placed to property owners in predominantly European American neighborhoods, the callers speaking AAVE or Chicano English are less likely to receive an appointment to inspect an advertised rental property. Nonstandard speech can thus arouse negative language attitudes and lead to discrimination. As with appearance and behavior associated with law enforcement, linguistic profiling may play an important role in impression formation and maintenance (Baugh, 2003). One can discern elements of socialization, consensus, and social identity in instances of profiling, and perhaps all three processes interact with and reinforce each other.

Stereotyping of European Americans

Before concluding this discussion on stereotyping, let us note some patterns in stereotyping of European Americans by African Americans. Although less extensively studied than racial stereotypes held by whites, there are important insights from the extant research in this area.

Fundamentally, African Americans in North America have often viewed European Americans as their oppressors. Indeed, a sense of shared oppression was a primary element in the emergence of African American culture and African nationalism (Stuckey, 1987). Turner (1993) notes the persistence of rumors among slaves that whites were ever ready to harm blacks and to employ tactics to prevent slaves from running away. Severe punishments of captured runaways served as examples of what would happen to those who tried to run away, thus slaveholders attempted to instill fear of punishment. Frederick Douglass, a former slave, notes that he was highly aware of his fugitive status and feared for his security (Douglass, 1968).

Part of the sentiment expressed by Douglass (1968) was related to his mistrust of whites, especially white men. An important sense of mistrust toward whites has long been a stereotypic viewpoint held by blacks. Turner (1993) describes numerous incidents over the years that have led to rumors in the African American community that white people could not be trusted to treat blacks fairly or honestly. Turner analyzes several recent rumors such as a belief that certain consumer foods and beverages contain chemicals that will sterilize black men, or that the murders of young black men in Atlanta in the 1980s were due to a conspiracy by the federal agency, the Centers for Disease Control (CDC), to extract interferon from the young men's bodies. One basis for the rumors about the CDC, as Turner (1993) notes, was the revelation that in the infamous Tuskegee experiments on treatment of syphilis in the 1930s, black volunteers were misled. The black participants were told they were being treated for the disease, when in actuality, they were merely being observed as the progression of the disease was studied. Even after the 1940s when penicillin was found to be an effective treatment for syphilis, the drugs were not administered to the black victims (Turner, 1993; see also, Fine & Turner, 2001). Beyond rumors and conspiracies, Watkins and Terrell (1988) note problematic issues of trust between blacks and whites in client-counselor relationships. As Watkins and Terrell observe, a main effect for mistrust emerges when blacks interact with a white counselor, during which expectations may further hinder effective counseling. For a variety of reasons, stereotyping and related beliefs have led to a continuing sense of mistrust toward whites on the part of blacks.

Several qualitative studies have examined blacks' stereotypic beliefs about whites in the context of retailing. McDermott's (2006) ethnographic study analyzes interaction between black and white customers and cashiers at convenience stores. Black cashiers often note that white customers are rude and sometimes place their money or credit cards on the counter, while seeming to deliberately refuse to put the cash or credit cards into the hands of the clerk. The black clerks interpret this behavior as signs of disrespect and reluctance to accommodate blacks. McDermott (2006) comments that race does, indeed, affect interactions in that a black cashier may react to a white customer's perceived negative attitude; however, black cashiers overlook the fact that black customers may also act rude in many instances. McDermott notes that socioeconomic class and regional variations complicate analyses of racial prejudice, and that expressions of prejudice, both by whites and blacks, have important situational constraints.

Lee (2002) has conducted in-depth interviews of Jewish, Korean, and African American shop owners and customers in Philadelphia and New York. Lee reports that blacks, particularly those shopping in white neighborhoods, feel they are not treated with respect by white clerks. Referring to opinions expressed by black interviewees, Lee (2002) states, "For instance, they say that sales associates greet and approach white customers more promptly than they do black customers, sometimes even skipping over blacks in line in order to help whites who were clearly behind them in line" (p. 170). Lee notes further that black shoppers, again in white neighborhoods, are closely followed by white clerks in a way that makes them feel they are being suspected of shoplifting. Essed (1991) also reports on interviews with black women from California and the Netherlands in regard to shopping experiences. In this study, women in both samples note personal as well as other reported accounts of being followed by white clerks while shopping, a pattern attributed to clerks' suspicions that black customers are more likely to shoplift. Essed (1991) presents additional data showing that accounts of racial discrimination associated with shopping are the third most reported category (after education and work). Similarly, Buttny (2004) finds that during black/white interaction in service encounters the communication of respect often becomes problematic.

More references to blacks' stereotypes of whites come from various anecdotal accounts. Barnes (2000) notes that, apart from being followed and not treated as kindly as white shoppers, blacks often feel stereotyped by white clerks who seem to question the ability of a black person to have funds to pay for an expensive item. Williams (2000) discusses beliefs among blacks that white people are incapable of acting "cool," dressing with style, or dancing well, and that whites acknowledge black acquaintances in private, but not in public while in the presence of their white friends. James (2004) describes beliefs and stereotypes revealed in stories told in her black family as she was growing up in Ohio in the 1950s and the 1960s. According to these family stories, common stereotypes blacks maintain toward whites include beliefs that whites are treacherous, whites feel inferior and, therefore, are motivated to derogate blacks, white men often rape black women, white men show interest in black women when the men expect to receive sexual favors, whites withhold approval for black achievement and accomplishments, most whites cannot be trusted (especially whites from the North), most white men are arrogant, most white women are lazy, and good whites are the exception (James, 2004).

Finally, results from quantitative research reveal additional instances of blacks' stereotyping of whites. Brigham (1993) conducted research on racial attitudes among college students, finding blacks expressing several negative beliefs related to how whites interact with blacks. Among the findings are beliefs that whites feel blacks are too demanding, that whites are not trustworthy and cannot understand blacks, and that whites have weaker character. Stephen, Boniecki, Ybarra, Bettencourt, Ervin, Jackson, McNatt, and Renfro (2002) examine the impact of perceived racist threats (realistic and symbolic) and intergroup anxiety on stereotyping. Based on university student participants, this study notes that negative contact experiences, strength of in-group identity, perceptions of intergroup conflict, perceived status inequality, and negative racial stereotyping are affected by racist threat variables. Measures of stereotyping include these twelve items: (1) hostility, (2) admiration, (3) dislike, (4) acceptance, (5) superiority, (6) affection, (7) disdain, (8) hatred, (9) approval, (10) sympathy, (11) rejection, and (12) warmth. Among the various findings in this study is the clear pattern that blacks maintain more negative stereotypes toward whites than do whites toward blacks. However, the antecedent conditions (racist threats and intergroup anxiety) account for more variance in the negative attitudes of whites toward blacks than in the negative attitudes of blacks toward whites.

Livingston's (2002) research examines the nature of black attitudes toward whites, finding differences between implicit and explicit attitudes. Based on a college student sample, Livingston finds that attitudes among African Americans displayed a pattern of in-group bias on explicit measures, but on implicit measures there was little evidence of in-group bias. This study also finds that out-group contact is correlated with negative attitudes towards whites, some of which may be due to a perceived negativity on the part of whites toward blacks.

Summary of Discussion of Racial Stereotypes

The point of this discussion has been to show how whites' stereotypes of African Americans have been unfair, harmful, and pervasive in the United States. Racial stereotypes have long existed and, although diminishing in many ways, have become instilled in American culture. Research also indicates that blacks' stereotypes of whites, albeit less extensively studied, are often negative. It should be noted that even though race-related stereotypes are often inaccurate and exaggerated, sometimes there is an element of truth to stereotypes (Schneider, 2004). For example, whites often stereotype blacks as being of lower economic status. Although there are growing numbers of middle, upper-middle, and upper income black families, it is true that, on average, family income for blacks is lower than family income for whites. Similarly, in health care contexts blacks may sometimes view with suspicion the treatments they are offered from white providers. Suspicion may stem from knowledge of actual conspiracies against blacks such as those occurring during the Tuskegee experiments of the 1930s and the 1940s. Although the conspiracies that occurred in the Tuskegee experiments took place many years ago, for at least some blacks there may remain an element of truth to fears associated with conspiracies.

Important as the cultural sources of stereotypes have been, historical and cultural trends are only part of the explanation for the persistence of racial stereotyping. Racial stereotypes are maintained and reinforced through the social cognitive influences of socialization, consensus, and social identity. Various ethnic minorities in the U.S. (e.g., Jews, Irish, Chinese) now enjoy a status that has made them susceptible to far less negative stereotyping than existed in the past. Thus, we find that over time, the cultural forms of racial stereotypes may be modified through social cognitive processes. The fact that racial stereotypes of blacks have proven more durable than stereotypes of certain other minorities may indicate that blacks' cultural and structural assimilation remains more limited compared to certain other ethnic groups. However, there is reason to expect that greater acceptance of African Americans in all sectors of American society will eventually lead to a decrease in negative racial stereotyping of blacks (Marger, 2009).

Discourse and Race

Over the course of American history there have been many periods when discussions of race have appeared with a particular set of meanings reflecting the current racial climate. It would be nearly impossible to examine all or even the main forms of racial discourse throughout American history. The present discussion will emphasize several of the more prominent patterns and themes in racial discourse that have been evident since the 1970s. One aim of this section is to examine patterns in discourse and how these patterns are interrelated with racial stereotypes. The major topics discussed are (1) color-blindness; (2) insults, slights, and political correctness; and (3) hate speech.

Color-blindness

It has been common to hear references to an ideal of a color-blind society in public and interpersonal discourse. Justice John M. Harlan used the term color-blind in his dissenting opinion in the 1896 *Plessy* case decided by the Supreme Court (Fireside, 2004). Harlan's use of color-blind was taken to mean that the Constitution recognizes basic rights for all individuals, regardless of color and, therefore, called attention to the extension of rights to black persons. A similar notion of color-blind was invoked by Martin Luther King, Jr., in his "I Have a Dream" speech in 1963. King referred to the goal of persons being granted rights based not on their color, but on the content of their character. Again, King was speaking in terms of extending rights to blacks. In the 1980s, President Ronald Reagan also stated the goal of color-blind policies that treat individuals without regard to color. Under President Reagan, the Civil Rights Division of the Department of Justice acted against racial quotas and promoted individual opportunity as opposed to group entitlements (O'Reilly, 1995). Thus, in this sense, color-blind was taken to mean that using skin color to benefit someone was just as misguided as using it to deprive one of opportunities. This sense of color-blind shifted away from emphasis on the extension of rights to blacks.

In Steele's (1990) analysis, affirmative action has led to unfortunate outcomes. Steele discusses how preferential treatment reinforces a counterproductive sense of white guilt, while simultaneously leading to the stigma that minority students and employees are not talented enough to succeed without such treatment. Steele and other observers, black and white, have thought of color-blindness as a way to move beyond the era of overt racism and toward a more meritocratic society. In this sense, preferential treatment underscores black inferiority and is ultimately harmful to blacks. Thus, taking a color-blind approach should help us recognize equal rights for all without regard for color. Such a perspective asks Americans to deemphasize and act without regard for color.

The foregoing examples help us see shifts in meanings of color-blindness and show how people with different value systems and/or political agendas can refer to color-blindness in different ways. As several researchers (e.g., Bonilla-Silva and Forman, 2000; Perry, 2002; Trepagnier, 2006) have concluded, one current function of the notion of color-blindness is to allow expression of one's apparent nonracist viewpoints. A sociocultural context has now arisen in which many white U.S. Americans reject racial prejudice and yet paradoxically maintain racist attitudes. Based on considerable empirical evidence from the 1970s and the 1980s, Gaertner and Dovidio (1986) argue that many whites in the United States maintain what is termed aversive racism, a belief in egalitarianism and a desire to think of oneself as nonprejudiced, while nevertheless harboring negative feelings toward blacks. Researchers hypothesize that aversive racists want to believe that they oppose racial discrimination and, therefore, often remove racist feelings from their awareness. It is argued that claims of color-blindness are a form of denying racist thoughts (Bonilla-Silva, 2003). A related but somewhat different concept, symbolic racism (Sears & Kinder, 1971; Sears, 1988) refers to political attitudes that show opposition to traditional, "old fashioned" racial prejudice. Nevertheless, symbolic racists regard blacks as not willing to work hard enough to succeed, not practicing self-reliance, and the beneficiaries of undeserved preferential treatment. Aversive and symbolic racism are two concepts that explain how someone can oppose racial prejudice and yet subscribe to negative attitudes toward blacks.

Survey data consistently show that most U.S. Americans now reject racial prejudice, especially in comparison to prevailing attitudes of the 1950s and earlier (e.g., Bonilla-Silva & Forman, 2000; Schuman, Steeh, Bobo, & Krysan, 1997). Yet, as noted in Chapter 4, interview data reveal a more complicated attitudinal framework. In their interviews with 41 college student participants, Bonilla-Silva and Forman find indirect but subtle expressions of racial prejudice among whites. To illustrate just one instance of such an expression, consider this exchange (Bonilla-Silva & Forman, 2000, p. 67):

Interviewer: Some Black people claim that they face a great deal of racism in their daily lives, and a lot of other people claim that that's not the case. What do you think?

Kara: I would think, presently speaking, like people in my generation, I don't think it's . . . as much that there is racism, *but Black people almost go into their experiences feeling like they should be discriminated against and I think that makes them hypersensitive.* (Interview. # 25:13; italics in the original).

In her response, Kara downplays the presence of racism in society today and engages in an argumentative strategy the researchers refer to as reversal, a form of blaming the victim (Bonilla-Silva & Forman, 2000). By holding blacks accountable for the discrimination they experience, the interviewee disavows her active role in racist behavior. On the surface, the speaker seems to affirm a color-blind attitude toward race and mentions that blacks face less racism today. However, she then states that some aspects of racism are actually caused by blacks themselves, thereby holding blacks responsible for racism.

For another example, consider the following excerpt from a focus group participant from a qualitative study of racial attitudes (Trepagnier, 2006):

I was explicitly told that racism is wrong, that they [her parents] are not racist, and that I shouldn't be racist, and that anyone decent wouldn't be. Yet at the same time I got the distinct feeling that they were uncomfortable about [the black neighbors]. If I just tried to picture them meeting a black person on the street, even though I can't really remember that, I'd know the look on their faces and the way their bodies would tense up . . . and no real explanation as to why. So I got, I think, a very deep message of underlying fear; that they intensely feared blacks. (pp. 23–24)

Trepagnier (2006) refers to this kind of talk as an example of silent racism. The participant's parents seemed to want their daughter to be opposed to racism. However, there was an informally communicated message that blacks are to be feared. Such mixed messages convey a sense that racism is to be avoided, yet, at the same time, there is the presence of a negative attitude toward blacks.

In the arena of public discourse, the U.S. Supreme Court ruled on a case in 2007 in which color-blind discourse was involved. As noted in Chapter 4, public school districts in Seattle and Louisville had been assigning students to schools on the basis of race, with the goal of achieving a racial balance and racial diversity within their districts. The school districts were sued and the cases eventually reached the Supreme Court. A critical issue for the court was whether there was a compelling state interest in employing assignments based on race for the purpose of achieving diversity in the schools. Chief Justice Roberts wrote the majority opinion in which he noted that the Fourteenth Amendment does not permit differential treatment on the basis of race. Chief Justice Roberts concluded his written opinion by stating, "The way to stop discrimination on the basis of race is to stop discriminating on the basis of race" (Greenhouse, 2007, p. A20). Whereas in earlier court rulings it was stated that race could be taken into account in issues involving education and diversity, now, in 2007, the court was stating that race should not be taken into account.

One sees multiple and conflicting meanings in instances of color-blind discourse. In some cases, color-blind means that individuals espouse a race-neutral stance and believe this will help us move beyond race as a stumbling block to improved race relations. To others, American society has not yet reached the point when we have fully accounted for race and that to ignore race is to act as if race no longer matters.

Insults, Slights, and Political Correctness

In February 2007, Senator Joseph Biden referred to fellow senator and presidential candidate Barack Obama as "the first mainstream African American who is articulate and bright and clean and a nice-looking guy" (Nagourney, 2007, p. 2). Later in 2007, radio personality Don Imus referred to the Rutgers University women's basketball players by stating, "That's some nappy-headed hos, there, I'm going to tell you that now" (Kosova, 2007, p. 26). One can identify a number of public statements like these, occurring frequently in the United States, when language is used in a way that invokes a negative stereotype of African Americans. In examples such as these, speakers are called to account for their utterances and then apologize, with the whole statement-criticism-apology sequence resembling a speech event or speech ritual. Senator Biden's position as U.S. senator was not jeopardized and his candidacy for president, although ultimately unsuccessful, was not derailed by this incident. Don Imus's indiscretion, however, led to a major public relations problem for him and he was forced to resign.

Several aspects of remarks like those of Biden and Imus are noteworthy. According to Biden, his comments were meant to refer to Obama in a positive sense as a talented public speaker with new ideas (Nagourney, 2007). To some, Biden's words were unfortunate and ill chosen, but not offensive, at least in the sense he intended. To others, the utterance was a reminder of similar phrases often heard before in American speech and represented negative and stereotypic thoughts on the intellect and verbal abilities of African Americans. Imus was known for his insults directed toward well-known political figures and others in business, sports, and entertainment (Kosova, 2007). However, the Rutgers University women's basketball team, successful and composed of a majority of black players, had performed admirably. The team was a source of pride to the university and had done nothing to merit negative publicity. In referring to the Rutgers team, Imus made a casual, off-hand comment that was similar to other references he often made as part of his style of insulting humor on the radio. In this case, his sexist and racist comments were completely unfair and inexcusable.

Both Biden and Imus later apologized. Senator Biden talked to Senator Obama who stated that he did not believe Biden intended to be offensive. Obama stated, "I didn't take Senator's Biden's comments personally, but obviously they were historically inaccurate" (Nagourney, 2007, p. A2). Obama then added that others such as Jesse Jackson, Al Sharpton, Shirley Chisholm, and Carol Moseley Braun were African Americans who had been candidates for major offices and could not be considered inarticulate. The Rutgers team held a press conference during which many of its members expressed sadness and anger over Imus's slur (Strauss, 2007). From the viewpoint of the team and its fans, the remarks detracted from what should have been a time to celebrate their success. Imus met with the Rutgers team and apologized for his remarks, and the team accepted his apology (Kelley, Starr, & Conant, 2007). As noted, Imus's position as radio host was terminated.

Another important characteristic of these incidents was that they occurred during an era of instant electronic communication. The controversial statements by Imus and Biden were covered widely by the media, and there was no way for the remarks to be ignored or denied. Biden's comments seemed to lose their news value within a few days. Moreover, his relationship with Obama was repaired, given that Biden was selected to run for the vice presidency and was ultimately elected to that office to serve with Obama. Imus's remarks were far more serious. The radio host's words were not only widely disseminated but also received continuing coverage for several days. As media outlets carry such stories, especially when the incidents involve well-known individuals, there is a tendency for media organizations to treat such events as sensational and tragic (Jacobs, 2000). This type of media coverage leads to feelings of an irreconcilable racial divide in the United States. However, reminders of a racial divide, in and of themselves, do little to encourage the kind of dialogue that would help people learn from problems, mistakes, and dilemmas of an interracial nature. By dwelling on the crisis aspects of race-related news stories, media coverage can end up short-circuiting interracial dialogue and do little to promote constructive discussions that could actually help us improve race relations.

Of utmost importance in incidents like this is that the individuals used language that is politically incorrect. Orbe and Harris (2008) offer this definition of political correctness: "A term popularized by the mass media to describe social movements to adopt a specific set of ideologies, concepts, and terms that reflect a sensitivity to issues of culture, power, and privilege, frequently abbreviated to 'PC' (p. 271)." PC came into being in the 1980s and was often described as a kind of speech code used on college campuses where students and faculty were trying to promote tolerance and standards for civil discourse. PC calls attention to the ability of language to stigmatize and, therefore, encourages avoidance of terms that negatively label individuals. Some commentators in the media ridiculed PC as both hypersensitive and trivial, as in substituting "chairperson" for chairman, or "chronologically advanced" for senior citizen (Lindsley, 1998). Critics contend that PC trivializes and calls undue attention to issues that may not be particularly significant, and, in any case, new address terms or labels will not ultimately change society's underlying sociopolitical dynamics (Hughes, 1993).

Outside of the media, other observers offer a more serious criticism of PC. To the extent PC has resulted in persons self-censoring their speech, we may find that true, honest feelings about race and related concerns are muted. When others are masking their racially oriented thoughts with PC expressions, there is a sense of mistrust that can lead to a form of racial paranoia (Jackson, 2008). Those claiming not to be racist may be hiding their inner feelings of racial animosity, which Jackson defines as *de cardio* racism (racism of the heart). For fear of being labeled as racist, whites may suppress their true feelings and speak in PC terms, and blacks may feel suspicious that what whites say about race cannot be trusted as genuine. As Jackson (2008) states:

> When dealing with such thorny topics today, we are forced to confront the impenetrability of other peoples' most secret views. Ultimately, we can only speculate about their inner feelings, even those of the folks we think we know best. De cardio racism uses that inescapable fact as the suspicious backdrop for any and all interracial communication in our politically charged and politically corrected present. (p. 90)

Of course, blacks may use PC language with the same effects as with whites, a masking of one's inner feelings and insincere expression. Although PC is dismissed by certain critics who make light of it as a convention for posturing and silliness, such critics overlook a greater concern, a sign of a breakdown in a basic level of trust in society. As with social capital (Putnam, 2000), levels of interracial trust in the United States may also be in decline due to insufficient achievement of social bonding between blacks and whites (Allen, 2004).

The remarks by Biden and Imus are contrasting examples of problematic communication resulting from politically incorrect speech. Biden's statements seemed less offensive, his apology was accepted, and the repercussions faded. The violation of PC was far more serious for Imus: although the persons he derogated accepted his apology, it became unacceptable for his employer to retain him and his freedom of expression was, temporarily at least, restricted. By considering how these two cases of racially oriented offenses were resolved, one can gain insight into the way discourse about race is operating in current events. Fairclough (2003) has called for new research emphases on PC and a need to theoretically examine how this kind of discourse relates to different spheres of social values. The main point here is to underscore the presence of PC and the impact it can have on discourse related to race. This much can be said: whether one finds merit in standards of PC or not, it seems clear that compared to 50 years ago, race-related discourse today reflects a heightened sensitivity to language that can stigmatize. It remains unclear, however, whether the benefits of PC have outweighed its costs.

Hate Speech

Finally, a third issue in racially oriented discourse concerns verbal expressions of hate. In noting significant issues in social science as well as the law, Leets and Giles (1997) refer to hate speech as verbal aggression that denigrates people on the basis of race, ethnicity, religion, gender, sexual orientation, age, disability, or membership in other social categories. Hate speech, along with hate crimes, has unfortunately been a not so uncommon occurrence in the United States. Torres (1999) reports that in the United States from 1992 to 1996 there was a 52 percent increase in hate crimes against African Americans. Sellas-Ferrer and Hutson (2004) note that of the 71,185 incidents of hate violence reported in the United States between 1992 and 2002, 62 percent of such incidents were motivated by race and 40 percent by anti-black prejudice. According to the Federal Bureau of Investigation (FBI), in 2006 there were 7,720 hate crimes in the United States (U.S. Department of Justice, 2007). The same

FBI report notes that of the incidents that were racially motivated, 66.2 percent were motivated by anti-black sentiments, and that intimidation was a common type of hate crime against persons (U.S. Department of Justice, 2007).

The study of hate offenses is complicated by the difficulty of obtaining reliable data. The FBI data may underreport hate crimes because victims are often reluctant to report transgressions against them (Rayburn, Earleywine, & Davison, 2003). Part of this reluctance stems from social desirability, a sentiment that a victim reporting a crime may feel the incident reflects negatively on him or her. To appear more socially desirable, victims may refrain from reporting a hateful act committed against them or avoid disclosing all details of the offense (Rayburn et al., 2003). In their study of reports of hate crimes involving college students, Rayburn et al. note that the largest category of hate crimes consists of verbal insults.

In a series of studies Leets and her colleagues (e.g., Leets & Giles, 1997; Leets, Giles, & Noels, 1999; Leets, 2001) have examined several important issues concerning hate speech in contemporary society. In their study of Anglo American offenses against Asian Americans, Leets and Giles (1997) note that direct racist speech is harmful, with the perceived harm increasing as racist threats become more severe. Interestingly, Leets and Giles observe that the Anglo American participants in their study view direct racist speech as more harmful than do the Asian American targets. However, the Anglo American participants view the indirect racist speech as less harmful than do the Asian Americans, a pattern attributed to the black sheep effect. In the context of intergroup relations, the black sheep effect explains how members of an in-group may preserve positive aspects of their identity by negatively judging certain behaviors attributed to fellow group members (Marques, 1990). Leets and Giles (1997) also find that the loss of dignity suffered due to racist speech results in psychological pain that is hard to endure and greater than physical pain.

One focus of the Leets and Giles study is to consider hate speech in its legal context. Victims of hate speech who wish to take legal action face the need to show that such speech is intentional, extreme, causes harm, and results in severe emotional distress (Leets & Giles, 1997). While it might seem that direct speech is more harmful and legally actionable, victims may actually experience greater harm from indirect acts of hate speech. Yet, the harm from indirect acts may be more difficult to demonstrate in court. In later research, Leets (2001) examines hate speech associated with three target groups: Asian Americans, African Americans, and Hispanic Americans. Among the findings of note, Leets affirms that social identity is an important part of the theoretical explanation for hate speech, and evidence again emerges for the black sheep effect. There is also the finding that hate speech perceived as most harmful to targets, regardless of ethnicity, leads to more moderate evaluations of harm among those who have the most experience as victims of racial slurs. Targets with less experience report more pronounced feelings of harm. Leets also comments that there are difficulties in taking legal action against hate speech, but that through restorative justice, repair of dignity can be promoted.

In the context of interracial communication, one particular instance of hate speech often occurs with the use of the word *nigger*. Kennedy (2002) explains how *nigger* is now being used by a variety of persons from a variety of ethnic backgrounds, and there is ongoing innovation in its usage. In a traditional sense, *nigger* has been used as a racial slur. More recently, in the presence of black and white audiences in public, the term has been put to various usages including connotations of endearment, respect, and ethnic pride.

As a slur, *nigger* has long been used by whites as an address term and label. In this sense, *nigger* is an epithet used with the intent to injure. It is this injurious meaning that was part of the experimental study conducted by Greenberg and Pyszczynski (1985). In this study black and white debaters were heard and then judged by white student participants. The student judges then overheard the black speakers referred to in either nonracist terms, or by including the word *nigger*. Greenberg and Pyszczynski find that referring to the black debaters as *niggers* leads to noticeably lower evaluations of their performances. The authors conclude that the racial slur seems to activate racist stereotypes and, therefore, directly facilitates prejudice (Greenberg & Pyszczynski, 1985; see also Kirkland, Greenberg, & Pyszczynski, 1987).

Kennedy (2002) examines several examples of *nigger* as a racial slur including court cases in which black employees found themselves in a hostile work environment due to supervisors using the word *nigger*. In two such cases, the employees successfully sued their employers, although in these cases the employees had lost in lower court rulings and had to seek redress through appeals. In both cases, the employees were able to show that usage of the word *nigger* constituted evidence of discriminatory treatment or the existence of a racially hostile workplace. Kennedy (2002) stresses that it is difficult to prove in court that conduct by an employer creates ongoing abusive conditions at work, and that litigation is always frustrating, expensive, and fraught with risk.

As a racial slur, *nigger* is most commonly (but not always) used by whites toward blacks. However, in many other situations, blacks may use *nigger* in communication with other blacks in ways that connote friendship, respect, or a kind of ethnic pride. Smitherman (2006) describes numerous examples of *nigger* being used by blacks to show affection toward fellow blacks and by black entertainers who show an appreciation for the many in-group meanings of the term. Smitherman also notes that the term formerly had a taboo status in public speech, but that over the last 30 to 40 years the term has been much more widely used in public by blacks. Kennedy states that *nigger* can be used to declare a defiant sense of ethnic pride, as demonstrated in the humor of the late Richard Pryor. In describing Pryor's comedic appeal Kennedy (2002) notes:

> He broke free, at least for a while, of all those — whites and blacks alike — who, sometimes for different reasons, shared an aversion to too much realism. He seemed radically unconcerned with deferring to any social conventions, particularly those that accepted black comedians as clowns but rejected them as satirists. Nothing more vividly symbolized his defiant, risk-taking spirit than his unprecedented playfulness regarding the explosive N-word in performances before racially mixed audiences. (p. 33)

As usage of *nigger* has become more common in comedy and especially in rap music lyrics, one may wonder whether the term has lost some of its stigmatizing force. Indeed, there is confusion from increased usage of *nigger*, with many whites feeling that blacks freely use the word while condemning whites for using it (Kennedy, 2002), and with some older blacks who feel strongly that the word should remain taboo (Smitherman, 2006). A double dilemma presents itself. On one hand and in a positive sense, recent usage has taken the word and its hateful impact away from white supremacists. On the other hand, when such a word loses its stigma, there is confusion over what it means, when it is allowed, and who can use it.

Another relevant issue is whether the word *nigger is* different from the word *nigga.* Kennedy (2002) is not clear on this point, but he suggests that the latter is basically a variation on the former and is not essentially different. Smitherman (2006) refers to the 19th century sense of *nigger* as a slur but notes that modern uses of *nigga* encode mostly positive meanings, typically when blacks are speaking to other blacks. Asim (2007) asserts that the case for the two words being different is not a convincing one. In stating his objections to anyone using *nigger*, Asim argues that in the historical context of American race relations, neither word honors the cultural heritage of African Americans who struggled mightily to attain freedom and equal rights.

Hate speech has clear pragmatic implications as it interferes with harmonious relations and civility. Furthermore, from a historical perspective, hate speech has not only led to intergroup tension, but it has also played a role in the rise of dangerous social movements (Tsesis, 2002). By invoking and reinforcing negative stereotypes, by harassing innocent people, and by benefiting from the difficulties of taking legal action against hate speech, our entire society is paying a price for this truly harmful form of communication.

Summary of Discussion of Discourse Themes

Many more forms of race-related discourse could be presented, and the three discussed here treat just a few of the more common themes. If one were to carefully compare discourse themes during different periods in history, one could trace how all sorts of issues concerning race have appeared, each time with shifts in emphasis, meaning, and rhetorical force. Inextricably bound with discourse themes are images and stereotypes that evoke strong and, at times, powerful feelings among those engaged in the discourse.

Conclusion

This chapter has discussed the nature of stereotyping and the origins of racial stereotypes in the United States; it has outlined some basic forms and functions of racial stereotyping and provided a framework for understanding how stereotypic thinking can influence interracial communication. And by briefly reviewing some features of race-related discourse, we have also seen how stereotypes and speech become interwoven and can affect each other. One underlying theme in the chapter is that stereotypes exist because humans communicate about them. In personal conversations, in group interaction, and in mass-communicated messages, the fundamental properties and processes of stereotyping are realized. In essence, stereotypes depend on consensus, and it is through communication that consensus is achieved.

Stereotypes are generalizations and as such are not necessarily good or bad. It must be noted, however, that stereotypes often interfere with clear thought processes and effective interracial communication. It is, therefore, incumbent upon us to recognize the harm that stereotypes can cause and to be on guard against faulty reasoning based on stereotypes.

CHAPTER 6

Prospects for Interracial Communication

Over the past five chapters, we have examined some basic features of interracial communication, the historical basis for certain patterns in race relations, aspects of race and language, the role of interracial communication in contexts such as education and employment, and how stereotyping and discourse function in interracial communication. In this concluding chapter, let us take account of the current state of interracial communication, discuss several models of race relations, and some approaches to and a model of greater effectiveness in interracial communication.

The Current State of Interracial Communication

In assessing the current status of interracial communication, one must locate the communication issues within the larger context of American race relations, in general. As we examine the state of race relations in the United States in the 21st century, there are reasons for both hope and despair.

Current U.S. Race Relations

Evidence is readily available showing that life is getting better for African Americans and that race relations are improving. As noted in Chapter 4, despite the fact that black/white income disparities remain, growing numbers of blacks have reached middle income levels and above. We must also note that as of 2006, 19 percent of African Americans at least 25 years old had earned a college degree, up from just 4 percent in 1970 (Pew Research Center, 2007). A recent poll finds that 60 percent of African Americans agree with the statement, "Things are getting better for me" and that 54 percent say they are confident about the future (Black America Today, 2008). A Pew Research Center survey (2007) reports that 80 percent of whites and 78 percent of blacks say they have a very or mostly favorable impression of the other race. When asked how well blacks and whites get along these days, 69 percent of blacks responded "pretty well" or "very well." Responding to the same question, 75 percent of whites said "pretty well" or "very well" (Pew Research Center, 2007). Presently, we also find that the vast majority of blacks and whites report that they have friends from the other race (Pew Research Center, 2007).

Not only are these encouraging signs, but some believe such news would garner even greater attention if it were more widely publicized. Several critics claim that progress in race relations is downplayed by biased scholars and journalists who are fixated on color, ignore or deemphasize evidence of socioeconomic progress for blacks, and prefer to view the United States as irredeemably racist (e.g., D'Sousa, 1995; McWhorter, 2005; Sleeper, 1997; Thernstrom & Thernstrom, 1997). Finally, we must recognize that for the first time in American history, an African American has been elected president. Obama's election will receive further comment later in this chapter. However, we can here note that this extraordinary event has brought pride to many African Americans and other minorities, as well as many European Americans. A black person being elected to the nation's highest office is a phenomenon that was simply unimaginable to many of us only a few years ago. Based on all these observations, one may conclude that race relations are improving and that life in the United States for African Americans has gotten better.

It is probably just as easy, if not easier, to find evidence that race relations are not improving and that life for blacks in the United States is not getting better. There is a flip side to most of the data mentioned in the preceding paragraphs. For every poll showing progress in race relations, there seems to be another poll, or even other responses within the same poll, indicating negative news on the racial front. The same Pew Research Center poll just mentioned also asked blacks about the state of black progress. Only 20 percent of blacks responded that things are better than five years ago, a lower figure than at any time since 1983 (Pew Research Center, 2007). A litany of dilemmas in race relations, continuing patterns of discrimination, and negative socioeconomic trends for blacks is apparent from a number of books (e.g., Brown et al., 2003; Feagin & McKinney, 2005; Massey & Denton, 1993). Other books and publications also document ongoing effects of racial discrimination across a range of contexts and show clear effects of individual and institutional racism. One legal scholar has written that integration has failed in virtually every sector of American society, and he proposes limited racial separation to achieve the goals of dignity, empowerment, and equality for blacks

(Brooks, 1996). Finally, Derrick Bell (1992), another legal scholar, has concluded that racism is a permanent feature of American society:

> Black people will never gain full equality in this country. Even those herculean efforts we hail as successful will produce no more than temporary "peaks of progress," short-lived victories that slide into irrelevance as racial patterns adapt in ways that maintain white dominance. This is a hard-to-accept fact that all history verifies. We must acknowledge it, not as a sign of submission, but as an act of ultimate defiance. (p. 12)

Thus, viewpoints and evidence pertaining to race relations reveal a truly mixed set of findings. If one wants to be optimistic about race relations, one can see signs of improvement that portend well for the future. Those taking a pessimistic view see progress that is so stunted as to be dismally unsatisfactory.

Models of Race Relations

In discussing current race relations, let us consider several theoretical models that can help organize our thoughts. Models of U.S. race relations have originated in all the social sciences and display great variety. Collapsing various models into a smaller, more manageable number is not easy. Nevertheless, for purposes of major comparisons and contrasts it is heuristically useful to group the many models of race relations into a small set and summarize their essential characteristics. Let us briefly discuss three main groupings of models: (1) ingrained racial stigma, (2) assimilation, and (3) multiculturalism.

Ingrained Racial Stigma

In an important analysis of racial inequality in the United States, Loury (2002) proposes that racial stigma is the main reason for the socially disadvantaged conditions for African Americans. To put it succinctly, identities are "raced" through an entrenched pattern in American history, and those who are construed as black are racially stigmatized (Loury, 2002; see also, Rawls, 2000). The primary effect of racial stigma is a profound sense of "otherness" resulting in the exclusion of blacks, especially those of lower socioeconomic status, from mainstream society and its socioeconomic opportunities. As Loury notes, "I want to suggest with the stigma idea that a withholding of the presumption of equal humanity is the ultimate mechanism of racism in American public life" (2002, p. 88). In Loury's analysis racial stigma is affected by two kinds of discrimination: contract and contact. Discrimination by contract can be addressed through legal action. Although legal action can be expensive, difficult, and result in varying degrees of success, there is at least a legal framework available for pursuing claims of contractual discrimination.

Discrimination by contact takes place in informal settings, neighborhoods, communities, schools, and other such places and includes friendship patterns, social networks, and various forms of voluntary associations. Unlike discrimination by contract, there is no institution or formal procedure for addressing claims of discrimination by contact. In effect, Loury (2002) is asserting that American society is racially segregated due to discrimination by contact, leaving many blacks feeling like outsiders. One notion stressed by Loury is that in early childhood education, in peer group interactions, and in the social atmosphere prevailing during the formative years, a development bias exists against racially stigmatized groups whose potential for leading productive lives thus becomes limited. Too often, according to Loury, those who are stigmatized are held responsible for their own condition.

The racial stigma framework parallels Blauner's (1969) colonization complex, according to which a group's forced entry into a society is followed by a significant alteration of the group's indigenous culture. The dominant group then continues to exert its influence as the subordinate-superior relationship is reinforced through a racist ideology. Marger (2009) notes that in the case of the United States, the status of blacks is due to a condition that can be termed internal colonization. Racial stigma is also related to a separatist model of race relations (Fredrickson, 1999). African Americans who identify with black nationalism may possess separatist orientations that diverge from mainstream American society, in part due to feelings of alienation.

Assimilation

An assimilationist approach posits that a subordinate group accepts important cultural features of the dominant group (Kim, 2005). Over time, subordinate groups conduct their lives in ways that are increasingly similar to the dominant group and, therefore, differences between the subordinates and the dominants recede. Complete assimilation can result in the disappearance of a subordinate group's outward cultural distinctiveness. One form of assimilation, a melting pot conceptualization, operates through widespread social interaction that leads to a homogenous society (Moghaddam & Solliday, 1991) and may also occur through amalgamation (Hollinger, 2006). The melting pot form of assimilation can lead to a blended society reflecting all groups, thus deviating from the one-way pattern of minorities always adapting to the majority.

Let us note that in the United States there are examples of various groups (e.g., Amish, Orthodox Jews, etc.) who choose not to assimilate or choose limited assimilation. As assimilation affects both dominant and subordinate groups, we may find a dialectical tension between assimilation and separation (Cook, 2003). Therefore, various groups may display degrees of assimilation that also reflect degrees of separation. A variation on the assimilationist/separatist dialectic is accommodation—a set of formally negotiated compromises between dominant and subordinate groups (Cook, 2003).

Marger (2009) describes an assimilationist model as comprising two forms of assimilation: cultural and structural. Cultural assimilation occurs when a subordinate group adopts cultural traits of the dominant group such as language, religion, food, music, and the like. It is also true that subordinate groups do not do all the adopting. As dominant and subordinate groups interact, both groups influence each other. In the intergroup context, accommodation by a minority group can result in convergence of cultural norms relevant to language and communication behavior (Shepard, Giles, & Le Poire, 2001). As noted in Chapter 3, there is ongoing discussion of convergence and divergence in the United States regarding speakers of SAE and AAVE.

Structural assimilation occurs at a primary level where social interaction takes place within families, small groups, social clubs, and other such intimate communities. At secondary levels of structural assimilation, relations occur within larger, nonintimate groupings such as those found at school, various organizations, and the workplace. Furthermore, secondary structural assimilation provides access to influential positions in major societal institutions such as government, finance, and law (Marger, 2009).

The greater the secondary structural assimilation, the greater will be the political and economic equality between the dominant and subordinate groups (Marger, 2009). Assimilation is usually conceptualized as a process occurring in stages. For African Americans, Marger claims that a moderately high degree of cultural assimilation has occurred, and there is also an unmistakable African American influence on mainstream American culture. To the extent we see maintenance of AAVE, tastes in music, religious preferences, and other such social elements, we may conclude that despite considerable cultural assimilation there remains a strong sense of ethnic identity for many blacks. Structural assimilation for African Americans has been more limited, particularly when one examines interracial patterns in housing, club membership, marriage, and the like. At the secondary level, structural assimilation for African Americans has been even more limited, with income disparities being only one clear indication. Even more revealing, in the major institutions of society and in comparison to certain other minority groups, African Americans have found restricted access to positions of influence such as managers, executives, and partners in firms.

Multiculturalism

A third model of race relations may be termed multiculturalism, an orientation that is similar to cultural pluralism. Multiculturalism essentially refers to a "set of ideas whose common theme is respect and toleration for cultural differences" (Schuck, 2003, p. 103). The United States has always had a culturally diverse population based on the early presence of African Americans, Native Americans, and European settlers. Immigrants in the 19th and early 20th centuries came mainly from Europe, with increasing numbers arriving from Eastern and Southern Europe. However, in the later 19th and the early 20th century, immigration from Asia increased, and later in the 20th century immigrants from Central America, the Caribbean, and Pacific islands became more numerous. By the latter 20th century, cities such as New York, Los Angeles, and Miami displayed cultural diversity to the point that European Americans were becoming a minority. Presently, along with New Mexico, Hawaii, and the District of Columbia, populations in Texas and California are now characterized as non-white majorities (Schuck, 2003). Moreover and as already noted, before the middle of the 21st century, European Americans will constitute less than 50 percent of the population in the United States. In a strict numerical sense, it appears to be only a matter of time until the European American majority will cease to exist, and the United States will become a nation of cultural minority groups.

Acknowledging the presence of cultural diversity in United States has become part of the promotion of multiculturalism in various settings such as schools, universities, government, and businesses. Those favoring multiculturalism have been defenders of affirmative action, have worked for curricular changes in schools and universities, and have promoted diversity training in many organizations. Supporters of multiculturalism argue that since the United States has become more culturally diverse and since employees and businesses now face a competitive global economy, there is a pressing need to raise awareness of cultural differences and facilitate ways for people from different ethnicities to work and live together. In all cases, a main theme in multiculturalism is appreciation and respect for the cultural and/or sociocultural distinct-iveness of others (Hornsey & Hogg, 2000).

Insights from the intergroup relations literature are relevant to the multiculturalism framework. For example, a superordinate identity (Gaertner et al., 1999; Wenzel, Mummendey, & Waldus, 2007) has been offered as a framework that can reduce intergroup conflict. The idea of a superordinate identity is that individual groups realize and respect their own identities through an all-inclusive group orientation. All individual groups view themselves and others as meaningful participants in and contributors to one superordinate group whose sociocultural orientations are not set according to the values of any preexisting, dominant group. With a superordinate identity, "us" vs. "them" orientations are replaced by a new "we" orientation. This and other models from the field of inter-group relations offer some of the more interesting theoretical approaches to multiculturalism.

Socioeconomic and Cultural Variables Affecting the Three Models

Before discussing interracial communication and models of race rela-tions, there is a need to comment on several significant variables. First, let us recall from Chapter 1 that among African Americans, as with all other groups, there is noticeable diversity. Regional, religious, political, and other influences make some segments of most groups different from other segments, sometimes significantly so. The Pew Research Center report mentioned at the start of this chapter refers to questions about di-versity within the African American community. When asked whether blacks can be thought of as a single race because they have so much in common, 53 percent said yes; however, a sizeable number, 37 percent, said no (Pew Research Center, 2007). One regional difference was strik-ing, as blacks from the Midwest were split with 46 percent saying there was no longer a single race, and 45 percent saying there was still a single race.

As with other groups, diversity among African Americans is often correlated with income as well as certain cultural factors. The Pew Re-search Center (2007) asked blacks and whites about values held by mid-dle-class and lower-class blacks. Fifty-four percent of whites and 61 percent of blacks reported that middle-class and poor blacks have grown more different over the past 10 years. Other signs of black diversity can be found in groups that vary according to education, age, and ancestral heritage. It is noteworthy that differences exist between blacks with North American slave ancestry and other blacks. Marger (2009) notes that over 3 percent of blacks in the United States are foreign-born, with a large number coming from the Caribbean. In comparing blacks of North American slave ancestry to blacks from the West Indies, there are clear differences in patterns of employment, education, and income, as well as differences in culture and, to some extent, language. Research has also identified conflict between blacks from the United States and blacks from the West Indies (Waters, 1999).

Considering diversity within ethnic groups raises the question of cultural identity in terms of socioeconomic status. While the median income for African American households in 2006 was $31,969, in 9.1 percent of black households the income level was at least $100,000, up from just 1.6 percent of black households in 1970 (U.S. Census Bureau, 2007). Thus, we see tremendous diversity among African Americans as measured by income. Overall, median black household income in 2006 was .61 of the median white household income of $52,423 (U.S. Census Bureau, 2007). Income represents access to goods and services, symbolizes what one has achieved, and, over time, can produce an accumulation of wealth. Income comparisons get at a crucial issue in race relations, namely, how should we regard ethnic identity in the face of persistent economic inequality?

Michaels (2006) offers an illuminating analysis of contemporary interethnic relations in the United States. He claims many groups and governmental programs have focused too often on efforts to achieve multicultural diversity and inclusiveness, yet these efforts have not significantly improved the socioeconomic status of various minority groups. In effect, asserts Michaels, we prefer fighting racism to fighting poverty. Highlighting one case in point, Michaels observes that a nation intent upon reducing inequality would fund all lower and secondary schools on an equal basis. In this scenario, students would succeed according to their individual efforts and not because of the unearned advantages of family wealth (Michaels, 2006). Similar approaches applying to health care, housing, and other such areas could also be considered. The main point is that a multicultural emphasis on ethnic identity and respect for ethnic heritage does not seem to significantly address issues of income inequality for African Americans and certain other minorities.

As a theoretical proposition, we may conclude that inequality can never be eliminated in the United States. The combined cultural, political, and social history of the United States shows that there is respect for equality of opportunity and protection of equal rights. Yet, in the United States there is no guarantee of equality of outcome in the socioeconomic sense. U.S. Americans tend to believe that persons can act autonomously on their own behalf, that individuals have equal opportunities, and that individual actions have consequences, both favorable and unfavorable (Loury, 2002; see also, Carbaugh, 1988). For many in the United States, the prevailing belief is that everyone has opportunities available to them, and it is difficult to understand why some are not taking advantage of their opportunities. How to interpret the persistence of socioeconomic inequality in the United States remains a vexing question.

Multiculturalism and Interracial Communication

In examining interracial communication within the more general context of race relations, one can see elements of all three models having important communication dimensions. We may conclude that racial stigma inflicts serious damages and that maintaining the stigma model is unacceptable. As a means to reduce racial stigma, this discussion will focus on multiculturalism with a view toward assimilation.

A major advantage of multiculturalism is its ability to raise consciousness of cultural differences and to foster respect for cultural minorities. Hornsey and Hogg (2000) assert that the greatest barrier to harmonious intergroup relations is subgroup identity threat. Multiculturalism is theoretically equipped to assist in identity development and help subgroups feel secure and become more tolerant of diverse cultures. Taylor (1991) also argues for the importance of cultural identity formation, an essential feature of which is heritage cultural maintenance.

By adopting a multicultural model of race relations it is argued that with its increasing diversity and decreasing European American dominance, the United States can benefit from a sociocultural state of inclusiveness. As noted, a superordinate group may facilitate a common, all-inclusive identity for all groups. All individual groups view themselves and others as meaningful participants in and contributors to one superordinate group whose sociocultural orientations are not set according to the values of any preexisting dominant group. Banks (2006) discusses the superordinate identity in the educational setting, noting the particular benefits from opportunities such as those available to students to belong to several extracurricular groups including intergroup dialogue associations. Banks sees great value as membership cuts across cultural boundaries and intergroup conflict is reduced, thus offering the potential to reduce stigma.

It is recognized that assimilation has been the principal means for immigrants to the United States to become full-fledged members of society. In terms of American race relations, assimilation may leave much to be desired, but, as Marger (2009) claims, not only has assimilation occurred among African Americans but also, over time, African Americans will reach levels of assimilation comparable to other non-European American ethnic groups. The key concern is how to employ multiculturalism as a means to manage, incorporate, and build upon the diversity now present in the United States.

By proposing multiculturalism with a view toward assimilation it is argued that a new kind of assimilation could be the result of a superordinate identity as discussed by Gaertner et al. (1999) and Wenzel et al. (2007). It would admittedly be difficult to balance ethnic identity needs with the values necessary for developing a superordinate identity. In place of an assimilation based on minority groups adapting to the dominant group, group identity would be shaped by members seeing themselves as vital participants in a new common identity. In this respect we need not necessarily discard the assimilation model entirely. Rather, we may find a way for a superordinate identity to function as the cultural mainstream has functioned in the traditional assimilation model.

Multiculturalism and Racial Stigma

Multiculturalism and racial stigma are intertwined in that the respect for African American identity has not been widely accepted by whites, in part due to racial stigma. In particular, many blacks perceive white society as being unwelcoming to the point of avoiding contact with blacks and offering few signs of respect or the granting of dignity. Furthermore, racial injustices from the past have a way of accumulating and their effects can become compounded (Blum, 2002).

One complicating factor in the adoption of multiculturalism is the influence of individualism in American culture. Among the most notable of cultural traits among U.S. Americans is a strong value placed on individualism and its orientations to personal liberty and autonomy. Even Loury (2002), who writes against racial stigma, observes that in a liberal society such as the United States, there must be a freedom to engage or not engage in personal contact. Otherwise, there is no true sense of liberty in the society. We can also recall instances in American history when personal choices were restricted through legal mandates (e.g., school integration in the 1950s, forced busing, applications of affirmative action). In such instances, individuals sometimes resisted and acted to avoid or circumvent the mandates, thus demonstrating their personal liberties.

Interracial Communication

There is a vital role for interracial communication in the practice of multiculturalism and the reduction of racial stigmatization. There is a tendency to regard racism and racial discrimination in the United States as existing at two levels: institutional and individual. Thus, some scholars have discussed social movements, public policy, and legal action to promote change within society's major institutions. At the individual level, efforts to combat racism have adopted methods through education and training that take a "one-person-at-a-time" or "one small group-at-a-time" approach. Scholars Essed (1991) and Trepagnier (2006) have argued that individual and institutional forms of racism are actually integral parts of the same process, and, therefore, we can address racism through a combined approach. Such an approach would potentially facilitate a superordinate identity and lessen the impact of racial stigma. The basic assumption behind the combined approach is that with a decrease in racial discrimination, participation in mainstream society would become more accessible to African Americans.

Essed (1991) argues that the greatest impact of racism occurs in everyday situations. It is through the events occurring in everyday life that racism is experienced, racial discrimination is enacted, and racism is seen to be tolerated. In effect, Essed is claiming that discrimination is conducted by individuals, not institutions. Trepagnier (2006) offers a similar perspective, noting that institutional racism is most often conducted by individuals who do not intend to act in a racist way. In Trepagnier's analysis, racial discrimination occurs through a process of silent racism, as noted in Chapter 5. Trepagnier (2006, p. 21) notes: "Silent racism predisposes white people to commit or collude with routine practices that are perceived by blacks as everyday racism. Silent racism is the cognitive aspect of everyday racism—in contrast to the behavioral aspect." Yet, silent racism is not formally learned and does not result from conscious behavior that is intended to be racist. What is important is the idea that people who are not consciously racist, nevertheless engage in behavior that produces racial discrimination. By certain actions (thought to be nonracist) and certain inactions (which show a passive tolerance for racism), people who think of themselves as not racist may produce and reproduce racial discrimination.

Essed and Trepagnier call attention to racism being enacted and reproduced through social structures. In a manner consistent with structuration theory (Giddens, 1979), individuals within organizations and institutions, and in settings of social communication, are prone to behave according to their understanding of local norms and procedures. Such behavior is largely routinized and, therefore, not consciously practiced. Communication plays a pivotal role as the behaviors, norms, and practices in social structures in society are primarily realized and reinforced through communication. Innumerable verbal and nonverbal behaviors serve to maintain stereotypes and race-related attitudes, and discourse themes allow individuals to explain their behaviors in ways that make sense according to locally accepted interpretations.

At the crux of many interracial dilemmas in the United States is a problematic negotiation of identity. A number of theories from the field of communication have focused on identity as a key element in explaining the way individuals from different cultural backgrounds interact. For example, Hecht (1993) has proposed the communication theory of identity as an explanation for how ethnic identity is shaped, enacted, negotiated, has semantic properties, and prescribes appropriate behavior for effective communication. Similarly, Orbe (1998) has developed co-cultural communication theory; Gallois, Ogay, and Giles (2005) have proposed current refinements in communication accommodation theory; Ting-Toomey (2005b) has formulated identity negotiation theory; and Jackson (2002) has explicated cultural contracts theory. All of these theories are different, have different emphases, and address somewhat different aspects of communication and identity. Yet, each of these theories supports the notions that through communication individuals enact and negotiate their identities, that identities emerge through groups and social networks, and that personal, social, and cultural identities are important in communication satisfaction.

For both blacks and whites, interracial communication often results in dissatisfaction as interactants experience a lack of identity affirmation from the other. It is proposed here that multiculturalism, facilitated through interracial communication, is likely the most viable option for improving race relations in the United States. As a means to foster more effective identity formation, multiculturalism seems capable of bringing about respect for the identities of self and others that would overcome racial stigma and its harms and lead to greater identity security for African Americans.

Correctives

From an interracial communication perspective, two main approaches are recommended that can help reduce the harms from racial discrimination in the United States and promote communication effectiveness. One approach could be termed applied diversity training, and the other, a community-based dialogic approach. By incorporating elements of multiculturalism, applied diversity training can raise awareness of racism as well as help participants appreciate cultural differences and realize that people who do not condone racism, nevertheless, contribute to the production of racism. The dialogic approach can reduce discrimination through the creation of social capital. Both approaches can be grounded in the principles of multiculturalism.

Applied Diversity Training

Insights from Educators and Observers

Orbe and Harris (2008) describe several applied approaches that can help overcome problems in race and communication, and that can be implemented in educational and organizational settings. Such applied approaches include

1. identifying unproductive assumptions about race and potential barriers to effective interracial communication,
2. identifying unproductive communication patterns such as apprehension and uncertainty that sometimes precede interracial interaction,
3. participating in race relations training,
4. participating in interracial dialogue.

From a practical perspective, here are some specific strategies proposed by Orbe and Harris (2008) that are beneficial in promoting interracial communication effectiveness:

1. Examine attitudes toward race with someone from another race or ethnicity.
2. European Americans should develop awareness of the privileges and benefits associated with their racial identities.
3. Demonstrate sensitivity in the use of language and nonverbal behaviors, with awareness of the ability of language to label and stigmatize
4. Develop an interracial friendship and openly discuss race and racial differences, including instances when conflict arises.
5. Interact with others from a different ethnic background without expecting them to act as spokespersons for their entire group.

Another set of practical guidelines come from Jacobs' (2006) book Race Manners for the 21st century. Jacobs, and African American who writes about racial issues, offers numerous suggestions for behaviors that promote effective interracial communication. Among the most useful are these (Jacobs, 2006):

1. If you behave unfairly toward someone, own it (p. 32).
2. Resist the intrusion of Rage Radio and TV into public space (p. 84).
3. Understand that people have the right to name themselves (p. 155).
4. Never try to talk "their" kind of English to a stranger (p. 189).
5. Never make ethnic assumptions based on telephone conversations (p. 190).
6. Don't tolerate casual racial slights. (p. 216).

To these lists of strategies may be added some important lessons based on the contents of the preceding chapters of this book. First, everyone in the United States shares a national heritage that includes the contributions of all groups. African Americans, along with all other minority groups, are just as much a part of American history as the dominant members of society. Second, everyone speaks a dialect and, knowing that it is a significant component of personal and social identity, we should show respect for different dialects and their speakers. This does not mean overlooking contexts in which SAE is necessary, but it does mean that we should not judge others negatively simply because of the way they speak. Third, negative stereotypes often affect us, even when we are not aware of them and/or we believe we are inhibiting them. Fourth, recognize that organizations often operate with their own particular (and sometimes peculiar) cultural norms and procedures. If you are a member of an organization, learn how its culture operates and work to change those aspects that result in unfair treatment of employees.

These lessons may not be easily accepted, nor can the strategies be easily applied. However, just considering them can help raise consciousness of race-related problems in communication. With heightened awareness, we can identify and begin to take action to break down racial barriers that interfere with effective communication.

Diversity Training in the U.S. Military

One specific example of applied diversity training is specially deserving of our attention: a program existing within the United States Department of Defense. As noted in Chapter 2, during the Korean War the United States military became racially integrated, although integration initially was limited to certain units. Later, in 1954, the Department of Defense abolished all segregated units in the Army (Dansby, Stewart, & Webb, 2001). Then, in 1971, following a race riot at Travis Air Force Base, a Department of Defense directive created the Defense Race Relations Institute (DRRI) (Dansby & Landis, 2001). The DRRI was later renamed the Defense Equal Opportunity Management Institute (DEOMI) and since the 1970s this organization's mission has been to systematically coordinate and evaluate intercultural and diversity training in the U.S. military. Through small group experiences, presentations, and classroom exercises, DEOMI has sought to ensure compliance with standards of fair treatment and equal opportunity. For over 35 years and during periods of increasing ethnic and gender diversity, the DEOMI has been hailed as a notable success in diversity training:

> Many would argue that this approach has made the military the most successful major institution in the United States in implementing the goal of EO [equal opportunity] for people of all racial/ethnic backgrounds. (Dansby & Landis, 2001, p. 22)

More recently, Lundquist (2007) has completed a comprehensive analysis of job satisfaction in the military. Her findings indicate that on measures of quality of life, compensation, and opportunities for advancement, women and minorities judge life in the military to be superior to civilian life. The U.S. military has many resources (e.g., housing, health care, etc.) that contribute to job satisfaction, and diversity training, in and of itself, is not necessarily the main reason for minorities' job satisfaction. Nevertheless, there is reason to believe diversity management in the Department of Defense has succeeded in significant ways in bringing about equal opportunity and more harmonious intergroup relations.

It must be emphasized that the Department of Defense has established a high priority for diversity training, in large part, because it contributes to combat readiness, especially in the sense of effective teamwork. Accordingly, the DEOMI has a clear focus, a strong organizational mandate, and also requires all personnel to undergo training. Taking the DEOMI as an example of a successful program for race relations training, it is interesting to question whether diversity training for military personnel could be a model for civilian organizations to adopt. When considering diversity training within organizational settings (e.g., schools, universities, workplaces), the methods of the DEOMI would appear to not only exemplify the benefits of diversity training but also show a strong, long-term commitment to the value of diversity training.

Intergroup Contact

To the extent the training methods of the DEOMI are effective, one reason for this is the opportunity for interracial (and intercultural) contact. The idea that intergroup contact can promote more effective intergroup relations has long been recognized as a valuable contribution from social science to the study of interethnic relations. Allport (1954) proposed the contact hypothesis, which maintains that cultural bias can be reduced when individuals from different groups come into contact in situations of equal status, a condition of cooperative intergroup interaction exists, there are opportunities for personal acquaintances between out-group members, and supportive egalitarian norms are present.

A great number of studies examining the contact hypothesis have discovered certain conditions under which intergroup bias is demonstrably reduced. Given the considerable body of extant research on the contact hypothesis, only a sampling of studies can be discussed here. Gaertner, Dovidio, and Bachman (1996) studied the experimental redirection of in-group members' positive regard for their own group members toward out-group members. In so doing, this research finds that a new group identity emerges resulting in lowered in-group bias toward the original out-group. Such an approach is termed the common in-group identity model (Gaertner et al., 1996). Brewer (1996) notes that intergroup contact succeeds when groups can attain cooperative interdependence in achieving mutual goals. In Brewer's framework, positive effects from contact can result from groups orienting toward an identity that balances inclusion and differentiation. Achieving this balance can lead to optimal distinctiveness, a state in which an individual's need for inclusiveness is met within one's group, and the need for differentiation is met through appreciation of intergroup differences.

As noted, a recent variation on the common in-group concept is the in-group projection model (Wenzel et al., 2007) through which a superordinate identity may emerge. The superordinate identity is a theoretical step forward in its approach to intergroup conflict and intergroup contact. One productive outcome of this approach is the respect groups show toward each other and tolerance for intergroup differences.

In his summary of contact hypothesis research, Pettigrew (1998) notes that the hypothesis has now developed into a more complete theory. Pettigrew's version of the more developed theory adds a fifth condition to Allport's hypothesis: friendship potential. In advocating for the study of long-term effects, Pettigrew is proposing that extended intergroup contact reduces prejudice and conflict through four processes: (1) learning about the out-group, (2) changing behavior, (3) generating affective ties, and (4) in-group reappraisal (Pettigrew, 1998). Intergroup friendship formation requires time, during which a process of recategorization can occur. Intergroup conflict exists, in the first place, because in-group and out-group members are socially categorized as having contrasting values, behaviors, and other characteristics (ethnicities, religion, political ideologies, etc.). Recategorization is possible and effective when contact occurs in pleasant circumstances, and the contact is based on persons who are viewed as representative of the out-group (Wilder, 1984).

Most recently, Pettigrew (2008) has reviewed the contact literature and offered suggestions for future research and applications. Pettigrew describes a meta-analysis of 516 experimental studies, finding clear evidence that intergroup contact reduces prejudice (Pettigrew & Tropp, 2006). Also noted are other studies, relatively few in number, that do not find a reduction of prejudice and actually show increases in anxiety and/or conflict between groups. While noting that no one claims intergroup contact works perfectly, especially in macro-level conflict, Pettigrew remains convinced that intergroup contact holds true potential to reduce prejudice and conflict.

Interracial Contact in the United States

Let us consider two important cases of interracial contact: housing and education. Analyses of the 2000 census data (Wilkes & Iceland, 2004) indicate that racial segregation exists in many metropolitan areas within the United States. The research by Wilkes and Iceland (2004) uses five dimensions of segregation:

1. Evenness (differential distribution of minority groups across neighborhoods)
2. Exposure (potential contact between groups)
3. Concentration (relative space occupied by the minority group)
4. Centralization (located near the center of an urban area)
5. Clustering (living in contiguous areas)

When several dimensions of segregation occur simultaneously, the condition is referred to as hypersegregation (Massey & Denton, 1989).

In a positive and overall sense, residential racial segregation is declining in the United States. Wilkes and Iceland note that between 1990 and 2000, the number of hypersegregated metropolitan areas decreased from 29 to 23. Furthermore, there are only two metropolitan areas where Hispanic/white hypersegregation exists, and no hypersegregated areas exist for Asian Americans and Native Americans. Therefore, black/white hypersegregation is, by far, the most common form of hypersegregation, and although hypersegregation remains, its levels have decreased.

Two other important points are noted by Wilkes and Iceland (2004). First, although many of the areas found to be hypersegregated in 1990 remained so in 2000, nine areas that were hypersegregated in 1990 were no longer hypersegregated in 2000. Second, a number of the most hypersegregated areas are in the Midwest and Northeast and include several of the largest cities in the United States. While it is also stated that a growing number of cities in the South have experienced increasing black hypersegregation, it is important to note that there are few hypersegregated areas in the West. Thus, hypersegregation is somewhat confined to certain regions of the United States and is less prominent outside of those regions. The data on hypersegregation offer some reasons to believe that interracial contact in residential settings may be increasing.

In addition to housing, education has been an important context for interracial contact. As a public policy in education, strategic interracial contact has been tried in the United States, most notably in the desegregation of schools in the 1950s and the 1960s, and later facilitated through forced busing in the 1970s and the 1980s. In an important sense, the Supreme Court ruling in the *Brown* case reflected the idea that segregated schools foster a feeling of inequality that is psychologically harmful to blacks (Thernstrom & Thernstrom, 1997). The proposed remedy in 1954 was to direct schools to educate black and white students together, within the same facilities. In effect, the court was acting to promote interracial contact. Unfortunately, from an academic outcomes perspective, the court-ordered school desegregation and busing produced mixed but mostly disappointing results (Brooks, 1996).

From a social science perspective, one can see that mandated desegregation had mixed results; however, these efforts were not planned and managed according to the conditions of the contact hypothesis (Cook, 1985; Schofield, 1991). Although there are noteworthy academic benefits from racially integrated education (Mickelson, 2005), these benefits seem to be underappreciated and not sufficiently attractive. Consequently, after a period of decreasing segregation from 1968 to 1980, resegregation steadily increased (Orfield, 1997). Aside from entire schools becoming resegregated, forms of segregation also exist due to tracking (see Chapter 4), which can occur even within individual schools that, overall, are racially balanced (Mickelson, 2005). School desegregation was theoretically capable of achieving far more positive outcomes than the results reveal (Cook, 1985). To some observers (e.g., Brooks, 1996) forced desegregation of public schools was unsuccessful as measured by learning outcomes. To other observers (see Schofield, 1991, for a review), interracial contact in integrated schools was more successful than many realized, and that when properly planned and managed, interracial education can yield important educational and social benefits. Unlike the prospects for interracial contact in residential areas, interracial contact in education seems to be more limited and has actually declined over the past 20 years.

Summary of Discussion on Diversity Training and Intergroup Contact

Applied diversity training holds the potential to raise awareness of attitudes and behaviors that can lead to discrimination. Sensitivity to racial and cultural differences, and specific communication strategies can facilitate interracial communication effectiveness. Furthermore, the review of the contact research and examples of interracial contact in the military, housing, and education show us the potential for contact to reduce prejudice and conflict. However, we must remember that there are conditions for successful intergroup contact to happen, without which positive results are negligible, insufficient, or even counterproductive. When the conditions specified by the contact hypothesis are met, one can argue that applied diversity training can be effective. The Department of Defense has recognized the need for and benefits of diversity training, the effectiveness of which is at least partly due to intergroup contact. In education, positive results from interracial contact have been realized but are viewed as limited. Again, when the conditions for the contact hypothesis are not met, results are constrained. Outside of controlled or semi-controlled contexts (as in the military and education), residential patterns reveal other insights into interracial contact. A number of factors enter into one's choice of residence (e.g., local services, schools, security, home values, etc.). Racially segregated housing remains common; however, looking on the bright side, there seems to be a decline in hypersegregation.

Community Dialogue

The second corrective approach is known as community dialogue on race, a special case of intergroup contact. Community dialogue is related to ongoing interest in social capital, an important current topic in social science. Putnam (2000) is one of a number of scholars (e.g., Coleman, 1990; Brehm & Rahn, 1977) who has written about social capital and its decline in the United States. Social capital may be defined as the capacity of a social network to collectively address public problems (Coleman, 1990).

A part of a longstanding pattern in U.S. American culture, social capital stems from a feeling that ordinary citizens can work together for the public good. Individuals can also join together to promote special interests, avocations, ethnic heritage, and other such causes. Ad hoc groups (e.g., aiding needy victims), civic groups (e.g., Rotary, Kiwanis), auxiliary groups (e.g., volunteers associated with health care, law enforcement, local education), lodges and fraternal groups, and innumerable other examples, all attest to the vitality of civic life in the United States as pursued through membership and activities in volunteer groups. One important aspect of the service-oriented civic groups is that their members have accomplished a great deal for the common good of their communities. However, they also represent important social networks that give individuals a sense of belonging and satisfaction from working together.

In his well-known book *Bowling Alone* (2000), Putnam claims that there has been a noticeable decline in involvement in volunteer groups in the United States, along with a general sentiment that "most Americans today feel vaguely and uncomfortably disconnected" (p. 402). One way to build social capital and address interracial problems at the same time is through a program of face-to-face meetings organized around community-level discussions of race and race-related concerns. Numerous scholars have studied the process of civic dialogue (e.g., Anderson, Baxter, & Cissna, 2004; Barge, 2002; Fernandez, 2001; Miller & Donner, 2000; Schoem & Hurtado, 2001), concluding that individuals engaging each other in dialogue can accomplish much to bridge their differences.

Walsh (2007) has studied 141 such groups in the United States and finds substantial benefits from ongoing dialogue. Walsh discusses two primary forms of discourse emerging in the dialogue groups: one oriented to unity and the other oriented to difference. The discourse of unity is a time-honored mode of talk that proceeds toward consensus and can lead to the de-emphasis of viewpoints of marginalized individuals. The discourse of difference is oriented to the expression of dissenting viewpoints and the broaching of conflict. These two discourses, which may also represent political dynamics, consider conflict as having contrasting qualities. In pursuit of unity, conflict is viewed as a temporary challenge to be overcome; whereas in pursuit of difference, conflict is a means of clarifying goals and questioning definitions of the common good. As Walsh (2007) states, "In very simple terms, a unity-focused conception of democracy treats conflict as something to be gotten past, while a difference-focused conception treats ongoing conflict as a means to avoid domination." (p. 249).

Walsh (2007) finds both forms of discourse useful and productive in the dialogue process. She also finds particular value in members' listening to others who feel they are being heard fully when they tell personal stories about racial incidents. Walsh is also impressed with the civility present in virtually all the groups, and the manner in which race is discussed in an atmosphere of friendship. An important quality of these dialogues is that people speak and listen to each other in a face-to-face setting, thereby facilitating the airing of conflict in a non-hostile manner. The context is more deliberative than confrontational.

Nagda's (2006) analysis of intergroup dialogues identifies four communication processes in intergroup dialogues: (1) appreciating difference, (2) engaging self, (3) critical self-reflection, and (4) alliance building. This research finds that the combined effect of the communication processes positively impacts the bridging of cultural differences among group members. Nagda emphasizes the importance of dialogic listening, therefore, complementing Walsh's (2007) conclusions on listening as a necessary quality of dialogue groups (see also Stewart & Thomas, 1995).

Contrary to views that discussion groups are symbolic displays of mere talk, there is evidence that the dialogue groups often accomplish something real. As Walsh (2007) notes, one group conducted a campaign against hate crimes that included public demonstrations in support of hate crime victims. Another group staged a public recognition ceremony for African American World War II veterans. Another group helped sponsor a supermarket in a low-income neighborhood as well as acted in other ways that led to tangible accomplishments. Walsh also finds an important benefit in the process of dialogue itself. Despite its limitations, individuals in dialogue can learn how to manage conflict, listen to each other, accept differences, and achieve a level of trust that fosters friendship and solidarity. The dialogues enable participants to overcome difficulties of identity negotiation that often arise in interracial encounters. In a counterintuitive sense, dialogue that produces conflict leads to group members coming together.

As a means of improving the effectiveness of interracial communication, community dialogue has much to recommend it. Any group can start a dialogue, and even though some have funding and are sanctioned by an agency of local government, others are more informal and structured more loosely. Although many of the community dialogue groups studied by Walsh are not necessarily organized with the contact hypothesis in mind, members nevertheless manage to reduce interracial conflict and prejudice. When successful, groups use a quality of talk about race that affirms the validity of diverging viewpoints. Scrutiny of diverging viewpoints not only allows for the expression of meaningful content but also enables participants to feel that their views are taken seriously. Therefore, a sense of identity confirmation is implicit in the talk during the dialogues.

Summary of Discussion on Community Dialogues

As a second approach to more effective interracial communication, community dialogues about race exemplify social networks whose members overcome racial barriers and reduce interracial prejudice and conflict. This approach can be messy and imperfect, yet dialogue groups are valuable in achieving more effective interracial communication, and they also help in the formation of social capital. In the spirit of participatory democracy, community dialogues represent one method that ordinary citizens can undertake, on their own, without elaborate bureaucratic support or public policy initiatives. What an effective dialogue on race needs, more than anything else, is a commitment to effective group communication and a civic-minded desire to act with the intent of improving interracial communication in one's community.

A Model of Effective Interracial Communication

Interracial communication effectiveness may be defined as an ongoing relational state between African Americans and European Americans who participate in mainstream society on a basis of social equality. This relational outcome can be conceptualized as a process involving three components: (1) contact, (2) mutual affirmation of identity, and (3) communication practices and relational maintenance.

Contact is the component emphasizing that meeting and interacting with persons of another ethnicity is the basis for interracial communication. All forms of communication and all means of conducting interracial communication begin with contact. Especially in public places such as neighborhoods and schools, contact is a necessary component. Based on interracial contact, interaction leads to the mutual affirmation of identity. Two main activities, applied diversity training and community dialogues, can provide a means to interact whereby individuals exhibit respect for and gain respect from each other. Mutual affirmation of identity requires rejecting stereotypes and approaching others by valuing what they have to say and what is important to them. Mutual affirmation of identity is also enhanced through friendship formation.

On the basis of mutual identity affirmation, individuals can then maintain interracial relationships by practicing useful verbal and nonverbal communication skills and by displaying a sensitivity to each other's communication style. Relationships may vary from intimate to nonintimate; however, it is important to nurture relationships regardless of intimacy. Relational maintenance can take place away from public spaces and include invitations to interact in home settings.

Chapter 1 argues that interracial communication with a black/white focus is important due to the historical significance of race and the ongoing presence of black exceptionalism in the United States. For these reasons, this book has emphasized the distinctive features of the black/white dynamic in intergroup relations. It is also true, however, that a number of other intergroup comparisons in the United States as well as other countries exhibit characteristics that are similar to black/white relations. Therefore, the model of effective interracial communication might also be termed a model of effective intergroup communication.

Figure 1. Components of Effective Intergroup Communication

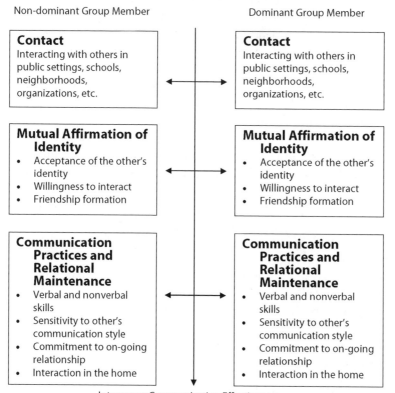

Figure 1 diagrams the components of effective intergroup communication, showing the presence of the components as well as the sequential relationship between components.

This model is a broad conceptualization of how effective intergroup communication can occur. It is not intended to be highly detailed; its simplicity stresses the basic, necessary features of interaction and communication that can offer an improvement over the current state of race and intergroup relations. It is important to stress that intergroup communication effectiveness requires intergroup contact, the mutual affirmation of identity, and the maintenance of relationships through communication practices.

Conclusion

Although one can see clear progress in race relations when comparing conditions of 100 or more years ago to the present, important barriers to effective interracial communication remain. This chapter has discussed how interracial communication is a component of several models of race relations in the United States. Multiculturalism is presented as the most viable model for improving race relations and that communication plays a vital role in multiculturalism, both by majority group members and by minority group members.

In arguing for a multiculturalist approach to improving race relations, it is acknowledged that there are significant difficulties and all parties may find costs and rewards. Some scholars (e.g., Hollinger, 2000; Schlesinger, 1992) conclude that multiculturalism can lead to the accentuation of cultural differences, a heightening of ethnic conflict, and can interfere with national cohesion. Another cost is weighed by those who see assimilation as a viable model for race relations. However flawed the assimilation process may be, in its melting pot form this model has brought benefits to significant numbers of immigrants who have effectively contributed to and derived satisfaction from participation in mainstream society. It has also been noted that African Americans have meaningfully participated in cultural and, to a lesser degree, structural assimilation. By advocating multiculturalism with a view toward assimilation, it is proposed that a new superordinate group identity could function similarly to the way assimilation has functioned previously in the United States.

Chief among the rewards of a successful multicultural approach would be healthy identity formation. Without pressures to assimilate to the dominant society, individuals and groups would be free to construct and maintain their own identities. The United States is still a long way from achieving ethnic and racial tolerance, thus we must view multiculturalism as a long-term goal. Presently, intermediate steps toward multiculturalism are already being undertaken through diversity training in many organizations, and through academic courses in secondary and higher education in intercultural and interracial communication. Over the long term, achieving the goals of improved race relations through multiculturalism will require concerted efforts and a commitment to equal rights. Interracial communication plays a vital role in both short-term and long-term outcomes.

Just as this book was undergoing final revisions, Barack Obama was elected president. His election to the presidency presents us with an intriguing question. Is it assimilation that his political success represents the triumph of, or is it multiculturalism? Some early reactions suggest that Obama's success is a sign that assimilation is viable. Viewed in one light, the election signifies "the vitality of America's most distinctive and powerful master trend—assimilation, an invincible force that selects from, absorbs and integrates difference, not always kindly, but always to the profit of the nation's mainstream" (Patterson, 2008, p. 40). Alternatively, others see in Obama a representative of the modern American cultural mosaic and a public figure who appeals to diverse groups. Obama's elective success demonstrated support from many ethnic groups, especially African American and Latino, voters from all regions of the country, and voters from both upper and lower income backgrounds. It has also been noted that racism was a minor factor in the motivations of voters (Seib, 2008). To some, Obama's election shows that U.S. Americans can accept a black person as president and that a new level of political and multicultural inclusiveness has been reached.

It remains to be seen how the election of Obama to the presidency will affect race relations. It seems quite possible that having an African American in such a visible role will bring about changes in racial stereotyping. Obama's image will be widely viewed and read about in the media; his activities will be much discussed by ordinary citizens, and we may find that he will be seen, not as a black president, but simply an American president. One may speculate that Obama's rise to the presidency is a symbolic shift to a post-ethnic era in the United States. However, it will be some time before there is any clear sense of a new post-ethnic climate. For many of us in the United States, the election of 2008 has captured our imagination and motivated us to examine and reexamine race relations as never before. People are thinking and talking about race, and in some ways, the election of 2008 has facilitated a national dialogue about race. Perhaps the time is right for the formation of a combined political, cultural, and social capital that will result in more meaningful participation in civic discourse.

Ultimately, the choice to promote multiculturalism and effective interracial communication in the United States is up to all U.S. Americans. The interracial contact that would help reduce bias, stigma, prejudice, and conflict is limited because there is too little effective interracial communication. In reviewing literature for this book, one important theme that kept occurring was that of strangers interacting together but not communicating. The book *A Country of Strangers* (Shipler, 1997) often refers to blacks and whites interacting on the basis of ignorance of each other as individuals. Shipler observes that whites do not know what blacks think of them:

> Few white Americans have much grasp of how they are seen by African-Americans because few whites ask the question—and if they do, most blacks would probably be more polite than honest. We do not converse across the racial line. (p. 562)

Shipler (1997) also comments that blacks often find it difficult communicating with whites, when utterances and gestures may be difficult to interpret:

> If you are black in America, you stand somewhere along a spectrum of assumptions about what is really happening behind the code of white behavior. ...in the middle of the spectrum, where most blacks seem to be, deciphering whites' comments and actions is an exhausting effort. Was it because of your blackness that you were denied the promotion, excluded from the meeting, treated rudely by the salesclerk, ignored by the professor? Was the unpleasant remark, glance, or laughter an encrypted expression of racial prejudice? (p. 448)

Shipler is getting at the idea that blacks and whites often have insufficient experience and insight into how to communicate with each other. It is as if we interact as strangers.

Coming at the issue of communicating with strangers from another perspective, Allen (2004) has written a book that discusses communication, friendship, and political involvement. In her book, *Talking to Strangers: Anxieties of Citizenship since Brown v. Board of Education*, Allen notes that a lack of interracial trust has left many Americans unable to form necessary political friendships. Allen (2004) refers to problems in other countries where distrust exists and then notes this about the United States:

An honest look at the political situation in the United States leads to a related recognition that among our core political problems is not racism, but interracial distrust. It flows always, but especially "both ways," across the black/white divide. Despite demographic change, the question "Whom can you trust?" keeps reconstituting the colorline. (Prologue, XIV)

Later in the book, Allen refers to Americans as strangers in the sense that low levels of trust have led to suspicions about government, politicians, and casual acquaintances. While underscoring the irony in the slogan, "Don't talk to strangers," Allen writes that many Americans have stepped back from opportunities to reach out to others and form political friendships based on trust. This is especially true for interracial friendships.

One purpose of this book is to examine the nature of interracial communication with a view toward encouraging greater interracial trust. If, indeed, we Americans have become strangers in our own land, the only way to foster familiarity and trust is to engage our fellow Americans in contact, communication, and the formation of interracial social networks. In the United States, inequality will always exist, race relations and multiculturalism remain problematic, and there are great differences among citizens due to not just race, but also class, gender, ethnicity, and other potentially divisive qualities. Communication cannot possibly bridge all the differences. However, in a nation devoted to self-government, it is incumbent upon ordinary citizens to construct, together, a civic environment where talk is practical and productive.

References

Aboud, F. (1984). Social and cognitive bases of ethnic identity constancy. *Journal of Genetic Psychology, 145*, 217-230.

Aboud, F., & Doyle, A. (1996). Parental and peer influences on children's racial attitudes. *International Journal of Intercultural Relations, 20*, 371-383.

Abrahams, R. (1989). Black talking in the streets. In R. Bauman & J. Scherzer (Eds.), *Explorations in the ethnography of speaking* (2d ed., pp. 240-262). Cambridge, UK: Cambridge University Press.

Adams, F., & Sanders, B. (2003). *Alienable rights: The exclusion of African Americans in a white man's land, 1619-2000*. New York: HarperCollins.

Ainsworth-Darnell, J., & Downey, D. (1998). Assessing the oppositional culture explanation for racial/ethnic differences in school performance. *American Sociological Review, 63*, 536-553.

Akinnaso, F., & Ajirotutu, C. (1982). Performance and ethnic style in job interviews. In J. Gumperz (Ed.), *Language and social identity* (pp. 119-144). Cambridge, UK: Cambridge University Press.

Allen, B. (1995). Diversity and organizational communication. *Journal of Applied Communication Research, 23*, 143-155.

Allen, B. (2008). Diversity in the workplace. In W. Donsbach (Ed.), *The international encyclopedia of communication* (Vol. IV, pp. 1392-1396). Malden, MA: Blackwell.

Allen, D. (2004). *Talking to strangers: Anxieties of citizenship since Brown v. Board of education*. Chicago: University of Chicago Press.

Allport, G. (1954). *The nature of prejudice*. Garden City, NY: Doubleday/Anchor.

Anderson, R., Baxter, L., & Cissna, K. (Eds.). (2004). *Dialogue: Theorizing difference in communication studies*. Thousand Oaks, CA: Sage.

Antonovics, K., & Knight, B. (2004). *A new look at racial profiling: Evidence from the Boston Police Department*. Cambridge, MA: National Bureau of Economic Research.

Armstrong, B., Neuendorf, K., & Brentar, J. (1992). TV entertainment, news, and racial perceptions of college students. *Journal of Communication, 42*, 153-176.

Ashcraft, K., & Allen, B. (2003). The racial foundation of organizational communication. *Communication Theory, 13*, 5-18.

Asim, J. (2007). *The n-word: Who can say it, who shouldn't, and why*. Boston, MA: Houghton Mifflin.

Atkins, C. (1993). Do employment recruiters discriminate on the basis of nonstandard dialect? *Journal of Employment Counseling, 30*, 108-118.

Augstein, H. (1996). *Race: The origins of an idea, 1760-1850*. Bristol, UK: Thoemmes.

Bailey, G., & Maynor, N. (1989). The divergence controversy. *American Speech, 64*, 12-38.

Bailey, R. (1998). Those valuable people, the Africans: The economic impact of the slave(ery) trade on textile industrialization in New England. In D. Roediger & M. Blatt (Eds.), *The Meaning of Slavery in the North* (pp. 3-31). New York: Garland.

Banks, J. (2006). Improving race relations in schools: From theory to research to practice. *Journal of Social Issues, 62*, 607–614.

Barge, J. (2002). Enlarging the meaning of group deliberation: From discussion to dialogue. In L. Frey (Ed.), *New directions in group communication* (pp. 159–178). Thousand Oaks, CA: Sage.

Barkley, C. (2005). *Who's afraid of a large black man?* New York: Penguin.

Barnes, A. (2000). *Everyday racism: A book for all Americans.* Naperville, IL: Sourcebooks.

Barnes, B., Palmary, I., & Durrheim, K. (2001). The denial of racism: The role of humor, personal experience, and self-censorship. *Journal of Language and Social Psychology, 20*, 321–338.

Baugh, J. (1983). *Black street speech: Its history, structure, and survival.* Austin, TX: University of Texas Press.

Baugh, J. (1998). Linguistics, education, and the law: Educational reform for African-American language minority students. In S. Mufwene, J. Rickford, G. Bailey, & J. Baugh (Eds.), *African-American English: Structure, history and use* (pp. 282–301). London: Routledge.

Baugh, J. (2000). *Beyond Ebonics: Linguistic pride and racial prejudice.* New York: Oxford University Press.

Baugh, J. (2003). Linguistic profiling. In S. Makoni, G. Smitherman, A. Ball, & A. Spears (Eds.), *Black linguistics: Language, society, and politics in Africa and the Americas* (pp. 155–168). London: Routledge.

Bayard, D., Weatherall, M., Gallois, C., & Pittam, J. (2001). Pax Americana?: Accent attitudinal evaluations in New Zealand, Australia, and America. *Journal of Sociolinguistics, 5*, 22–49.

Behrendt, S. (1999). Transatlantic slave trade. In K. Appiah & H. Gates (Eds.), *Africana: The encyclopedia of the African American experience* (pp. 1865–1877). New York: Basic Civitas.

Bell, D. (1992). *Faces at the bottom of the well: The permanence of racism.* New York: Basic Books.

Bennett, E. (1999). Rap. In K. Appiah & H. Gates (Eds.), *Africana: The encyclopedia of the African and African American experience* (pp. 1589–1591). New York: Basic Civitas.

Berlin, I. (1998). *Many thousands gone: The first two centuries of slavery in North America.* Cambridge, MA: Belknap Press of Harvard University Press.

Berlin, I. (2003). *Generations of captivity: A history of African-American slaves.* Cambridge, MA: Belknap Press of Harvard University Press.

Bernstein, D. (2001). *Only one place of redress: African Americans, labor regulations, and the courts from reconstruction to the new deal.* Durham, NC: Duke University Press.

Biernat, M. (2003). Toward a broader view of social stereotyping. *American Psychologist, 58*, 1019–1027.

Billig, M. (1988). The notion of prejudice: Rhetorical and ideological aspects. *Text, 8*, 91–110.

Black America Today (2008). General Highlights. *Religion and social views.* Retrieved July 1, 2008, from http://www.BlackAmericaStudy.com.

Blackshire-Belay, C. (1996). The location of Ebonics within the framework of the Africological paradigm. *Journal of Black Studies, 27,* 5–23.

Blauner, R. (1969). Internal colonialism and ghetto revolt. *Social Problems, 16,* 393–408.

Blom, J., & Gumperz, J. (1972). Social meaning in linguistic structure: Code-switching in Norway. In J. Gumperz & D. Hymes (Eds.), *Directions in sociolinguistics: The ethnography of communication* (pp. 407–434). New York: Holt, Rinehart Winston.

Blubaugh, J & Pennington, D. (1976). *Crossing difference . . .Interracial communication.* Columbus, OH: Charles E. Merrill.

Blum, J. (1991). *Years of discord: American politics and society, 1961–1974.* New York: Norton.

Blum, L. (2002). *"I'm not a racist, but . . .": The moral quandary of race.* Ithaca, NY: Cornell University Press.

Blumenbach, J. (1969). *On the natural varieties of mankind* (T. Bendyshe, Trans). New York: Bergman. (Original work published 1865).

Blumenthal, S. (2003). *The Clinton wars.* New York: Farrar, Straus and Giroux.

Bodenhausen, G., & Macrae, C. (1998). Stereotype activation and inhibition. In R. Wyer, Jr. (Ed.), *Stereotype activation and inhibition: Advances in social cognition XI,* (pp. 1–52). Mahwah, NJ: Erlbaum.

Bogle, D. (1996). *Toms, coons, mulattoes, mammies, and bucks: An interpretive history of blacks in American films* (3rd ed.). New York: Continuum.

Bogle, D. (2001). *Prime time blues: African Americans on network television.* New York: Farrar, Straus and Giroux.

Bolgatz, J. (2005). *Talking race in the classroom.* New York: Teachers College Press.

Bonilla-Silva, E. (2003). *Racism without racists: Color-blind racism and the persistence of racial inequality in the United States.* Lanham, MD: Rowman & Littlefield.

Bonilla-Silva, E., & Forman, T. (2000). "I am not a racist but . . .": Mapping White college students' racial ideology in the USA. *Discourse and Society, 11,* 50–85.

Borstelmann, T. (2001). *The cold war and the color line: American race relations in the global arena.* Cambridge, MA: Harvard University Press.

Boskin, J. (1986). *Sambo: The rise & demise of an American jester.* New York: Oxford University Press.

Braddock II, J. H., & McPartland, J. M. (1987). How minorities continue to be excluded from equal employment opportunities: Research on labor market and institutional barriers. *Journal of Social Issues, 43*(1), 5–39.

Brehm, J., & Rahn, W. (1997). Individual level evidence for the causes and consequences of social capital. *American Journal of Political Science, 41,* 999–1023.

Brewer, M. (1996). When contact is not enough: Social identity and intergroup cooperation. *International Journal of Intercultural Relations, 20,* 291–303.

Brigham, J. (1993). College students' racial attitudes. *Journal of Applied Social Psychology, 23,* 1933–1967.

Brooks, R. (1996). *Integration or separation? A strategy for racial equality.* Cambridge, MA: Harvard University Press.

Brown, M., Carnoy, M., Currie, E., Duster, T., Oppenheimer, D., Shultz, M., & Wellman, D. (2003). *Whitewashing race: The myth of a color-blind society*. Berkeley: University of California Press.

Bryant, J., & Thompson, S. (2002). *Fundamentals of media effects*. Boston: McGraw-Hill.

Bugental, D., & Grusec, J. (2006). Socialization processes. In N. Eisenberg (Ed.), *Handbook of Child Psychology* (6th ed., pp. 366–428). Hoboken, NJ: John Wiley & Sons.

Buttny, R. (1997). Reported speech in talking race on campus. *Human Communication Research, 23*, 477–506.

Buttny, R. (2004). *Talking problems: Studies of discursive construction*. Albany: State University of New York Press.

Buzzanell, P. (1999). Tensions and burdens in employment interviewing processes: Perspectives of non-dominant group applicants. *The Journal of Business Communication, 36*, 134–162.

Carbaugh, D. (1988). *Talking American: Cultural discourses on Donahue*. Norwood, NJ: Ablex.

Cargile, A., & Bradac, J. (2002). Attitudes toward language: A review of speaker-evaluation and a general process model. In W. Gudykunst (Ed.), *Communication Yearbook 25* (pp. 347–382). Mahwah, NJ: Erlbaum.

Chriss, J. (2007). *Social control: An introduction*. Cambridge, UK: Polity.

Cobb, W. (2007). *To the break of dawn: A freestyle on the hip-hop aesthetic*. New York: New York University Press.

Cole, P., & Taylor, O. (1990). Performances of working class African American children in three tests of articulation. *Language, Speech, and Hearing Services in Schools, 21*, 171–176.

Coleman, J. (1990). *Foundations of social theory*. Cambridge, MA: Belknap Press of Harvard University Press.

Collins, P. (1998). *Fighting words: Black women and the search for justice*. Minneapolis: University of Minnesota Press.

Conrad, C., & Poole, M. (2002). *Strategic organizational communication in a global economy*. Fort Worth, TX: Harcourt College.

Cook, P., & Ludwig, J. (1997). Weighing the burden of "acting white": Are there race differences in attitudes toward education? *Journal of Policy Analysis and Management*, Spring, 256–278

Cook, S. (1985). Experimenting on social issues: The case of school desegregation. *American Psychologist, 40*, 452–460.

Cook, T. (2003). *Separation, assimilation, or accommodation: Contrasting ethnic minority policies*. Westport, CT: Praeger.

Cox, T. (2001). *Creating the multicultural organization: A strategy for capturing the power of diversity*. San Francisco: Jossey-Bass.

Craig, H., & Washington, J. (1995). African American English and linguistic complexity in preschool discourse: A second look. *Language, Speech, and Hearing Services in Schools, 26*, 87–93.

Cripps T. (1993a). *Slow fade to black: The Negro in American Film, 1900–1942*. Oxford, UK: Oxford University Press.

Cripps, T. (1993b). *Making movies Black: The Hollywood message movie from World War II to the civil rights era.* New York: Oxford University Press.

Crosby, F. (2004). *Affirmative action is dead: Long live affirmative action.* New Haven, CT: Yale University Press.

Cukor-Avila, P., & Bailey, G. (2001). The effects of the race of the interviewer on sociolinguistic fieldwork. *Journal of Sociolinguistics, 5,* 254–270.

Curtin, P. (1969). *The Atlantic slave trade: A census.* Madison, WI: University of Wisconsin Press.

Dalby, D. (2003). The African element in black American English. In N. Norment (Ed.), *Readings in African American language: Aspects, features, and perspectives* (pp. 5–23). New York: Peter Lang.

Daniel, J., & Smitherman, G. (1976). How I got over: Communication dynamics in the black community. *Quarterly Journal of Speech, 62,* 26–39.

Dansby, M., & Landis, D. (2001). Intercultural training in the United States Military. In M. Dansby, J. Stewart, & S. Webb (Eds.), *Managing diversity in the military: Research perspectives from the Defense Equal Opportunity Management Institute* (pp. 9–28). New Brunswick, NJ: Transaction.

Dansby, M., Stewart, J., & Webb, S. (2001). Overview. In M. Dansby, J. Stewart, & S. Webb (Eds.), *Managing diversity in the military: Research perspectives from the Defense Equal Opportunity Management Institute* (pp. xvii–xxxii). New Brunswick, NJ: Transaction.

Dillard, J. (1972). *Black English: Its history and usage in the United States.* New York: Random House.

Dixon, T. (2006). Psychological reactions to crime news portrayals of black criminals: Understanding the moderating roles of prior news viewing and stereotype endorsement. *Communication Monographs, 73,* 162–187.

Dixon, T., & Azocar, C. (2007). Priming crime and activating blackness: Understanding the psychological impact of the overrepresentation of blacks as lawbreakers on television news. *Journal of Communication, 57,* 229–253.

Dixon, T., Schell, T., Giles, H., & Drogos, K. (2008). The influence of race in police-civilian interactions: A content analysis of videotaped interactions taken during Cincinnati police traffic stops. *Journal of Communication, 58,* 530–549.

Doob, C. (1999). *Racism: An American cauldron* (3rd ed.). New York: Longman.

Dougherty, C. (2008, Aug. 14). Nonwhites to be majority in U.S. by 2042. *Wall Street Journal,* p. A3.

Douglass, F. (1968). *Narrative of the life of Frederick Douglass, an American slave.* New York: Signet.

D'Sousa, D. (1995). *The end of racism: Principles for a multicultural society.* New York: Free Press.

Du Bois, W. (1903). *The souls of black folk.* Chicago: A. C. McClurg & Company. Published in 1996 by Penguin Books.

Dyson, M. (2005). *Is Bill Cosby right?: Or has the black middle class lost its mind?* New York: Basic Civitas.

Eltis, D. (2000). *The rise of African slavery in the Americas*. Cambridge, UK: Cambridge University Press.

Entman, R. (1992). Blacks in the news: Television, modern racism, and cultural change. *Journalism Quarterly, 69*, 341–361.

Entman, R., & Rojecki, A. (2000). *The black image in the white mind: Media and race in America*. Chicago: University of Chicago Press.

Essed, P. (1991). *Understanding everyday racism: An interdisciplinary theory*. Newbury Park, CA: Sage.

Eze, E. (Ed.). (1997). *Race and the Enlightenment: A reader*. Cambridge, MA: Blackwell Publishers.

Fairclough, N. (2003). "Political correctness": The politics of culture and language. *Discourse and Society, 14*, 17–28.

Feagin, J., & McKinney, K. (2005). *The many costs of racism*. Lanham, MD: Rowman & Littlefield.

Fehrenbacher, D. (1978). *The Dred Scott case: Its significance in American law and politics*. New York: Oxford University Press.

Fehrenbacher, D. (2001). *The slaveholding republic: An account of the United States government's relations to slavery*. Oxford, UK: Oxford University Press.

Fein, S., & Spencer, S. (1997). Prejudice as self-image maintenance: Affirming self through derogating others. *Journal of Personality and Social Psychology, 73*, 31–44.

Fenton, S. (1999). *Ethnicity: Racism, class, and culture*. Lanham, MD: Rowman & Littlefield.

Fernandez, T. (2001). Building "bridges" of understanding through dialogue. In D. Schoem & S. Hurtado (Eds.), *Intergroup dialogue: Deliberative democracy in school, college, community and workplace* (pp. 45–58). Ann Arbor, MI: University of Michigan Press.

Fine, G., & Turner, P. (2001). *Whispers on the color line: Rumor and race in America*. Berkeley: University of California Press.

Finkelman, P. (2001). *Slavery and the founders: Race and liberty in the age of Jefferson* (2nd ed.). Armonk, NY: M. E. Sharpe.

Fireside, H. (2004). *Separate and unequal: Homer Plessy and the Supreme Court decision that legalized racism*. New York: Carroll & Graf.

Fleming, J., Darling, J., Hilton, J., & Kojetin, B. (1990). Multiple-audience problem: A strategic perspective on social perception. *Journal of Personality and Social Psychology, 58*, 593–609.

Fogel, R. (1989). *Without consent or contract: The rise and fall of American slavery*. New York: W.W. Norton & Company.

Fogel, R. (2003). *The slavery debates: A retrospective*. Baton Rouge, LA: Louisiana State University Press.

Fogel, R., & Engerman, S. (1974). *Time on the cross*. Boston: Little, Brown & Co.

Foner, E. (1988). *Reconstruction: America's unfinished revolution, 1863–1877*. New York: Harper & Row.

Ford, R. (2008). *The race card: How bluffing about bias makes race relations worse*. New York. Farrar, Straus and Giroux.

Fordham, S., & Ogbu, J. (1986). Black students' school success: Coping with the "burden of 'acting white.'" *The Urban Review, 18*, 176–206.

Frankenburg, R. (1993). *White women, race matters: The social construction of whiteness*. Minneapolis: University of Minnesota Press.

Fredrickson, G. (1988). *The arrogance of race: Historical perspectives on slavery, racism, and social inequality*. Middletown, CT: Wesleyan University Press.

Fredrickson, G. (1999). Models of American ethnic relations: A historical perspective. In D. Prentice & D. Miller (Eds.), *Cultural divides: Understanding and overcoming group conflict* (pp. 23–34). New York: Russell Sage Foundation.

Fredrickson, G. (2002). *Racism: A short history*. Princeton, NJ: Princeton University Press.

Gaertner, S., & Dovidio, J. (1986). The aversive form of racism. In J. Dovidio & S. Gaertner (Eds.), *Prejudice, discrimination, and racism* (pp. 61–89). Orlando, FL: Academic Press.

Gaertner, S., Dovidio, J., & Bachman, B. (1996). Revisiting the contact hypothesis: The induction of a common ingroup identity. *International Journal of Intercultural Relations, 20*, 271–290.

Gaertner, S., Dovidio, J., Nier, J., Ward, C., & Banker, B. (1999). Across cultural divides: The value of a superordinate identity. In D. Prentice & D. Miller (Eds.), *Cultural Divides: Understanding and overcoming group conflict* (pp. 173–212). New York: Russell Sage Foundation.

Gallois, C., Ogay, T., & Giles, H. (2005). Communication accommodation theory: A look back and a look ahead. In W. Gudykunst (Ed.), *Theorizing about intercultural communication* (pp. 121–148). Thousand Oaks, CA: Sage.

Gardner, M. (2002). *Harry Truman and civil rights: Moral courage and political risks*. Carbondale, IL: Southern Illinois University Press.

Garner, T. (1983). Playing the dozens: Folklore as strategies for living. *Quarterly Journal of Speech, 69*, 47–57.

Garner, T., & Rubin, D. (1986). Middle class Blacks' perceptions of dialect and style shifting: The case of southern attorneys. *Journal of Language and Social Psychology, 5*, 33–48.

Gates, H., & McKay, N. (Eds.). (1997). *The Norton anthology of African American literature*. New York: Norton.

Giddens, A. (1979). *Central problems in social theory: Action, structure, and contradiction in social analysis*. Berkeley: University of California Press.

Gilens, M. (1999). *Why Americans hate welfare: Race, media, and the politics of antipoverty policy*. Chicago: University of Chicago Press.

Giles, H., & Bourhis, R. (1976). Voice and racial categorization in Britain. *Communication Monographs, 43*, 108–114.

Giles, H., & Johnson, P. (1987). Ethnolinguistic identity theory: A social psychological approach to language maintenance. *International Journal of the Sociology of Language, 68*, 69–99.

Glaser, J., & Banaji, M. (1999). When fair is fair and foul is foul: Reverse priming in automatic evaluation. *Journal of Personality and Social Psychology, 77*, 669–687.

Goldfield, D., (1990). *Black, white, and southern: Race relations and southern culture, 1940 to the present.* Baton Rouge: Louisiana State University Press.

Gorham, B. (2006). News media's relationship with stereotyping: The linguistic intergroup bias in response to crime news. *Journal of Communication, 56,* 289–308.

Gould, S. (1996). *The mismeasure of man.* New York: W. W. Norton & Co.

Graham, L. (1995). *Member of the club: Reflections on life in a racially polarized world.* New York: HarperPerennial.

Graves, J. (2004). *The race myth: Why we pretend race exists in America.* New York: Dutton.

Gray, H. (1995). *Watching race: Television and the struggle for "blackness."* Minneapolis, MN: University of Minnesota Press.

Green, L. (2002). *African American English: A linguistic introduction.* Cambridge, UK: Cambridge University Press.

Greenberg, B., & Collette, L. (1997). The changing faces on TV: A demographic analysis of network television's new seasons, 1966–1992. *Journal of Broadcasting & Electronic Media, 41,* 1–13.

Greenberg, B., Mastro, D., & Brand, J. (2002). Minorities and the mass media: Television into the 21st century. In J. Bryant & D. Zillmann (Eds.), *Media effects: Advances in theory and research* (pp. 333–351). Hillsdale, NJ: Erlbaum.

Greenberg, J., & Pyszczynski, T. (1985). The effects of an overheard ethnic slur on evaluations of the target: How to spread a social disease. *Journal of Experimental Social Psychology, 21,* 61–72.

Greenberg, K. (1996). *Honor & slavery: Lies, duels, masks, dressing as a woman, gifts, strangers, humanitarianism, death, slave rebellions, the pro-slavery argument, baseball, hunting and gambling in the old South.* Princeton, NJ: Princeton University Press.

Greenhouse, L. (2007, June 29). Justices, 5-4, limit use of race for school integration plans. *New York Times,* pp. A1, A20.

Gumperz, J. (1982). *Discourse strategies.* Cambridge, UK: Cambridge University Press.

Halberstam, D. (1993). *The fifties.* New York: Villard.

Hale, G. (1998). *Making whiteness: The culture of segregation in the south, 1890–1940.* New York: Pantheon.

Hale, J. (1994). *Unbank the fire: Visions for the education of African American children.* Baltimore, MD: Johns Hopkins University Press.

Hamilton, D. (2005). Activation of cognitive structures: Introduction and preview. In D. Hamilton (Ed.), *Social cognition* (pp. 147–153). New York: Taylor & Francis.

Hamilton, D., & Gifford, R. (1976). Illusory correlation in interpersonal perception: A cognitive basis of stereotypic judgments. *Journal of Experimental Social Psychology, 12,* 392–407.

Hardin, C., & Higgins, E. (1996). Shared reality: How social verification makes the subjective objective. In R. Sorrentino & E. Higgins (Eds.), *Handbook of motivation and cognition: Vol. 3. The interpersonal context* (pp. 28–84). New York: Guilford.

Hargrove, H. (1988). *Black Union soldiers in the Civil War.* Jefferson, NC: McFarland & Company.

Harris, T., & Kalbfleisch, P. (2004). Interracial dating: The implications for initiating a romantic relationship. In R. Jackson (Ed.), *African American communication and identities* (pp. 125–136). Thousand Oaks, CA: Sage.

Hart, B., & Risley, T. (1995). *Meaningful differences in the everyday experience of young American children*. Baltimore: Brookes.

Haslam, S., Oakes, P., Reynolds, K., & Turner, J. (1999). Social identity salience and the emergence of stereotype consensus. *Personality and Social Psychology Bulletin, 25,* 809–818.

Hecht, M. (1993). 2002: A research odyssey toward the development of a communication theory of identity. *Communication Monographs, 60,* 76–82.

Hecht, M., Collier, M., & Ribeau, S. (1993). *African American communication: Ethnic identity and cultural interpretations*. Newbury Park, CA: Sage.

Hecht, M., Jackson, R., & Ribeau, S. (2003). *African American communication: Exploring identity and culture* (2nd ed.). Mahwah, NJ: Erlbaum.

Higgins, E., Rholes, W., & Jones, C. (1977). Category accessibility and impression formation. *Journal of Experimental Social Psychology, 13,* 141–154.

Hirschfeld, L. (1996). *Race in the making: Cognition, culture, and the child's construction of human kinds*. Cambridge, MA: MIT Press.

Hochschild, J. (1995). *Facing up to the American dream: Race, class, and the soul of the nation*. Princeton, NJ: Princeton University Press.

Hochschild, J., & Scovronick, N. (2003). *The American dream and the public schools*. New York: Oxford University Press.

Hogg, M., & Abrams, D. (2001). Intergroup relations: An overview. In M. Hogg & D. Abrams (Eds.), *Intergroup relations: Essential readings* (pp. 1–14). Philadelphia: Taylor & Francis.

Hollinger, D. (2000). *Post-ethnic America*. New York: Basic Books.

Hollinger, D. (2006). *Cosmopolitanism and solidarity: Studies in ethnoracial, religious, and professional affiliation in the United States*. Madison, WI: University of Wisconsin Press.

Hollinger, D. (2008, February 29). Obama, blackness, and postethnic America. *The Chronicle Review,* B7–B10.

Holm, J. (1988). *Pidgins and Creoles: Theory and structure* (Vol. 2). Cambridge, UK: Cambridge University Press.

Holt, G. (1977). Stylin' outta the black pulpit. In T. Kochman (Ed.), *Rappin' and stylin' out: Communication in urban black America* (pp. 189–204). Urbana: University of Illinois Press.

Hopper, R. (1977). Language attitudes in the employment interview. *Communication Monographs, 44,* 346–352.

Hopper, R., & Williams, F. (1973). Speech characteristics and employability. *Speech Monographs, 40,* 296–302.

Hornsey, M., & Hogg, M. (2000). Assimilation and diversity: An integrative model of subgroup relations. *Personality and Social Psychology Bulletin, 4,* 143–156.

Hughes, D., & Chen, L. (1997). When and what parents tell children about race: An examination of race-related socialization among African American families. *Applied Developmental Science, 1*, 200–214.

Hughes, R. (1993). *Culture of complaint: The fraying of America.* New York: Oxford University Press.

Hurwitz, J., & Peffley, M. (Eds.). (1998). *Perception and prejudice: Race and politics in the United States.* New Haven, CT: Yale University Press.

Husband, C. (1977). News media, language, and race relations: A case study in identity maintenance. In H. Giles (Ed.), *Language, ethnicity, and intergroup relations* (pp. 211–240). London: Academic Press.

Hymes, D. (1974). *Foundations in sociolinguistics: An ethnographic approach.* Philadelphia: University of Pennsylvania Press.

Irons, P. (2002). *Jim Crow's children: The broken promise of the Brown decision.* New York: Viking.

Jablin, F. (2001). Organizational entry, assimilation, and disengagement/exit. In F. Jablin & L. Putnam (Eds.), *The new handbook of organizational communication: Advances in theory, research, and methods* (pp. 732–818). Thousand Oaks, CA: Sage.

Jackson, J. (2008). *Racial paranoia: The unintended consequences of political correctness.* New York: Basic Civitas.

Jackson, L., Sullivan, L., & Hodge, C. (1993). Stereotype effects on attributions, predictions, and evaluations: No two social judgments are quite alike. *Journal of Personality and Social Psychology, 65*, 69–84.

Jackson, R. (2002). Cultural contracts theory: Toward an understanding of identity negotiation. *Communication Quarterly, 50*, 359–367.

Jackson, S. & Roberts, J. (2001). Complex syntax production of African American preschoolers. *Journal of Speech, Language, and Hearing Research, 44*, 1033-1096.

Jacobs, B. (2006). *Race manners for the 21st century: Navigating the minefield between black and white Americans in an age of fear* (2nd ed.). New York: Arcade.

Jacobs, J., & Labov, T. (2002). Gender differentials in intermarriage among sixteen race and ethnic groups. *Sociological Forum, 17*, 621–646.

Jacobs, R. (2000). *Race, media, and the crisis of civil society: From Watts to Rodney King.* Cambridge, UK: Cambridge University Press.

James, E. (2000). Race-related differences in promotions and support: Underlying effects of human and social capital. *Organization Science: A Journal of the Institute of Management Sciences, 11*, 493–508.

James, N. (2004). When Miss America was always white. In A. Gonzalez, M. Houston, & V. Chen (Eds.), *Our voices: Essays in culture, ethnicity, and communication* (4th ed., pp. 61–65). Los Angeles: Roxbury.

Jamieson, K. (1992). *Dirty politics: Deception, distraction, and democracy.* New York: Oxford University Press.

Jemie, O. (Ed.). (2003). *Yo' mama!: New raps, toasts, dozens, jokes and children's rhymes from urban black America.* Philadelphia: Temple University Press.

Johnson, D., & Campbell, R. (1981). *Black migration in America: A social demographic history.* Durham, NC: Duke University Press.

Johnson, F. (2000). *Speaking culturally: Language diversity in the United States*. Thousand Oaks, CA: Sage.

Johnson, F., & Buttny, R. (1982). White listeners' responses to "sounding Black" and "sounding White": The effects of message content on judgments about language. *Communication Monographs, 49*, 33–49.

Kant, I. (1963). Idea for a universal history from a cosmopolitan point of view (L. Beck, Trans.). In L. Beck (Ed.), *On history: Immanuel Kant* (pp.11–26). Indianapolis, IN: Bobbs-Merrill. (original work published 1784)

Kelley, R. (1997). *Yo' mama's dysfunktional: Fighting the culture wars in urban America*. Boston: Beacon Press.

Kelley, R., Starr, M., & Conant, E. (2007, April 23). A team stands tall. *Newsweek*, pp. 32–33.

Kennedy, R. (1997). *Race, crime, and the law*. New York: Vintage Books.

Kennedy, R. (2002). *Nigger: The strange career of a troublesome word*. New York: Vintage.

Kennedy, R. (2003). *Interracial intimacies: Sex, marriage, identity, and adoption*. New York: Pantheon.

Kern-Foxworth, M. (1994). *Aunt Jemima, Uncle Ben, and Rastus: Blacks in advertising, yesterday, today, and tomorrow*. Westport, CT: Greenwood.

Kim, C., & Tamborini, C. (2006). The continuing significance of race in the occupational attainment of whites and blacks: A segmented labor market analysis. *Sociological Inquiry, 76*, 23–51.

Kim, Y. (2005). Adapting to a new culture: An integrative communication theory. In W. Gudykunst (Ed.), *Theorizing about intercultural communication* (pp. 375–400). Thousand Oaks, CA: Sage.

Kinder, D., & Sanders, L. (1996). *Divided by color: Racial politics and democratic ideals*. Chicago: University of Chicago Press.

King, W. (1995). *Stolen childhood: Slave youth in nineteenth century America*. Bloomington: Indiana University Press.

Kirkland, S., Greenberg, J., & Pyszczynski, T. (1987). Further evidence of the deleterious effects of overheard derogatory ethnic labels: Derogation beyond the target. *Personality and Social Psychology Bulletin, 13*, 216–227.

Klinkner, P., & Smith, R. (1999). *The unsteady march: The rise and decline of racial equality in America*. Chicago: University of Chicago Press.

Koch, L., & Gross, A. (1997). Children's perceptions of Black English as a variable in interracial perception. *Journal of Black Psychology, 23*, 215–226.

Kochman, T. (1981). *Black and white styles in conflict*. Chicago: University of Chicago Press.

Kolchin, P. (1993). *American slavery, 1619–1877*. New York: Hill and Wang.

Kosova, W. (2007, April 23). The power that was. *Newsweek*, pp. 24–31.

Kozol, J. (2005). *The shame of the nation: The restoration of apartheid schooling in America*. New York: Three Rivers.

Kretzschmar, W. (Ed.) (1998). Editor's Note. *Journal of English Linguistics, 26*, 93–94.

Labov, W. (1972a). *Language in the inner city: Studies in Black English Vernacular*. Philadelphia: University of Pennsylvania Press.

Labov, W. (1972b). *Sociolinguistic patterns*. Philadelphia: University of Pennsylvania Press.

Labov, W. (1982). Objectivity and commitment in linguistic science: The case of the Black English trial in Ann Arbor. *Language in Society, 11*, 165–201.

Labov, W. (1998). Co-existent systems in African-American Vernacular English. In S. Mufwene, J. Rickford, G. Bailey, & J. Baugh (Eds.), *African-American English: Structure, history and use* (pp.110–153). London: Routledge.

Leacock, E. (1985). The influence of teacher attitudes on children's classroom performance: Case studies. In K. Borman (Ed.), *The social life of children in changing society* (pp. 47–64). Norwood, NJ: Ablex.

Lee, C. (1993). *Signifying as a scaffold for literary interpretation: The pedagogical implications of an African American discourse genre*. Urbana, IL: National Council of Teachers of English.

Lee, J. (2002). *Civility in the city: Blacks, Jews, and Koreans in urban America*. Cambridge, MA: Harvard University Press.

Leets, L. (2001). Explaining perceptions of racist speech. *Communication Research, 28*, 676–706.

Leets, L., & Giles, H. (1997). Words as weapons: When do they wound? Investigations of harmful speech. *Human Communication Research, 24*, 260–301.

Leets, L., Giles, H., & Noels, K. (1999). Attributing harm to racist speech. *Journal of Multilingual and Multicultural Development, 20*, 209–215.

Lewontin, R. (1995). *Human diversity*. New York: Scientific American Library.

Lindsley, S. (1998). Communicating prejudice in organizations. In M. Hecht (Ed.), *Communicating prejudice* (pp. 187–205). Thousand Oaks, CA: Sage.

Litwack, L. (1961). *North of slavery: The Negro in the free states, 1790–1860*. Chicago: University of Chicago Press.

Livingston, R. (2002). The role of perceived negativity in the moderation of African Americans' implicit and explicit racial attitudes. *Journal of Experimental Social Psychology, 38*, 405–413.

Locke, J. (1960). *Two treatises of government* (P. Laslett Ed.). Cambridge, UK: Cambridge University Press. (Original work published 1690)

Loury, G. (2002). *The anatomy of racial inequality*. Cambridge, MA: Harvard University Press.

Lundquist, J. (2007). Ethnic and gender satisfaction in the military: The effect of a meritocratic institution. *American Sociological Review, 73*, 477–495.

Lundy, G. (2003). The myths of oppositional culture. *Journal of Black Studies, 33*, 450–467.

Maass, A., Salvi, D., Arcuri, L., & Semin, G. (1989). Language use in intergroup contexts: The linguistic intergroup bias. *Journal of Personality and Social Psychology, 57*, 981–993.

MacDonald, J. (1983). *Blacks and white TV: Afro-Americans in television since 1948*. Chicago: Nelson-Hall.

Majors, R. (1991). Nonverbal behaviors and communication styles among African Americans. In R. Jones (Ed.), *Black psychology* (3rd ed., pp. 269–294). Hampton, VA: Cobb & Henry.

Majors, R., & Billson, J. (1992). *Cool pose: The dilemmas of black manhood in America.* New York: Simon & Schuster.

Manring, M. (1998). *Slave in a box: The strange career of Aunt Jemima.* Charlottesville: University Press of Virginia.

Marable, M. (2002). *The great wells of democracy: The meaning of race in American life.* New York: Basic Civitas.

Marger, M. (2009). *Race and ethnic relations: American and global perspectives* (8th ed.). Belmont, CA: Wadsworth.

Marques, J. (1990). The black sheep effect: Outgroup homogeneity in social comparison settings. In D. Abrams & M. Hogg (Eds.), *Social identity theory: Constructive and critical advances* (pp. 131–151). London: Harvester Wheatsheaf.

Martin, J., Hecht, M., & Larkey, L. (1994). Conversational improvement strategies for interethnic communication: African American and European American perspectives. *Communication Monographs, 61,* 236–255.

Massey, D., & Denton, N. (1989). Hypersegregation in U.S. metropolitan areas: Black and Hispanic segregation. *Demography, 26,* 373–393.

Massey, D., & Denton, N. (1993). *American apartheid: Segregation and the making of the underclass.* Cambridge, MA: Harvard University Press.

Massood, P. (2003). *Black city cinema: African American urban experiences in film.* Philadelphia: Temple University Press.

McCullough, D. (1992). *Truman.* New York: Simon & Schuster.

McDavid, R., & McDavid, V. (1951). The relationship of the speech of American Negroes to the speech of whites. *American Speech, 26,* 3–17.

McDermott, M. (2006). *Working-class white: The making and unmaking of race relations.* Berkeley: University of California Press.

McPherson, J. (1982). *Ordeal by fire: The Civil War and reconstruction.* New York: Alfred A. Knopf.

McPherson, J. (1988). *Battle cry of freedom: The Civil War era.* Oxford, UK: Oxford University Press.

McWhorter, J. (1998). *The word on the street: Fact and fable about American English.* New York: Plenum.

McWhorter, J. (2005). *Winning the race: Beyond the crisis in black America.* New York: Gotham.

Menocal, M. (2002). *The ornament of the world: How Muslims, Jews, and Christians created a culture of tolerance in medieval Spain.* Boston: Little, Brown.

Michaels, W. (2006). *The trouble with diversity: How we learned to love identity and ignore inequality.* New York: Metropolitan.

Mickelson, R. (2005). How tracking undermines race equity in desegregated schools. In J. Petrovich & A. Wells (Eds.), *Bringing equity back: Research for a new era in American educational policy* (pp. 49–76). New York: Teachers College Press.

Miller, J., & Donner, S. (2000). More than just talk: The use of racial dialogues to combat racism. *Social Work with Groups, 23*, 507–524.

Mills, C. (1997). *The racial contract.* Ithaca, NY: Cornell University Press.

Milroy, J., & Milroy, L. (1985). *Authority in language: Investigating standard English.* London: Routledge.

Milroy, L., & Muysken, P.(1995). Introduction: Code-switching and bilingualism research. In L. Milroy & P. Muysken (Eds.), *One speaker, two languages: Cross-disciplinary perspectives on code-switching* (pp. 1–14). Cambridge, UK: Cambridge University Press.

Mitchell-Kernan, C. (1972). Signifying, loud-talking and marking. In T. Kochman (Ed.), *Rappin and stylin' out: Communication in urban black America* (pp. 315–335). Urbana: University of Illinois Press.

Moghaddam, F., & Solliday, E. (1991). "Balanced multiculturalism" and the challenge of peaceful coexistence in pluralistic societies. *Psychology and Developing Societies, 3,* 51–71.

Montagu, A. (1997). *Man's most dangerous myth: The fallacy of race* (6th ed.). Walnut Creek, CA: Altamira.

Montesquieu, C. (1989). *The spirit of the laws,* A. Cohler, B. Miller, & H. Stone, (Trans., Eds.). Cambridge, UK: Cambridge University Press. Original work published in 1748.

Morgan, M. (1993). The Africanness of counter-language among Afro-Americans. In S. Mufwene (Ed.), *Africanisms in Afro-American language varieties* (pp. 423–435). Athens: University of Georgia Press.

Morgan, M. (2002). *Language, discourse, and power in African American culture.* Cambridge, UK: Cambridge University Press.

Morton, S. (1849). Observations on the size of the brain in various races and families of man. *Proceedings of the Academy of Natural Sciences Philadelphia, 4,* 173–175.

Moss, P., & Tilly, C. (1996). "Soft" skills and race: An investigation of black men's employment problems. *Work and Occupations, 23,* 252–276.

MSNBC.com (2008, July 10). *AMA apologizes to black doctors.* Retrieved July 10, 2008, from http://www.msnbc.com/id/25614966.

Mufwene, S. (2003). The shared ancestry of African American and American White English: Some speculations dictated by history. In S. Nagle & S. Sanders (Eds.), *English in the southern United States* (pp. 64–81). Cambridge, UK: Cambridge University Press.

Mufwene, S., Rickford, J., Bailey, G., & Baugh, J. (Eds.). (1998). *African American English: Structure, history, and use.* London: Routledge.

Myrdal, G. (1944). *An American dilemma.* New York: Harper and Brothers.

Nagda, B. (2006). Breaking barriers, crossing borders, building bridges: Communication processes in intergroup dialogues. *Journal of Social Issues, 62,* 553–576.

Nagourney, A. (2007, February 1). Biden unwraps his bid for '08 with an oops! *New York Times,* pp. A1, A16.

Nakayama, T., & Martin, J. (Eds.). (1999). *Whiteness: The communication of social identity.* Thousand Oaks, CA: Sage.

National Public Radio (2008, March 24). *Understanding Rev. Jeremiah Wright*. Retrieved November 4, 2008, from http://www.npr.org/templates/story/storry.php?storyId=88941182.

Nelson, L. (1990). Code-switching in the oral life narratives of African-American women: Challenges to linguistic hegemony. *Journal of Education, 172,* 142–155.

O'Connor, L., Brooks-Gunn, J., & Graber, J. (2000). Black and white girls' racial preferences in media and peer choices and the role of socialization for black girls. *Journal of Family Psychology, 14,* 510–521.

Ogbu, J. (2003). *Black American students in an affluent suburb: A study of academic disengagement*. Mahwah, NJ: Erlbaum.

Oliver, M., Jackson, R., Moses, I., & Dangerfield, C. (2004). The face of crime: Viewers' memory of race-related facial features of individuals pictured in the news. *Journal of Communication, 54,* 88–104.

Omi, M., & Winant, H. (1994). *Racial formation in the United States: From the 1960s to the 1990s*. New York: Routledge.

Orbe, M. (1998). *Constructing co-cultural theory: An explication of culture, power, and communication*. Thousand Oaks, CA: Sage.

Orbe, M., & Harris, T. (2001). *Interracial communication: Theory into practice*. Belmont, CA: Wadsworth.

Orbe, M., & Harris, T. (2008). *Interracial communication: Theory into practice* (2nd ed.). Thousand Oaks, CA: Sage.

O'Reilly, K. (1995). *Nixon's piano: Presidents and racial politics from Washington to Clinton*. New York: Free Press.

Orfield, G. (1997). *Metropolitics: A regional agenda for community and stability*. Washington, DC: Brookings Institution.

Orfield, G., & Lee, C. (2005, January). *Why segregation matters: Poverty and educational inequality*. The Civil Rights Project, Harvard University. Retrieved Nov. 1, 2008 from http://www.civilrightsproject.harvard.edu.

Paludan, P. (1988). *A people's contest: The Union and the Civil War. 1861–1865*. New York: Harper & Row.

Patterson, O. (2008, November 10). The new mainstream. *Newsweek*, pp. 40–41.

Patton, J. (1998). The disproportionate representation of African Americans in special education: Looking behind the curtain for understanding and solutions. *Journal of Special Education, 32,* 25–31.

Peffley, M., & Hurwitz, J. (1998). Whites' stereotypes of blacks: Sources and political consequences. In J. Hurwitz & M. Peffley (Eds.), *Perception and prejudice: Race and politics in the United States* (pp. 58–99). New Haven, CT: Yale University Press.

Perry, P. (2002). *Shades of white: White kids and racial identities in high school*. Durham, NC: Duke University Press.

Pettigrew, T. (1998). Intergroup contact theory. *Annual Review of Psychology, 49,* 65–85.

Pettigrew, T. (2008). Future directions for intergroup contact theory and research. *International Journal of Intercultural relations, 32,* 187–199.

Pettigrew, T., & Martin, J. (1987). Shaping the organizational context for black American inclusion. *Journal of Social Forces, 43,* 41–78.

Pettigrew, T., & Tropp, L. (2006). A meta-analytic test of intergroup contact theory. *Journal of Personality and Social Psychology, 90*, 751–783.

Pew Research Center (2007, November 13). Optimism about black progress declines. *Blacks see growing values gap between poor and middle class.* Retrieved March 10, 2008, from http://pewsocialtrends./org/pubs/700/black-public-opinion

Pew Research Center (2008, July 10). Candidates race, age, experience and religion. *Likely rise in turnout bodes well for Democrats.* Retrieved October 30, 2008, from http://people-press.org/report/?pageid=1339

Philipsen, G. (1992). *Culturally speaking: Explorations in social communication.* Albany: State University of New York Press.

Pollock, M. (2004). *Colormute: Race talk dilemmas in an American school.* Princeton, NJ: Princeton University Press.

Poplack, S. (Ed.) (2000). *The English history of African American English.* Malden, MA: Blackwell Publishers.

Purnell, T., Idsardi, W., & Baugh, J. (1999). Perceptual and phonetic experiments on American English dialect identification. *Journal of Language and Social Psychology, 18*, 10–30.

Putnam, R. (2000). *Bowling alone: The collapse and revival of American community.* New York: Simon & Schuster.

Ransom, R. (1989). *Conflict and compromise: The political economy of slavery, emancipation, and the American Civil war.* Cambridge, UK: Cambridge University Press.

Rawls, A., (2000). "Race" as an interaction order phenomenon: W.E.B. Du Bois's "Double Consciousness" thesis revisited. *Sociological Theory, 18*, 241–274.

Ray, G. (2004, May). *Language attitudes and African American Vernacular English: New directions for research.* Paper presented at the annual meeting of the International Communication Association, New Orleans, LA.

Rayburn, N., Earleywine, M., & Davison, G. (2003). Base rates of hate crime victimization among college students. *Journal of Interpersonal Violence, 18*, 1209–1221.

Reagan, R. (1983). *A time for choosing: The great speeches of Ronald Reagan, 1961–1982.* Chicago: Regnery Gateway.

Reiss, O. (1997). *Blacks in colonial America.* Jefferson, NC: McFarland & Co.

Rich, A. (1974). *Interracial communication.* New York: Harper & Row.

Richards, L. (2000). *The slave power: The free North and southern domination, 1780–1860.* Baton Rouge, LA: Louisiana State University Press.

Richardson, E. (1998). The anti-Ebonics movement: "Standard English only." *Journal of English Linguistics, 26*, 156–169.

Rickford, J. (1997). Unequal partnership: Sociolinguistics and the African American speech community. *Language in Society, 26*, 161–197.

Rickford, J. (1999). *African American Vernacular English: Features, evolution, educational implications.* Malden, MA: Blackwell.

Rickford, J., & Rickford, R.(2000). *Spoken soul: The story of black English.* New York: John Wiley & Sons.

Rogan, R., & Hammer, M. (1998). An exploratory study of message affect behavior: A comparison between African Americans and Euro-Americans. *Journal of Language and Social Psychology, 17*, 449–464

Rogin, M. (1996). *Blackface, white noise: Jewish immigrants in the Hollywood melting pot.* Berkeley: University of California Press.

Rose, T. (1994). *Black noise: Rap music and black culture in contemporary America.* Hanover, NH: University Press of New England.

Rothbart, M., & John, O. (1985). Social categorization and behavioral episodes: A cognitive analysis of the effects of intergroup contact. *Journal of Social Issues, 41*, 81–104.

Rousseau, J. (1950). *The social contract and discourses* (G. Cole, Trans). New York: E. P. Dutton. (Original work published 1762)

Ruscher, J. (2001). *Prejudiced communication: A social psychological perspective.* New York: Guilford.

Sachdev, I., & Bourhis, R. (2001). Multilingual communication. In W. Robinson & H. Giles (Eds.), *The new handbook of language and social psychology* (pp. 407–428). Chichester, UK: John Wiley.

Sellas-Ferrer, M.I., & Hutson, H.R. (2004). A review of hate violence in the United States from 1992 to 2002 and its implications for emergency physicians. *Annals of Emergency Medicine, 44*, S96, S97.

Schlesinger, A. (1992). *The disuniting of America.* New York: Norton.

Schmidt, P. (2007, August 31). Michigan. *The Chronicle of Higher Education: Almanac Issue, 2007–08*, p. 64.

Schnake, S., & Ruscher, J. (1998). Modern racism as a predictor of the linguistic intergroup bias. *Journal of Language and Social Psychology, 17*, 484–491.

Schneider, D. (2004). *The psychology of stereotyping.* New York: Guilford.

Schoem, D., & Hurtado, S. (2001). *Intergroup dialogue: Deliberative democracy in school, college, community and workplace.* Ann Arbor, MI: University of Michigan Press.

Schofield, J. (1986). Causes and consequences of the colorblind perspective. In J. Dovidio & S. Gaertner (Eds.), *Prejudice, discrimination, and racism* (pp. 231-253). Orlando, FL: Academic Press.

Schofield, J. (1991). School desegregation and intergroup relations: A review of the literature. In G. Grant (Ed.), *Review of Research in Education* (Vol. 17, pp. 335–409). Washington, DC: American Education Research Association.

Schuck, P. (2003). *Diversity in America: Keeping government at a safe distance.* Cambridge, MA: Harvard University Press.

Schuman, H., Steeh, C., Bobo, L., & Krysan, M. (1997). *Racial attitudes in America: Trends and interpretations.* (Rev. ed.), Cambridge, MA: Harvard University Press.

Scott, K. (2000). Crossing cultural borders: "girl" and "look" as markers of identity in Black women's language use. *Discourse and Society, 11*, 237–248.

Sears, D. (1988). Symbolic racism. In P. Katz & D. Traylor (Eds.), *Eliminating racism: Profiles in controversy* (pp. 53–84). New York: Plenum.

Sears, D., Citrin, J., Cheleden, S., & van Laar, C. (1999). Cultural diversity and multicultural politics: Is ethnic balkanization psychologically inevitable? In D. Prentice

& D. Miller (Eds.), *Cultural divides: Understanding and overcoming group conflict* (pp. 35–79). New York: Russell Sage Foundation.

Sears, D., & Kinder, D. (1971). Racial tensions and voting in Los Angeles. In W. Hirsch (Ed.), *Los Angeles: Viability and prospects for metropolitan leadership* (pp. 51–88). New York: Praeger.

Sechrist, G., & Stangor, C. (2001). Perceived consensus influences intergroup behavior and stereotype accessibility. *Journal of Personality and Social Psychology, 80,* 645–654.

Seib, G. (2008, November 6). The changed contours of America. *The Wall Street Journal,* p. A9.

Seymour, H., & Roeper, T. (1999). Grammatical acquisition of African American English. In O. Taylor & L. Leonard (Eds.), *Language acquisition across North America: Cross-cultural and cross-linguistic perspectives* (pp. 109–152). San Diego, CA: Singular.

Shelton, J., & Richeson, J. (2005). Intergroup contact and pluralistic ignorance. *Journal of Personality and Social Psychology, 88,* 91–107.

Shelton, J., Richeson, J., & Salvatore, J. (2005). Expecting to be the target of prejudice: Implications for interethnic interactions. *Personality and Social Psychology Bulletin, 31,* 1189–1202.

Shepard, C., Giles, H., & Le Poire, B. (2001). Communication accommodation theory. In W. Robinson & H. Giles (Eds.), *The new handbook of language and social psychology* (pp. 33–56). Chichester, UK: John Wiley.

Shipler, D. (1997). *A country of strangers: Blacks and whites in America.* New York: Alfred A. Knopf.

Simon, B., & Brown, R. (1987). Perceived intragroup homogeneity in minority-majority contexts. *Journal of Personality and Social Psychology, 53,* 703–711.

Skolnick, J. (1966). *Justice without trial: Law enforcement in democratic society.* New York: Wiley.

Skrentny, J. (2002). *The minority rights revolution.* Cambridge, MA: Harvard University Press.

Sleeper, J. (1997). *Liberal Racism.* New York: Penguin.

Sloat, B. (2006, July 22). Discrimination issue resurfaces for Honda. *The Plain Dealer,* pp. C1,3.

Smedley, A. (1993). *Race in North America: Origin and evolution of a worldview.* Boulder, CO: Westview.

Smith, Arthur. (1973). *Transracial Communication.* Upper Saddle River, N.J.: Prentice-Hall.

Smitherman, G. (1977). *Talkin' and testifyin': The language of black America.* Boston: Houghton Mifflin.

Smitherman, G. (Ed.) (1995). *African American women speaking out on Anita Hill–Clarence Thomas.* Detroit: Wayne State University Press.

Smitherman, G. (2000). *Talkin that talk: Language, culture, and education in African America.* London: Routledge.

Smitherman, G. (2006). *Word from the mother: Language and African Americans*. New York: Routledge.

Spears, A. (1982). The black English semi-auxiliary come. *Language, 58,* 850–872.

St. Jean, Y., & Feagin, J. (1998). *Double burden: Black women and everyday racism.* Armonk, NY: M.E. Sharpe.

Stangor, C. (2000). Volume overview. In C. Stangor (Ed.), *Stereotypes and prejudice: Essential readings* (pp. 1–16). Philadelphia: Taylor & Francis.

Stangor, C., & Schaller, M. (1996). Stereotypes as individual and collective representations. In C. Macrae, C. Stangor, & M. Hewstone (Eds.), *Stereotypes and stereotyping* (pp. 3–40). New York: Guilford.

Steele, C., & Aronson, J. (1995). Stereotype threat and the intellectual test performance of African Americans. *Journal of personality and social psychology, 69,* 797–811.

Steele, S. (1990). *The content of our character: A new vision of race in America*. New York: St. Martin's Press.

Stephen, W., Boniecki, K., Ybarra, O., Bettencourt, A., Ervin, K., Jackson, L., McNatt, P., & Renfro, C. (2002). The role of threats in the racial attitudes of blacks and whites. *Personality and Social Psychology Bulletin, 28,* 1242–1254.

Stewart, J., & Thomas, M. (1995). Dialogic listening: Sculpting mutual meanings. In J. Stewart (Ed.), *Bridges not walls*, (6th ed., pp. 184–210). New York: McGraw-Hill.

Stockman, I. (1999). Semantic development of African American children. In O. Taylor & L. Leonard (Eds.), *Language acquisition across North America: Cross-cultural and cross-linguistic perspectives* (pp. 61–106). San Diego, CA: Singular.

Stockman, I., & Vaughn-Cooke, F. (1986). Implications of semantic category research for the language assessment of nonstandard speakers. *Topics in Language Disorders, 6,* 15–25.

Stohl, C. (2001). Globalizing organizational communication. In F. Jablin & L. Putnam (Eds.), *The new handbook of organizational communication: Advances in theory, research, and methods* (pp. 323–375). Thousand Oaks, CA: Sage

Strauss, R. (2007, April 11). Rutgers women show anger, but agree to meet Imus. *New York Times*, p. C19.

Stuckey, S. (1987). *Slave culture: Nationalist theory and the foundations of black America.* New York: Oxford University Press.

Sullivan A. (2008, May 28). Jeremiah Wright goes to War. *Time*. Retrieved Nov. 10, 2008 from http://www.time. com/time/politics/article/0,8599,1735662,00.html.

Sullivan, P. (1996). *Days of hope: Race and democracy in the New Deal era*. Chapel Hill: University of North Carolina Press.

Sweet, J. (1997). The Iberian roots of American racist thought. *The William and Mary Quarterly, 54,* 1997, 143–166.

Tajfel, H. (1978). Social categorization, social identity, and social comparison. In H. Tajfel (Ed.), *Differentiation between social groups: Studies in the social psychology of intergroup relations* (pp. 61–76). London: Academic.

Tajfel, H., Billig, M., Bundy, R., & Flament, C. (1971). Social categorization and intergroup behavior. *European Journal of Social Psychology, 1,* 149–178.

Tajfel, H., & Forgas, J. (1981). Social categorization: Cognitions, values, and groups. In J. P. Forgas (Ed.), *Social cognition: Perspectives on everyday understanding* (pp. 113–140). New York: Academic.

Tajfel, H., & Turner, J. (2001). An integrative theory of intergroup conflict. In M. Hogg & D. Abrams (Eds.), *Intergroup relations: Essential readings* (pp. 94–109). Philadelphia: Psychology Press.

Tarone, E. (2003). Aspects of intonation in black English. In N. Norment (Ed.), *Readings in African American language* (pp. 97–105). New York: Peter Lang.

Tatum, B. (1997). *Why are all the black kids sitting together in the cafeteria?* New York: Basic Books.

Tatum, B. (2007). *Can we talk about race?: And other conversations in an era of school resegregation.* Boston: Beacon.

Taylor, D. (1991). The social psychology of racial and cultural diversity: Issues of assimilation and multiculturalism. In A. Reynolds (Ed.), *Bilingualism, multiculturalism, and second language learning: The McGill conference in honour of Wallace E. Lambert* (pp. 1–19). Hillsdale, NJ: Erlbaum.

Thernstrom, A. & Thernstrom, S. (2003). *No excuses: Closing the racial gap in learning.* New York: Simon & Schuster.

Thernstrom, S., & Thernstrom, A. (1997). *America in black and white: One nation, indivisible.* New York: Simon & Schuster.

Thomas, C. (2007). *My grandfather's son: A memoir.* New York: Harper.

Thomas, H. (1997). *The slave trade: The story of the Atlantic slave trade: 1440–1870.* New York: Simon & Schuster.

Ting-Toomey, S. (2005a). The matrix of face: An updated face-negotiation theory. In W. Gudykunst (Ed.), *Theorizing about intercultural communication* (pp. 71–92). Thousand Oaks, CA: Sage.

Ting-Toomey, S. (2005b). Identity negotiation theory: Crossing cultural boundaries. In W. Gudykunst (Ed.), *Theorizing about intercultural communication* (pp. 211–233). Thousand Oaks, CA: Sage.

Toll, R. (1974). *Blacking up: The minstrel show in nineteenth-century America.* New York: Oxford University Press.

Torres, S. (1999). Hate crimes against African Americans: The extent of the problem. *Journal of Contemporary Criminal Justice, 15*, 48–63.

Tracy, K. (2002). *Everyday talk: Building and reflecting identities.* New York: Guilford.

Trepagnier, B. (2006). *Silent racism: How well-meaning white people perpetuate the racial divide.* Boulder, CO: Paradigm.

Tsesis, A. (2002). *Destructive messages: How hate speech paves the way for harmful social movements.* New York: New York University Press.

Tucker, G., & Lambert, W. (1969). White and Negro listeners' reactions to various American-English dialects. *Social Forces, 47*, 463–468.

Turner, L. (1949). *Africanisms in the Gullah dialect.* Chicago: University of Chicago Press.

Turner, P. (1993). *I heard it through the grapevine: Rumor in African American culture.* Berkeley: University of California Press.

Tuttle, K. (1999). Television and African Americans. In K. Appiah & H. Gates (Eds.), *Africana: The encyclopedia of the African and African American experience* (pp. 1830–1834). New York: Basic Civitas.

Tyson, K., Darity, Jr., W., & Castellino, D. (2005). It's not a "black thing": Understanding the burden of acting white and other dilemmas of high achievement. *American Sociological Review, 70,* 582–605.

U.S. Census Bureau (2000). Selected occupational groups by race and Hispanic origin for the United States: 2000. *Census 2000, Sample Edited Detail File. Summary File 1.* Washington, DC: U.S. Government Printing Office.

U.S. Census Bureau (2003). America's families and living arrangements: 2003. *Annual social and economic supplement: 2003 current population reports, series P20–553.* Washington, DC: U.S. Government Printing Office.

U.S. Census Bureau (2007). Selected social characteristics in the United States: 2006. American Community Survey. Retrieved Nov. 15, 2008 from http://factfinder.census.gov/.

U.S. Department of Education (2003). Reading highlights 2003. *National Assessment of Educational Progress.* Washington, DC: U.S. Government Printing Office.

U.S. Department of Education (2005). Reading highlights 2005. *National Assessment of Educational Progress.* Washington, DC: U.S. Government Printing Office.

U.S. Department of Justice (2007, November). *Federal Bureau of Investigation: Uniform Crime Report: Hate Crime Statistics.* Washington, DC: U.S. Government Printing Office.

U.S. Equal Employment Opportunity Commission (2000). *Occupational employment in private industry by race/ethnic group/sex, and by industry, United States, 2000.* Job patterns for Minorities and women in private industry, 2000. Retrieved December 17, 2008, from http://www.eeoc.gov/stats/jobpat/2000/index/html.

Van DeBurg, W. (2004). *Hoodlums: Black villains and social bandits in American life.* Chicago: University of Chicago Press.

van den Berghe, P. (1978). *Race and racism: A comparative perspective* (2nd ed.). New York: John Wiley & Sons.

Van Dijk, T. (1987). *Communicating racism.* Newbury Park, CA: Sage.

Walker, M. (2000). The acquisition of African American English: Social-cognitive and cultural factors. In O. Taylor & L. Leonard (Eds.), *Language acquisition across North America: Cross-cultural and cross-linguistic perspectives* (pp. 41–58). San Diego, CA: Singular.

Walsh, K. (2007). *Talking about race: Community dialogues and the politics of difference.* Chicago: University of Chicago Press.

Washington, J., & Craig, H. (1992). Performances of low-income, African American preschool and kindergarten children on the Peabody Picture Vocabulary Test. *Language, Speech and Hearing Services in Schools, 23,* 329–333.

Washington Post (2004, July 27). *Transcript: Illinois Senate candidate Barack Obama.* Retrieved July 15, 2006 from washingtonpost.com.http//www.washingtonpost.com/wedyn/articles/A1975-2004. html.

Waters, M. (1999). *Black identities: West Indian immigrant dreams and American realities.* New York: Russell Sage Foundation.

Watkins, C., & Terrell, F. (1988). Mistrust and its effects on counseling expectations in black client-counselor relationships: An analogue study. *Journal of Counseling Psychology, 35,* 194–197.

Welchman, J. (1995). Locke on slavery and inalienable rights. *Canadian Journal of Philsophy, 25,* 67-81.

Wells, A., & Crain, R. (1997). *Stepping over the color line: African-American students in white suburban schools.* New Haven: Yale University Press.

Wenzel, M., Mummendey, A., & Waldus, S. (2007). Superordinate identities and intergroup conflict: The ingroup projection model. *European Review of Social Psychology, 18,* 331-372.

Wharry, C. (2003). Amen and hallelujah preaching: Discourse functions in African American sermons. *Language in Society, 32,* 203–225.

White, S., & White, G. (1998). *Stylin': African American expressive culture from its beginnings to the zoot suit.* Ithaca, NY: Cornell University Press.

White, T. (1965). *The making of the president: 1964.* New York: Atheneum.

Wilder, D. (1984). Intergroup contact: The typical member and the exception to the rule. *Journal of Experimental Social Psychology, 20,* 177–194.

Wilkes, R., & Iceland, J. (2004). Hypersegregation in the twenty-first century. *Demography, 41,* 23-36.

Williams, L. (2000). *It's the little things: Everyday interactions that anger, annoy, and divide the races.* New York: Harcourt.

Williams, M., & Eberhardt, J. (2008). Biological conceptions of race and the motivation to cross racial boundaries. *Journal of Personality and Social Psychology, 94,* 1033–1047.

Wilson, W. (1978). *The declining significance of race: Blacks and changing American institutions.* Chicago: University of Chicago Press.

Wolfram, W. (1969). *A sociolinguistic description of Detroit Negro speech.* Washington, DC: Center for Applied Linguistics.

Wolfram, W., & Schilling-Estes, N. (1998). *American English: Dialects and variation.* Malden, MA: Blackwell.

Wolfram, W., & Schilling-Estes, N. (2006). *American English: Dialects and variation* (2nd ed.). Malden, MA: Blackwell.

Wolfram, W., & Thomas, E. (2002). *The development of African American English.* London: Blackwell.

Wood, J. (2009). *Gendered lives: Communication, gender, and culture* (8th ed.). Boston: Wadsworth Cengage.

Wood, J., & Pearce, W. (1980). Sexists, racists, and other classes of classifiers: Form and function of "...IST" accusations. *Quarterly Journal of Speech, 66,* 239–250.

Woodward, C. (1974). *The strange career of Jim Crow* (3rd rev. ed.). Oxford, UK: Oxford University Press.

Wright, D. (1990). *African Americans in the colonial era: From African origins through the American revolution.* Arlington Heights, IL: Harlan Davidson.

Wright, D. (1993). *African Americans in the Early Republic: 1789–1831*. Wheeling, IL: Harlan Davidson.

Zweigenhaft, R., & Domhoff, G. (2003). *Blacks in the white elite: Will the progress continue?* Lanham, MD: Rowan & Littlefield.

Author Index

Subject Index

Language
as SOCIAL
ACTION ▶

Howard Giles,
GENERAL EDITOR

This series explores new and exciting advances in the ways in which language both reflects and fashions social reality—and thereby constitutes critical means of social action. As well as these being central foci in face-to-face interactions across different cultures, they also assume significance in the ways that language functions in the mass media, new technologies, organizations, and social institutions. Language as Social Action does not uphold apartheid against any particular methodological and/or ideological position, but, rather, promotes (wherever possible) cross-fertilization of ideas and empirical data across the many, all-too-contrastive, social scientific approaches to language and communication. Contributors to the series will also accord due attention to the historical, political, and economic forces that contextually bound the ways in which language patterns are analyzed, produced, and received. The series will also provide an important platform for theory-driven works that have profound, and often times provocative, implications for social policy.

For further information about the series and submitting manuscripts, please contact:

Howard Giles
Dept of Communication
University of California at Santa Barbara
Santa Barbara, CA 93106-4020
HowieGiles@aol.com

To order other books in this series, please contact our Customer Service Department at:

(800) 770-LANG (within the U.S.)
(212) 647-7706 (outside the U.S.)
(212) 647-7707 FAX

Or browse online by series at:

www.peterlang.com